INTRODUCTION TO THE NEW TESTAMENT

INTRODUCTION
TO THE NEW TESTAMENT

An Approach to its Problems

BY

W. MARXSEN

*Professor of New Testament Theology
in the University of Münster/Westphalia*

TRANSLATED BY

G. BUSWELL

1970

FORTRESS PRESS

PHILADELPHIA

© in this translation Basil Blackwell, Oxford, 1968

Library of Congress Catalog Card No. 68-15419

First published 1968
Second impression 1970

A translation of the third edition of
EINLEITUNG IN DAS NEUE TESTAMENT
published by © Gütersloher Verlagshaus Gerd Mohn,
Gütersloh, Germany 1964

Reproduced by photo-lithography and made in Great Britain at
the Pitman Press, Bath

CONTENTS

VI. APOCALYPTIC LITERATURE

PREFACE

The traditional manuals of New Testament Introduction contain an abundance of historical details which have been brought to light as the result of many years of investigation, and thus they are often overcrowded with facts. The beginner especially—but not only the beginner—often finds it impossible to grasp the vast amount of material that is presented, nor can he see the importance of 'Introduction' for exegesis, and even the manuals tend to leave this aspect out of account. The result is that this particular discipline has become divorced from the field of theology proper, which was surely not the intention of its representatives. Anyone who is only slightly acquainted with most 'practical exegesis'—or exegesis in practice—nowadays cannot but admit that 'Introduction' is almost completely ignored. The reason for this lies not least in the fact that the theological student usually studies Introduction for his first examinations, but then lays it aside because he has never really grasped the point of it.

The aim of this book is to try to remedy this particular situation. Detail has been strictly limited, in order to bring out more clearly the most significant elements which serve the purpose of really 'introducing' the New Testament. There is of course room for difference of opinion as to the choice of material and the points emphasized. The general approach of the work cannot—and does not seek to—conceal the author's own standpoint. Discussion of other viewpoints has been restricted as much as possible in order to keep the material within reasonable proportions, and in many instances it is more implicit than explicit. In contrast to most manuals the various sections are not uniformly arranged. This has been done intentionally, as the problems presented by the various writings are often quite different, which means that each case demands its own approach. For the same reason the contents of the various writings have been set out in different ways: in some instances there is a brief summary, in others commentary and paraphrase, particularly where the problems of Introduction are elucidated by study of the content.

The book is limited to so-called special Introduction. References to other literature have been kept brief, and in general only those books have been mentioned which are easily available and which lead on to further reading.

The presentation is intentionally that of a 'reader', for the aim is to set out the problems New Testament Introduction has to face and at the same time to show the necessity of this discipline for all exegesis. In other words, the book really seeks to 'introduce' the reader to the New Testament, by giving him an insight into the history of the Gospel, by indicating the important issues and by encouraging a more precise grasp—through careful exegesis—of the various problems that arise.

Münster, Spring 1963   WILLI MARXSEN

ABBREVIATIONS

ASNU	*Acta Seminarii Neotestamentici Uppsaliensis*
ATR	*Anglican Review*
Bauer	W. Bauer, *Griechisch-deutsches Wörterbuch zu den Schriften des Neuen Testaments und der übrigen urchristlichen Literatur* (5 ed., 1958). (E.T. *A Greek-English Lexicon of the N.T. and other Early Christian Literature* (from 4 ed.), University of Chicago Press, 1957).
BJRL	*Bulletin of the John Rylands Library*
Black	Black's New Testament Commentaries
Blaß-Debrunner	F. Blaß, *Grammatik des neutestamentlichen Griechisch*, edited by A. Debrunner (9 ed., 1954). (E.T. *A Greek Grammar of the New Testament and other Early Christian Literature*, with supplementary notes by A. Debrunner, revised and translated by R. W. Funk (from 9 and 10 ed., 1959), Cambridge University Press; University of Chicago Press, 1961).
CGTC	Cambridge Greek Testament Commentary
ET	*Expository Times*
EvTh	*Evangelische Theologie*
HTR	*Harvard Theological Review*
ICC	International Critical Commentary
JBL	*Journal of Biblical Studies*
JR	*Journal of Religion*
JTS	*Journal of Theological Studies*
Lietzmann	Handbuch zum Neuen Testament, series of volumes begun by H. Lietzmann. General editor G. Bornkamm
Meyer	Kritisch-exegetischer Kommentar über das Neue Testament, series of volumes begun by H. A. Meyer
Moffatt	The Moffatt New Testament Commentary
NTD	Das Neue Testament Deutsch, Neues Göttinger Bibelwerk, edited by P. Althaus and G. Friedrich
NTS	*New Testament Studies*
Pelican	The Pelican Gospel Commentaries
Prophezei	Schweizerisches Bibelwerk für die Gemeinde

RGG	*Die Religion in Geschichte und Gegenwart,* edited by K. Galling, 6 vols.+index (3 ed. 1957–63). This edition is referred to, except where indicated.
ThBl	*Theologische Blätter*
ThLZ	*Theologische Literaturzeitung*
ThR	*Theologische Rundschau*
ThStKr	*Theologische Studien und Kritiken*
ThWNT	*Theologisches Wörterbuch zum Neuen Testament,* begun by G. Kittel, edited by G. Friedrich and others (1933 ff.)
TU	Texte und Untersuchungen zur Geschichte der altchristlichen Literatur
VE	*Vox Evangelica*
ZNW	*Zeitschrift für neutestamentliche Wissenschaft und die Kunde der älteren Kirche*
ZThK	*Zeitschrift für Theologie und Kirche*

THE THEOLOGICAL APPROACH TO NEW TESTAMENT
INTRODUCTION

It is usual when considering New Testament Introduction to distinguish between special and general Introduction. Special Introduction is concerned with the origin of the documents—author, time and place of writing, occasion and purpose, the readers for whom it was intended, integrity and sources. General Introduction deals with the transmission of the documents—the history of the text and translations, and with the way in which they are assembled—the origin and history of the Canon. It is clear that in all these problems we are concerned with historical questions. In what sense therefore can we speak of New Testament 'Introduction'?

The name is of course the traditional one, and we should not make the mistake of reading too much into it. Nevertheless, the word suggests that this kind of introductory study does give us access to the documents, so that the person who is familiar with its findings can be brought at best to a correct understanding or at least to a better understanding of the documents. It must be admitted, however, that we are not always prepared to admit that New Testament Introduction has this part to play, and this is understandable. But is it immediately obvious that one can arrive by means of historical investigation at findings that are theologically relevant? Can Introduction—in the sense of a historical discipline—be at all the object of theological study, or is it not rather only an ancillary study?

It cannot really be disputed that the writings comprised within the Canon of the New Testament are also products of their time. It follows from this that in principle it must be possible to examine them also by historical means. But can this method lead us to the essence of the problem? If it should be shown, for example, that the authors of the Gospels were not eye-witnesses and that we do not even know their names, that the Pastoral Epistles were not written by Paul and that Hebrews was included in the Canon by mistake, then these would be first and foremost historical findings. They contradict—at least in part—the tradition of the Church. But we could hardly conclude from this alone that these documents should no longer be used in preaching or that they should be omitted in Bible-reading. Then the question arises whether the study of New Testament Introduction is of any consequence

B

at all for the theological assessment, application and interpretation of the documents. The historical question could no doubt be considered parallel to the theological. In this case New Testament Introduction would lead to a better historical understanding—but what would be its theological relevance?

We could try to bring out its relevance by indicating that both— theological and historical interpretation—are concerned with the same object, and this in fact is what is usually done nowadays. For if other documents than the canonical writings of the New Testament are studied from the standpoint of New Testament Introduction, this is called 'the history of literature', but this difference of name is basically misleading. If our approach is the historical one, we must always use the historical method. The question of authorship of a canonical writing cannot be answered in a different manner from that of a non-canonical writing, and the same is true of the other problems dealt with under 'Introduction'. What we call 'Introduction' is therefore concerned simply with a history of primitive Christian literature (special Introduction) to which is added an account of the transmission of this literature (general Introduction). The difficulty is merely that the group of documents is limited to the twenty-seven writings in the New Testament Canon. Viewed from this angle, we could therefore abandon the term 'Introduction'.

The concept itself is not of great importance. The study of Introduction has no special method, and yet it ought not to be too hastily dismissed from theology. Rightly or wrongly, the name implies the claim that Introduction seeks to 'introduce', and thereby lead to understanding. It is worth examining this claim because, if it is a sound one, the study of Introduction would indicate a help which we should not lightly abandon.

The theologian who is studying the New Testament writings from the standpoint of Introduction needs to bear in mind that they have been deliberately selected. For all these writings have been recognized as having at least implicitly a special theological quality. But is this special quality recognizable? Certainly not by a study of Introduction from the purely historical angle.

The concept of the 'Word of God' can help to clarify this point. It needs to be made clear whether and in what way this idea can be applied to the New Testament. For our purpose it is enough to point out that it is used and that it is meant to express the special position of the Canon as distinct from other literature. This means that writings such as 1 Clement or the Didache, which originated about the same time as the latest of the New Testament documents, would never be described as the

'Word of God' in the same sense, for example, as Jude or 2 Peter. So we could say that the study of Introduction is concerned with the literary history of the Word of God and with the history of the transmission of the Word of God. In this case this 'Word of God' would be examined merely from its human, historical and 'secular' side, regardless of the fact that it is the Word of God. But is this possible?

Now one could seek to avoid answering this question by saying that it is not the Word of God that is being examined, but only the outward form which it has adopted, its cloak or garment or some such term. This would mean that we are concerned with the formal statement of the Word of God in the New Testament: the Word of God in the word of man. Here again we shall not argue whether this is an acceptable definition, and yet as regards our problem we must ask whether it is theologically permissible to draw such a distinction. The Divine Word would then be excluded from the 'Word of God' and only the human word would be examined from the historical standpoint. Even if this were possible, what would be the theological consequences? The 'secularization' which had already been systematically carried out could not be in any way undone.

There are therefore two aspects of the situation to be borne in mind. If we start by considering the question of method, it is not possible to distinguish New Testament Introduction from what otherwise is called the history of literature. From the standpoint of method, the Canon does not hold any special position. If on the other hand we start from the idea of the Word of God in the word of man, from the particular characteristics of the New Testament, from the Canon, and at the same time take our own presuppositions seriously, we can certainly pursue the study of Introduction from the 'secular' angle, but as a result cannot avoid losing the theological relevance from the outset. It has already become clear, therefore that the study of Introduction is certainly possible as a historical discipline, as history of literature; but it does not seem to be an undertaking that is theologically necessary, nor are we yet in a position to say whether—and even less how—its findings can be made significant for theology.

The study of New Testament Introduction, at least in the form in which it is at present undertaken, had its origin in the Enlightenment. It is only since that period that we can speak of historical science in our sense of the term. Nevertheless there are two earlier examples to which we ought to refer. The name of our subject first appears in a work of the otherwise unknown Greek writer Adrianos. He was a theologian of the

Antiochene school who wrote· an *Introduction to the Divine Writings* about the year 450, in which he set out his method, which deals among other things with principles of exposition and gives an exegesis of several difficult passages. This was therefore, in the true sense of the word, a real Introduction, as it was meant to help towards a correct reading and better understanding. Since that time the word has been used in the same sense in a number of other works. We should also remember Luther's Prefaces to his 1522 translation of the Bible, although he does not actually use the term 'Introduction'. Best known is his statement that James is 'an epistle full of straw'.

It is worth spending a little time analysing this passage. Luther names as the main books of the New Testament John and 1 John, the Epistles to the Galatians, Romans and Ephesians and 1 Peter. Apart from these he holds that none of the other books is really essential. Then he continues: 'In comparison with these, the epistle of St. James is an epistle full of straw, because it contains nothing evangelical.'[1] Luther's criterion therefore is the 'evangelical' quality. Where he finds this characteristic specially marked he designates the document as one of the principal books, and where it is lacking he relegates it to a secondary position. In other words, he is drawing distinctions within the Canon, and he is using a *dogmatic* criterion as the key to an understanding of the New Testament. This means that we are confronted here with the question of Introduction in the original sense of the word. The important thing is to see the 'evangelical' quality or—as Luther put it elsewhere—it is a question of whether a writing 'presents Christ', which is what it should do. This is the way in which the New Testament writings are to be read and judged. We cannot of course call this 'Introduction' in the modern sense, and yet the essence of it is there. Instead of the historical question there is the dogmatic. The dogmatic problem is one of interpretation. It was to be solved later in the Enlightenment by the historical problem—which was itself again a problem of interpretation.

The Enlightenment brought about a great change in the doctrine of Scripture, laid down on the Roman side by the Council of Trent and on the Protestant side by the old orthodoxy. The English Deists as part of their critical approach to religion demanded that the Bible should be examined by the same methods as secular literature, and they adopted this approach themselves. This led not only to the breaking up of the unity of the Old and New Testaments, but the separate books of the two

---

[1] B. L. Woolf, *Reformation Writings of Martin Luther*, II (Lutterworth Press; Philosophical Library, 1956), p. 283.

Testaments were also put in their own historical context and interpreted in the light of it. By introducing the historical question scholars were forced to make up their minds on the question of inspiration, the 'Divine' nature of Scripture and the Canon. And it is here that the historical approach became relevant to the problem of interpretation.

A number of different procedures were possible. Richard Simon (1638–1712), a member of the French Oratory, was the first to examine the New Testament from the standpoint of literary history. In his criticism (which was moderate for the most part) he was able to go against the traditional conceptions because his aim—indirectly, at least—was to demonstrate the necessity for the Catholic doctrine of the Church. On account of the doubts concerning its transmission, he considered the Bible a somewhat unreliable foundation for faith. For this reason he held that one could not do without the doctrine of the Church for a correct use of the Bible. This conception admitted unrestricted historical investigation, and its findings did not need to affect the Church's use of Scripture, for this was based on the Church's dogma.

These developments, which from the outset prevented the historical findings from having any bearing on theology, did not apply on the Protestant side. Here the historical question had a direct impact on the dogmatic aspect. J. S. Semler (1725–1791), who translated Simon's works into German, himself published an *Abhandlung von freier Untersuchung des Canons* (1771–1775) in which he drew a distinction between the Word of God and the Bible. The two are not identical, but as the Canon came into being as a result of human agreement, the relationship of a book to the Canon can be and should be examined by historical criticism.

This point was developed by Semler's contemporary, J. D. Michaelis (1717–1791). His *Einleitung in die göttlichen Schriften des neuen Bundes* published in 1750 and several times revised (4th ed., 1788), made him the real founder of the science of New Testament Introduction. He was not content with historical investigations alone, but combined with them theological judgements. The apostolic authorship of a book was his criterion for canonicity. In this way the questions raised by Introduction came to be dogmatically relevant, for its findings determined which books were to be considered as inspired, and therefore Divine, and which were not. But this was bound to have consequences for the Church's use of the New Testament. To this extent Introduction was more than literary history, and had become pre-eminently a theological task, but nevertheless consciously employed 'secular' methods. We can see here the similarity to Luther's attitude, but also the difference. Both Luther and

Michaelis adopted a critical attitude to the Canon, but it arose in the one case from a dogmatic viewpoint, in the other from a historical viewpoint. It is not hard to understand how this new approach inevitably led to a feeling of great uncertainty, as it forced scholars to face the question of a revision of the Canon. It did not in fact come to this, but it is significant to see how the problem was dealt with.

Although the historical method, once discovered, had a great influence on future investigations, the theological questions which were raised were not investigated, but excluded. The two disciplines became separated and so J. P. Gabler (1753–1826), for example, distinguished between Biblical and dogmatic theology. The former can be understood purely from the historical standpoint, and therefore always remains the same, whereas the latter has a didactic character and changes according to its particular context and the philosophical views of the individual theologians. Is there any bridge between the two? Gabler distinguishes between the divine and the human in Scripture. As far as dogmatic theology is concerned the human element plays no part, for dogmatic theology is more interested in the divine element, as only this is of permanent value for the 'Christian religion of all times'. In order to develop this idea, Gabler introduces an interesting distinction. An exegesis which deals with what the writer meant must be supplemented by an explanation of the nature of the material. This explanation says more than the writers wished to say or could say if, for example, they took stories clothed in myth to be actual happenings. This calls for a critical 'exposition', and only in this way can the material that has been examined historically be made theologically fruitful. It is clear that by this means the theological aspect was once again kept separate from the historical study. The question that arises is whether it will be possible in the future to achieve a reconciliation.

First, however, a new discipline emerged. Under the influence of Gabler and J. G. Eichhorn (1752–1827), G. L. Bauer (1755–1806) wrote a *Biblische Theologie des Neuen Testaments* (1800–1802) in which he dealt in turn with the 'theory of the Christian religion' of the Synoptics, John, Revelation, Peter, etc. In view of the arrangement of this work and the fact that Bauer had already written a Theology of the Old Testament, so that for the first time ever the Old and New Testaments appeared to be separated in theology also, one might gain the impression that the historical question had now been introduced into theology and that Bauer had written something approaching a history of the Biblical message. But this was not really the case, for the dogmatic approach was retained. Bauer arranged his material according to doctrinal concepts and therefore in the last resort his Biblical theology kept a theological orientation. But the break-through had now taken place and new lines of approach could be discerned which could be profitably pursued. At the same time it became clear that the theological relevance of the secular science of Introduction had to be demonstrated not from the standpoint of this science itself but from that of New Testament theology.

We must refer at this point to F. C. Baur (1792–1860), who brought this development to its climax, but also to a temporary halt. In presenting his views we must bear in mind that they evolved slowly. They cannot therefore simply be deduced from his various writings, but must be evaluated in the light of the whole tendency of his research. First he used the method of Introduction in a critical examination of the Canon. This had already been done by Michaelis, but in this case with a positive purpose insofar as his main concern was to strengthen the argument for the 'Divine' nature of Scripture by proving apostolic authorship. Baur subjects the concept of the Canon itself to critical examination by examining the dogmatic element in the concept and asking whether this element could be brought out by means of historical criticism. He did not arrive at a final judgement on this matter, but he carried the question over into New Testament theology. Here he saw various forces at work. Over against Gentile Christianity (represented by the 'genuine' Pauline epistles—Rom., 1 and 2 Cor., Gal.) there stands Jewish Christianity (Rev.). Baur sees a synthesis between the two in, for example, the Pastoral Epistles, Heb. and 1 Pet. Although this so-called 'Tendenzkritik' is fundamentally influenced by Hegel's philosophy of history and although a pattern is imposed upon primitive Christianity from outside into which it cannot be forced as easily as Baur imagined, still we cannot overlook the vitally important recognition that every single document can be fitted into a specific historical context by reference to which it must be interpreted. Every document stands at a particular point in the story of the early Christian Church. Baur accordingly defined New Testament theology as 'the history of Christian dogma as it develops within the New Testament'.

We have touched here upon one of Baur's most important insights which, however, did not bear as much fruit in subsequent research as it could and ought to have done. For if we see the New Testament writings as records of early Church history and the history of dogma, which begin not after but before the New Testament, then historical research is set free from the burden implied in the dogmatic concept of the 'Canon'.

But does this not mean that it also loses its theological reference? It has to be admitted that, compared with earlier conceptions of the Canon, this does mean the beginning of a historical relativism. If Church history and the history of dogma begin not after, but before, the New Testament, then the New Testament is not simply a counterpart of the Church from its very beginning, but is part of its early history. Then, however, the problem of the norm, which is of course linked with the Canon acquires a new aspect. Baur saw this clearly. He did not adopt a purely historical approach to the Scriptures as though this were adequate by itself, while leaving the question of the bearing of this research upon theology to a second, independent course of study; on the contrary, he pursues his line of thought to its logical conclusion. As he sees the writings as the outcome of a theological development, he is obliged to give an account of the beginnings of this development. Therefore, he attempts to arrive at the 'earliest period' in this development, which he sees in the 'teaching of Jesus'. In Baur's view this is 'not yet theology, but religion'.

It would make it harder for us to appreciate the full force of Baur's view if we were to attempt at this point to set out his understanding of the teaching of Jesus. His findings here are as disputable as those of his 'Tendenzkritik', but his insights as regards method are of decisive importance. No subsequent work of New Testament Introduction has made any advance upon these insights, at least as far as basic principles are concerned. Because attention was directed almost exclusively to Baur's findings (and those of his 'Tübingen school'), people have often been prevented from fully appreciating his basic conception. His great achievement was that he pointed out the way in which New Testament Introduction could free itself from a false theological orientation and yet remain of pre-eminently theological significance.

We have already pointed out that a direct theological connection of this work cannot derive from the historical method of Introduction. If, on the other hand, we start from its subject matter as theologically defined—i.e., the 'Word of God' or the 'Canon'—then the historical question never catches sight of the real theological element at all.

It now appears doubtful whether we have described correctly what it is that is investigated in New Testament Introduction. If Baur's assertion is correct (and I do not know any argument against it), that New Testament theology is 'the history of Christian dogma as it develops within the New Testament', then the writings are records of this early history of dogma. As such they are of course 'theological' documents, but only as part of a particular tradition, and not independently of it. They are theological as actualizations of the unique revelation that preceded them.

Let us consider again the concept of 'the Word of God'. We can no longer say that the object of our study is the human side of a Word of God that is now speaking to *us* in the Canon, but must rather say that the writings to be investigated are proclamations (in the broadest sense of the word) addressed to an actual situation in the *past*. The writings therefore *were* the Word of God or, to be more precise, they *claimed* to be the Word of God for the people for whom they were written at the time.

They derive this claim themselves (partly implicitly, partly explicitly) from the fact that they testify to the people of their time to the revelation of God that took place in Jesus. They start out therefore from this 'once-for-all' activity of God in history and seek to declare this Divine activity to their contemporaries in such a way that they will now be confronted with it. But from this it becomes plain that every new period, every new environment, every different linguistic area, every concrete situation in which those who are being addressed find themselves necessitates a restatement of the message. It presents itself, therefore in ever-renewed 'modern' forms, yet without losing contact with the once-for-allness. Its content and its theological relationship to the norm cannot be separated from its historically conditioned form. The pattern of 'kernel and shell' or 'content and form' is quite inapplicable in this case. For the same reason we cannot make a division between the historical and the theological aspects. We always find the proclamations in *historically conditioned* forms, and therefore, the historical method is the only one adequate in view of the nature of the sources.

At the same time we must bear in mind what this method is able to achieve. It can help us to achieve a historical understanding of *those* proclamations, but no more. There is one question that must remain open: every proclamation, every sermon (including those in the New Testament) can be true or false proclamation. It is correct, and therefore theologically legitimate, when it declares the 'substance' of revelation in such a way that this—corresponding to the historical situation at the time—is preserved. A variation in the concepts, in the ideas that are employed, in language, in argument or in the material that is used need in no way mean an alteration in the original matter, but it may do. This has to be tested each time, but this testing is not a task for New Testament Introduction; indeed, strictly speaking, it does not concern New Testament studies but rather systematic theology.

However, Introduction can render valuable help here. By clarifying the historical situation of the various writings, it helps us to understand why the message was formulated in a particular way and why variations from earlier proclamation were introduced. In this way it offers decisive viewpoints without which an objective examination would be impossible. Ignoring the findings of New Testament Introduction there is always the danger that the so-called 'inner-canonical criticism', which is necessary in view of the inconsistency of the various proclamations, might be carried out in an unhistorical way. To take a classic example, we cannot place Rom. iii. 28 and Jas. ii. 24 alongside each other and compare them, for each statement has to be understood in its own historical context, and in making a comparison the historical sequence has to be remembered. In this respect the science of Introduction can help us to use the writings properly—and it thereby proves to be a real 'Introduction'.

New Testament Introduction, however, seeks to be of direct service in the work of exegesis, which takes the writings for what they are—the documents of an author who is seeking to address a particular circle of readers. Exegesis can therefore be defined as the repetition in my language of what an author wanted to say to his readers. For the most part the documents contain only the statement itself: of the author we often learn nothing more than his name, and at times not even that. The direct references to the readers, too, are mostly very brief; often there are only indirect references. For an understanding of the message, however, which is always 'directed' to a more or less definite circle of people, a knowledge of both the writer and addressee (or intended circle of readers) is of vital importance. It is precisely this that Introduction is concerned with, as it seeks to clarify the occasion behind the production of a particular writing, to set out the situation and to investigate the material used to express the message, and so makes it possible for us even to arrive at a correct understanding of the message at the time it was written, and as a result, at the only correct exegesis for today. 'Introduction' understood in this sense really deserves its name.

We need to remember, however, that not all the twenty-seven writings in the New Testament have *direct* contact with the once-for-allness of revelation. They belong rather to certain lines of tradition, which can be distinguished, for example, as far as the Gospels are concerned, as independently existing traditions of the Synoptics, collections of material, logia source, Mark, Matthew, Luke—two sources theory and, as far as Paul is concerned, as pre-Pauline material, Pauline and pseudo-Pauline epistles. We shall have to trace these lines in greater detail.

And this is how the present approach is arranged. If we take the separate writings in the order in which they stand in the Canon or if we arrange them according to literary categories this will hardly make clear the history of proclamation or the various lines of tradition. The better procedure is to examine the writings in the order in which they appeared, for only in this way do the various lines of tradition emerge. We can then in the case of each writing investigate the origin of the message it contains, which will bring out its relation to the beginnings in Christ and also the form and terms which the author employs in order to 'reach' his readers.

All this of course applies not only to Introduction, but also to the theology of the New Testament. In fact we cannot really separate the two disciplines. It is only the emphasis that is different. We can express the difference by saying that Introduction is primarily concerned with the *material* in which the authors have embedded the message, whereas theology unfolds the *message* by interpreting the material. Introduction is therefore 'the other aspect of theology'—and vice-versa.

The material that is presented to us in the literary form of the writings themselves—and of their sources as well—is extremely varied. If we were to begin by making only a rough distinction, we should have to list: letter, epistle, gospel, apocalypse, which in turn contain further material of various kinds—liturgical material, confessional formulae, lists of family duties, paranetic material, concepts borrowed from the cultural environment, Old Testament quotations, etc. Occasionally one whole document forms the source for another.

It is not enough, however, just to explain, define and classify this material. The material is not an end in itself, but is used to express the message. If we concern ourselves only with the material we shall certainly see the stones, but we shall overlook the fact that these stones were part of a building. Introduction therefore always leads over into theology, but it is important for the latter to take note of the findings of Introduction, otherwise it runs the risk (to maintain the metaphor) of considering the building as the sum of its stones, but of overlooking that what is necessary is to perceive the purpose of these stones.

New Testament Introduction can therefore help in many ways to achieve a correct use of the documents. We have already referred to one essential point—that the documents should not be read as addressed to the present as 'God's Word to us', but as witnesses to their own particular time. Introduction therefore helps us to interpret the later writings in the light of those that come earlier in the line of tradition. We cannot, for example, really understand Matthew's account if we do not see his work in relation to Mark's, and we cannot interpret the pseudo-Pauline writings properly unless we see them in the light of the Pauline tradition. There are also many of Paul's statements that we cannot understand correctly unless we see the part played in his writings by older material and Old Testament quotations. Sometimes the apostle uses such material as his basis and then builds his thoughts on it, whilst at other times he includes already formulated material in his line of thought and uses it in circumstances independent of its earlier meaning.

If it is possible to allot the separate writings their p⁻ce in the various lines of tradition and to understand them in their historical context, then a problem which has often been hotly disputed becomes considerably less important—that of pseudonymity. So long as we assume the traditional idea of canonicity and accept as permanently normative only what derives from the apostles or the disciples of the apostles, as did the early Church, 'not genuine' is a serious charge to make. Apostolic authorship of course still remains important, for it expresses proximity to the origins of the tradition; but all the writings—including the 'apostolic' writings—are in the first place documents belonging to the history of dogma. If, for example, we establish that 2 Thess. cannot have been written by Paul, we cannot go on to assert that this 'does not make any great difference' (Jülicher-Fascher). On the contrary, we must draw the opposite con-clusion, that we cannot really understand 2 Thess. in its old sense (as a Pauline epistle) and that all attempts to do so have proved to be forced and to my mind have failed. But if we admit its pseudonymity we are far more likely to place the letter in its particular historical context and to be able to understand it. We can therefore state quite simply that it was when the Pauline authorship was seen to be untenable and no longer formed any obstacle to exegesis that we were able for the first time to 'grasp' the full meaning of the letter.

The question of the *recipients* is however far more important than the question of authorship. It is not enough to define the recipients from the geographical point of view; in fact this is often of very little help. It is more important in every case to discover the situation of the recipients, for in this way we can see the needs that are present in the different communities, the problems with which they are faced, the questions to which they can find no answer, etc. For it is to these situations that the various writings are directed. As we shall see, this applies not only to the letters, but it naturally comes out particularly clearly in their case. We can imagine, for example, what would have happened if Paul had sent

Phil. to Galatia and Gal. to Philippi! However correct the statements in both letters were, they would not have been understood. This point is of enormous practical importance both for the liturgical use of Scripture and for private Bible reading. Such considerations certainly make the reading of the Bible more difficult, but this is the only correct method by which it can be done. The choice is quite simple: either we read by the wrong method but take the easier way or we read by the correct method and face the difficulties. There can be no doubt that if we read by the wrong method we have little chance of coming to a correct understanding. We need to remember, however, that New Testament Introduction can render service in dealing with these new difficulties.

We must say a final word on the question of which writings have to be examined in the study of Introduction. In theory the answer should be: all proclamations from the apostolic period to our own day. If we select twenty-seven writings out of this complex, the only theological significance of this is that we are concerned with the earliest writings, with those that stand nearest in time to the once-for-allness of revelation. As we have no other access to revelation except by following back the line of tradition at the end of which we stand, we shall always arrive ultimately at one of the lines that had their origin then. To this extent these beginnings can never be ignored. Whether we draw the line at the beginning of the second century or earlier is simply a matter of choice. If we make the cut at the beginning of the second century, we are faced with a relatively compact body of literature. We could perhaps exchange 2 Pet. for the Didache and Jude for 1 Clem., but this is of no significance as far as basic principles are concerned, and we should therefore not make it a problem.

BIBLIOGRAPHY

W. G. Kümmel, *Das Neue Testament, Geschichte der Erforschung seiner Probleme* (1958)—historical survey of the different approaches to the various problems, with extensive quotations from the most important authors.

E. Dinkler, 'Bibelkritik' in *RGG*, cols. 1188 ff.

W. G. Kümmel, 'Bibelwissenschaft des NT', *ibid.*, cols. 1236 ff.

Among recent books on New Testament Introduction the following should be noted:

P. Feine–J. Behm, *Einleitung in das Neue Testament* (11 ed., 1956). A further edition, completely revised by W. G. Kümmel, appeared in 1963, but it was too late to be taken into account in the present book. All references to Feine–Behm therefore are to the eleventh edition. (E.T. *Introduction to the New Testament* (from 14 ed., 1965), SCM; Abingdon Press, 1966).

A. Jülicher–E. Fascher, *Einleitung in das Neue Testament* (7 ed., 1931).

W. Michaelis, *Einleitung in das Neue Testament* (3 ed., 1961).

A. Wikenhauser, *Einleitung in das Neue Testament* (3 ed., 1959—Catholic). (E.T. *New Testament Introduction* (from 2 ed., 1956), Herder, 1958).

The following should also be noted:

M. Albertz, *Die Botschaft des Neuen Testamentes*, I, 1 and 2; II, 1 and 2 (1947 ff.).

M. Dibelius, *Geschichte der urchristlichen Literatur* (2 vols., 1926).

On the history of New Testament Interpretation:

R. H. Fuller, *The New Testament in Current Study* (1963).

R. M. Grant, *A Short History of the Interpretation of the Bible* (1965).

A. M. Hunter, *Interpreting the New Testament, 1900–1950* (1951).

S. Neill, *The Interpretation of the New Testament, 1861–1961* (1964).

Introductory to the study of the New Testament:

R. H. Fuller, *Critical Introduction to the New Testament* (1966).

R. M. Grant, *A Historical Introduction to the New Testament* (1963).

D. Guthrie, *New Testament Introduction* (1961–5).

E. C. Hoskyns and N. Davey, *The Riddle of the New Testament* (2 ed., 1936).

A. H. McNeile, *An Introduction to the Study of the New Testament* (2 ed., 1953).

C. F. D. Moule, *The Birth of the New Testament* (2 ed., 1966).

H. F. D. Sparks, *The Formation of the New Testament* (1952).

Much important material in:

C. H. Dodd, *New Testament Studies* (1953).

T. W. Manson, *Studies in the Gospels and Epistles* (1962).

On the recurrent question of Aramaic sources:

M. Black, *An Aramaic Approach to the Gospels and Acts* (3 ed., 1967).

I. The Pauline Epistles

At least seven of the New Testament writings were written by Paul—
1 Thess., Gal., Phil., Phm., 1 and 2 Cor. and Rom. This raises a
number of common problems which we will consider first.

1. PAUL

Apart from questions such as the special situation of the recipients, which will be referred to at the appropriate times, it is important for the exegesis of the Pauline epistles to see in what order and in connection with which events in his life the apostle wrote his letters. We must therefore try to fit them into the chronology of Paul's life, then later we shall be able to draw conclusions concerning the development in the apostle's theological views. Then we shall make a preliminary survey of the literary character of these writings, of the forms used by Paul and also the traditional material (sources) and the way the apostle uses it.

(1) *The Chronology of Paul's Life.* As no date has come down to us in any of Paul's letters (neither the date of the letter itself nor of any event mentioned in any of the letters) the best we can do is to draw up a relative chronology of Paul's life which merely indicates the order of the events that are known to us and the period of time that elapsed between them. We ought to be able to achieve a relatively accurate account in this way; and if we could determine the date of only one event, this would turn the relative chronology into an absolute one.

Our sources, however, contain many gaps. The Pauline letters themselves need to be considered first. The information they provide has to be supplemented by the information contained in other documents, particularly in Acts. We shall notice straightaway certain discrepancies which show (for reasons we shall go into later—section 15) that the information in Acts cannot always be depended on. The rule therefore is that when there is a discrepancy, the evidence of the Pauline letters is to be preferred, and we shall therefore turn to them first. We can recognize fairly clearly the general pattern of three periods in the apostle's activities—the beginning, a brief middle section and the end.

We learn from Gal. i. 13–ii. 3 that Paul has previously persecuted the Christian communities (cf. 1 Cor. xv. 8), but that God then revealed his Son in him (the so-called Damascus experience), after which the apostle did not go straight to Jerusalem, but went first to Arabia and from there later back to Damascus.

It is possible that the information in 2 Cor. xi. 32 f. points to this period, as there is no definite reference to the time the events occurred.

C

The ethnarch of king Aretas is besieging Damascus and trying to capture Paul, who escapes from a window in the wall by being let down in a basket. Acts ix. 20–25 suggests that this event took place during the apostle's second stay in Damascus, although some of the details are presented differently there. It should be noted that Acts omits the stay in Arabia, and here the persecution is instigated by the Jews. This is an example of Luke's stylized treatment, whereby in Acts he traces every persecution, even those carried out by the political authorities, back to a Jewish intrigue.

Paul goes from Damascus to Jerusalem in order to meet Cephas, and he stays there for fifteen days. This took place 'after three years' (Gal. i. 18), reckoning from Paul's conversion. As in the ancient world parts of a year were included in such reckonings, we would probably be right in counting this as about two years. Afterwards, Paul goes to the regions of Syria and Cilicia and returns to Jerusalem after about thirteen years (Gal. ii. 1) for the so-called Apostolic Council. From this whole period not only do we not have a single letter by Paul, but there is also no indication that he wrote one.

At this point information about the course of events in Paul's life, as far as his own statements are concerned, breaks off, and the continuity is not resumed until we come to the last phase of his activities. Paul wrote 1 Cor. from Ephesus (1 Cor. xvi. 8) and tells of his plan to come to Corinth via Macedonia. He intends to send a mission from the church at Corinth (under his direction) to take the money that has been collected to Jerusalem (1 Cor. xvi. 3 f.). Paul seems in fact to have taken this course of action (cf. section 9). In Rom. xv. 25 he writes (presumably from Corinth) that he intends to travel to Jerusalem and then via Rome to Spain (Rom. xv. 23 ff.). For reasons which we shall deal with in connection with 2 Cor. (which itself is a collection of several Pauline letters written to Corinth partly from Ephesus and partly from Macedonia—cf. section 8) we can assume that the apostle went on a short visit to Corinth from Ephesus.

For the final phase of Paul's activity therefore the following stages emerge: Ephesus— Corinth — Ephesus — Macedonia — Corinth — Jerusalem—Rome. We do not know how long this period lasted, but if we assume that Paul was arrested in Jerusalem, taken to Rome as prisoner and there presumably executed, then it is important from the point of view of the overall picture to note that the three great Pauline letters that have come down to us (1 and 2 Cor. and Rom.) were written towards the end of his period of freedom.

When we remember that Phil. and Phm. are captivity letters, the date of which is difficult to determine (cf. sections 5 and 6), the question arises whether 1 Thess. and Gal. can be used to fill the gap between the Apostolic Council and Paul's stay in Ephesus. Gal. only raises further difficulties, for several possible theories can be applied here (section 4), but 1 Thess. does provide some clues.

Paul came from Philippi (1 Thess. ii. 2) to Thessalonica, where he founded the church. After his departure he several times planned a further visit, but 'Satan' prevented him (1 Thess. ii. 17 f.). From Athens Paul sent Timothy to Thessalonica (1 Thess. iii. 1 f.), a route which he had already taken himself, when he travelled from Ephesus (1 Cor.) via Macedonia (parts of 2 Cor.) to Corinth. The route could have led through Thessalonica and Athens, but this 'collection journey' cannot be identical with the route indicated in 1 Thess. as it presupposes a collection made in already established churches (2 Cor. viii. f.).

This is all the direct information we have from Paul himself. It is extremely sparse, for even a relative chronology can be deduced only for the first section, whilst even the connection between the three sections remains far from clear.

Against the background of the information we have gained so far we can now try to fill in the picture from the Acts of the Apostles. Paul spent about thirteen years in Syria and Cilicia (Gal. ii. 1), in the region around Antioch and Tarsus (according to Acts this was Paul's native place—cf. e.g. ix. 11). Acts introduces at this point the so-called *first missionary journey*. The starting-point is Antioch (Acts xiii. 1), then the route passes through Cyprus (xiii. 4) to Perga in Pamphylia (xiii. 13), from there northwards to Pisidian Antioch (Acts xiii. 14), then south-eastwards through Iconium (xiii. 51) to Lystra and Derbe (xiv. 6, 8, 20). On the way back he first takes the same route via Lystra, Iconium and Antioch (xiv. 21) to Perga, but from there he goes via Attalia (xiv. 25) to the starting-point, Antioch (xiv. 26). The next stage is then the Apostolic Council at Jerusalem (xv. 2).

As Paul is essentially concerned in Gal. only with his visits to Jerusalem, and the reference to the thirteen years (Gal. ii. 1) in Syria and Cilicia is no doubt to be taken as a summary account, we can call this period the first missionary journey. We cannot decide for certain whether the place references are consistent, as the question of sources is not entirely clear. It is possible that Luke is constructing here a 'model journey' in order to fill this period. Some statements which are certainly unhistorical support this view, as, for example, that Paul appointed elders in the churches he

visited (Acts xiv. 23)—an arrangement which is not to be found in the
Church until much later (section 15).

According to the account in Acts Paul comes to Jerusalem (xv. 2, 4)
for a third time (cf. ix. 26; xi. 30; xii. 25). This certainly contradicts the
account in Gal., according to which up to the composition of this letter
Paul had been in Jerusalem only twice. The best explanation appears to
be that Luke was familiar with a tradition that referred to no date,
according to which Paul once brought a collection to Jerusalem. He
linked this with the other tradition of Agabus' announcement of a famine
(xi. 28) and inserted it here—incorrectly from the historical point of view.
Errors such as this remind us of the need for caution in trying to ascertain
historical evidence from Acts.

After the Apostolic Council Paul returns to Antioch (xv. 30), from
where he soon sets out on the *second missionary journey* (xv. 36). He first
visits already established churches in Syria and Cilicia (xv. 41), and then
goes on to Derbe and Lystra (xvl. 1). His route then takes him across
Asia Minor (Phrygia and Galatia) to Troas (xvi. 8) and on to Macedonia
(xvi. 9 ff.), with calls at Samothracia, Neapolis and Philippi (xvi. 11 f.).
After his deliverance from prison he passes through Amphipolis and
Apollonia to Thessalonica (xvii. 1), where he once again meets opposition. He proceeds to Beroea (xvii. 10) where he leaves Silas and Timothy
behind (xvii. 14), then goes on to Athens (xvii. 18) and sends for the two
companions he had left behind to join him. He goes on to Corinth
(xviii. 1), where he stays a year and six months (xviii. 11) and then (after
an incident involving the proconsul Gallio) begins the return journey by
ship via Ephesus (xviii. 19) to Caesarea, from where he continues to
Jerusalem, but departs again after a short stay and returns to Antioch
(xviii. 22).

On this so-called second missionary journey we see once again the
intermediate section which we have already noted as emerging from
1 Thess.: Philippi—Thessalonica—Athens. Again, however, a number of
detailed accounts raise problems, as, for example, the Areopagus speech
(Acts xvii. 22 ff.). The account of a return to Jerusalem (xviii. 22) is also
almost certainly incorrect, for if Gal. was written after two visits to
Jerusalem (cf. section 4), it cannot be attributed to the second missionary
journey, but must have been written much later.

The so-called *third missionary journey* begins after a short stay in Antioch
(xviii. 23). Its route (according to Acts) leads through Galatia and
Phrygia (xviii. 23) to Ephesus (xviii. 24), where Paul stays exactly three
years (cf. xix. 8, 10, 22; xx. 31). It is to be noted that we are told here of

the plan to travel through Macedonia and Achaia to Jerusalem and then to Rome (xix. 21). Paul goes through Macedonia to Greece, where he stays three months (xx. 1 f.). The return journey takes him through Macedonia (xx. 3), Philippi and Troas (xx. 6) to Assos (xx. 14), from there by sea via Mitylene, Chios and Samos to Miletus (xx. 15); after a short stay he continues to Tyre (xxi. 3), Ptolemais (xxi. 7) and finally to Caesarea (xxi. 8), from where he completes the journey to Jerusalem (xxi. 15).

This account agrees essentially with those we have from Paul himself. We can assume a fairly long stay in Ephesus in the light of 1 Cor. xvi. 8, although no statement is made about the length of time (cf. also 1 Cor. xv. 32). Paul then went through Macedonia to Corinth. He does not say which return route he took to Jerusalem, but it could well be the one indicated in Acts.

Although we have brought together the many scattered details, we have not succeeded in drawing up a complete relative chronology. This makes the attempt to achieve an absolute chronology somewhat questionable. The so-called Gallio inscription,[1] which is to be found in a letter carved in stone from the Emperor Claudius to the city of Delphos, might be of assistance here. The Emperor names Gallio as the proconsul of Achaia and mentions his own 26th acclamation as ruler. As the period of office of a proconsul in a senatorial province lasted one year, and the 27th acclamation was on 1st August in the year 52, we can assume that Gallio was proconsul from about June 51 to May 52. As according to the account in Acts, Paul was in Corinth eighteen months (xviii. 11) and Gallio is mentioned in this connection (xviii. 12 f.), Paul probably left Corinth in the spring of 52, and therefore probably arrived there in the autumn of 50.

It is very difficult to work backwards from this point, because the time from the start of the second missionary journey to the arrival at Corinth can only be estimated, but it is generally assumed to be a year and a half. Compared with the thirteen years of the first missionary journey this seems very brief, but on the one hand it is doubtful whether we can make a comparison here, and on the other hand we cannot go much beyond a year and a half, as this would mean putting the Damascus experience too early. An absolute chronology therefore remains hypothetical. With this proviso we might suggest the following dates:

---

[1] Text in C. K. Barrett, *The New Testament Background: Selected Documents* (S.P.C.K., 1956), pp. 48 ff.

33/34   Damascus;
           About two years in Arabia; Damascus (Gal. i, 17 f.);
  36   Jerusalem;
           About thirteen years in Syria and Cilicia (Gal. i, 21;
           ii. 1);
           According to Acts, first missionary journey;
  49   Apostolic Council;
           Second missionary journey;
Autumn 50 to Spring 52—Corinth;
           Return to Antioch.

To fix the other events chronologically is even more difficult. The attempt has occasionally been made to construct a framework from the scattered information in Acts, which often refers to the length of stay at some of the places on the third missionary journey. The accounts in Acts have also been compared with the information available from extra-Biblical sources, but no agreement has been reached, nor could any really be expected. We cannot be certain even when Paul arrived in Rome. The theories vary between 56 and 62. According to Acts Paul had two years of relatively lenient imprisonment.

What happened afterwards is an open question. Did Paul still go to Spain, as he had planned? We find ourselves in a dilemma here. If the Pastorals were written by Paul, they can have been written only after his visit to Rome; in this case Paul must have been set free once again and it is possible that he did visit Spain, but he must also have paid another visit to the East. Paul can only have written the Pastorals (apart from other evidence which points to the contrary) if he was once again set free from imprisonment in Rome. It is impossible to put forward any definite proof. However, most of the arguments are against the Pauline authorship of the Pastorals (section 18); it is a surprising fact that we have no direct evidence of any of Paul's later activities.

Some later traditions do speak of a renewed activity in the East by the apostle, especially that in the so-called Muratorian Fragment (c. 180),[2] which refers to a journey to Spain. It is possible to deduce this also from a passage in 1 Clem. (v. 5–7), which was written in Rome about 96. But the exegesis here is debatable. In any case this passage in 1 Clem. is the earliest evidence for Paul's martyrdom in Rome, but we cannot be sure whether this was connected with the Neronian persecutions. So the course of Paul's life is lost in the mists of history. Only a short stretch of it

[2] Text in H. Bettenson, *Documents of the Christian Church* (2 ed., 1963), pp. 40 ff.

is reasonably accessible, in essence the period in which he wrote his letters.

BIBLIOGRAPHY

G. Bornkamm, 'Paulus' in *RGG*, V, cols. 166 ff.

R. Bultmann, 'Paulus' in *RGG* (2 ed.), IV, cols. 1019 ff.

M. Dibelius, *Paulus*, edited by W. G. Kümmel (2 ed., 1956). (E. T. *Paul* (from 1 ed.), Longmans, Green & Co.; Westminster Press, 1953).

G. B. Caird, *The Apostolic Age* (1955).

W. D. Davies, 'The Apostolic Age and the Life of Paul' in Peake's *Commentary on the Bible*, Ed. M. Black and H. H. Rowley (1962).

G. Ogg, 'The Chronology of the New Testament' (ibid.).

(2) *Paul's Use of Letters as a Means of Proclamation.* (a) *Letters in the Framework of Early Christian Literature.* It was by no means a matter of course that literature came into being in the early Church. Indeed there were three important factors standing in the way of its production. In the first place, the early Church had its strongest hold in the lower social strata, where one does not generally expect much literary activity. In addition, the early Church did not develop in a closed cultural sphere, and therefore an essential condition for the emergence of literature is missing. The main obstacle, however, is presented by an actually anti-literary factor, namely the understanding of history that prevailed in the early Christian communities, the main feature of which was the expectation of an imminent *parousia*. In these circumstances one does not write, but proclaims directly by word of mouth. The literary documents assembled in the New Testament are therefore preceded by a broad stream of oral tradition, which later flows into the Gospels. We can therefore speak—in a qualified sense at least—of 'literature' to the extent that the oral tradition was subject to certain formal patterns, which prevented any violent distortion of what was handed down.

The circumstances behind the growth of occasional literature are a little different. It could well be more necessary (despite the expectation of an early *parousia*) that answers should be given to inquiries and that difficulties that arose in the churches should be dealt with quickly. For this reason primitive Christian literature—insofar as its records have been preserved—began in letter-form. It is in this form that we find twenty-one out of the twenty-seven books of the New Testament.

There are certain distinctions we need to make here. Not all these letters are very early, and they are not all real letters. Sometimes an author uses the letter just as a literary art-form, which was very popular in the ancient world, but there is very little evidence of this kind of influence in the New Testament. A much stronger influence is that of the Pauline letters. This is true at least for the pseudo-Pauline letters, but also for some of the Church epistles, although the problems to which they give rise are different.

Deißmann[3] made the suggestion that we should make a distinction in terminology between letter and epistle, 'letter' being taken to mean a real letter, and 'epistle' a literary document which uses the letter form. This distinction has been widely adopted, and it can be valuable, although it is not always possible to make an exact division. For example, if we describe Eph. as an epistle (section 17), we cannot go on to describe Col. as an epistle with the same certainty, although they are closely related in many respects (section 18). The boundary between the two is therefore fluid. Quite apart from this, however, these descriptions are not adequate. Heb. for example has the form of a homily, but its form changes into that of a letter in the closing verses (section 19). 1 Pet. presents similar problems (section 21). Each case has to be decided separately. The question—letter or epistle?—is significant in so far as the author has particular recipients in mind or is writing quite generally for his contemporaries. One thing that is certain is that according to this distinction the 'genuine' Pauline letters are to be regarded as letters.

Paul uses the form of the letter that prevailed in the ancient world. He begins with the Greek pattern, but varies it and approaches very close to the oriental pattern. In the Greek type the opening consists of one sentence. The sender is mentioned first (Nominative), followed by the recipient (Dative), and then comes—elliptically—a χαίρειν. λέγει or ἐπέστειλεν is understood.[4] In other words: A says 'Hail' to B, or A sends B greetings. We find this formula in the New Testament, in Acts xiv. 23, xxiii. 26 and Jas. i. 1. The two passages in Acts do not contain actual letters, but letters used as a stylistic device by Luke to give liveliness to his account. He still retains the Greek pattern. The shortest example is in Acts xxiii. 26: Κλαύδιος Λυσίας τῷ κρατίστῳ ἡγεμόνι Φήλικι χαίρειν ('Claudius Lysias unto the most excellent Governor Felix, greeting').

It is possible for the χαίρειν to be omitted, and there is an example of this in Rev. i. 4. Paul however, always replaces the χαίρειν with a full greeting beginning with χάρις ὑμῖν . . . ('Grace be with you . . .'). In

---

[3] *Bibelstudien* (1895), pp. 189 ff. (E.T. *Bible Studies*, T. & T. Clark, 2 ed., 1903, pp. 3 ff.); *Licht vom Osten* (4 ed., 1923), pp. 194 ff. (E.T. *Light from the Ancient East*, pp. 228 ff., Doran 1927; reissued Baker Book House, n.d.).

[4] Blaß-Debrunner, sect. 389; 480, 5. Bauer, art. χαίρω.

this he approaches the oriental pattern, which has two sentences in the introduction—the sender writes to the recipient: May blessings be multiplied upon you. There are echoes of this in 1 Pet. i. 1–2, though considerably expanded.

Both types could be expanded in a similar way, but there are no parallels in ancient literature to the way in which Paul expands his introductions. He describes himself as sender more precisely, and also the recipient; and we can sometimes trace a certain correspondence between the phrasing of the introduction and the subsequent content of the letter. We can see therefore from the pattern he uses for his letters that although Paul adopts traditional forms, he fills them with new content by means of the changes he makes. It was customary for a brief farewell greeting to come at the end of a letter, but Paul changes this into an expression of blessing.

(b) *Literary Problems Presented by Paul's Letters.* As the writings of Paul that we have to consider are real letters which were written for specific reasons to particular recipients, we would expect to find that the apostle expresses himself freely and independently, and this is in fact the case for the most part. However, a careful examination of the documents from the literary and stylistic standpoint shows that Paul on the one hand occasionally incorporated into his letters existing material, and on the other hand from time to time uses stylistic devices which we find in contemporary literature and are in fact adopted from it. It is important to recognize this, as otherwise there is the danger of taking these traditions and devices he has adopted as Pauline and of coming to an exaggerated or in some other way mistaken estimate of what Paul says. The problems arise in the individual letters and are different in each case, and therefore cannot be set out here in full, but we can refer to some of the main factors.

We can recognize where Paul is taking over an already formulated *kerygma* relatively easily when he indicates it by the 'framework' terminology, as, for example, when he says that he has received and delivered the tradition of the Lord's Supper (1 Cor. xi. 23–25). The terms used here (παραλαμβάνειν and παραδιδόναι) correspond to the Rabbinic terminology for the passing on of tradition (קִבֵּל מִן—received by and לְ מָסַר ?—delivered to). The same applies to the *kerygma* set out in 1 Cor. xv. 3 ff., though we cannot be altogether certain here just where Paul is using his own phraseology, particularly in v. 6 and v. 8 onwards. Paul also took over the so-called Christ-hymn (Phil. ii. 5–11), but a careful analysis shows that the apostle made alterations in the text.

Whilst the extent of the traditional material in these cases is relatively large and the fact that such material is present is easily recognized, this becomes much more difficult in the passages where there are shorter, mostly confessional-type phrases, for example in Rom. x. 9, 1 Cor. xii. 3 (κύριος Ἰησοῦς—the Lord is Jesus) or Rom. i. 3 f. (an early confessional or possibly baptismal formula).

The aphoristic or paranetic material adopted by Paul is more easily recognizable. This includes, for example, the so-called catalogues of virtue and vice, which occur quite frequently (catalogue of virtue: Phil. iv. 8; Rom. xii. 2; catalogue of vice: 1 Cor. v. 11, vi. 9 f.; 2 Cor. xii. 20; Rom. i. 29–32; catalogue of vice and virtue together: Gal. v. 19–22). This last example shows very clearly how Paul uses the traditional material. He introduces the list of vices with 'works of the flesh' and the list of virtues with 'fruits of the spirit'. This is a case of Pauline interpretation of tradition. In making an exegesis of the passage therefore we have to remember that Paul is not concerned here with the individual virtues or vices, and that we should not look for any deliberate arrangement of the material. What is decisive for the arrangement is often the stylistic consideration, whilst the material itself is interchangeable. On the other hand it is important to bear in mind that for Paul the 'vices' are not really vices but works of the flesh, and that the 'virtues' are not really virtues but fruits of the spirit. In making an exegesis we have to start from this point.

Another kind of catalogue is the so-called 'peristatic' catalogue (from περίστασις=circumstance, condition). Here the circumstances which someone has had to face are listed, as for example in Rom. viii. 35. It is rather different in 2 Cor. xi. 21 ff., because although Paul uses the form of the peristatic catalogue, he lists the events which have actually taken place in his life.

In the pseudo-Pauline writings, finally, we find the lists of household responsibilities (Eph. v. 22 ff.; Col. iii. 18 ff.; 1 Tim. ii. 8 ff.; 1 Pet. ii. 13 ff.). What we find here are catalogues of duties (in form and content pre-Christian) for the different members of the household, husband, wife, children, slaves, etc. We can sometimes see from these lists the way in which the ethics of the ancient world were christianized. This is done from the point of view of form by interpretative additions such as 'in Christ', etc.; as far as exegesis is concerned, the same applies as was said above with reference to the catalogues of virtue and vice.

As far as Old Testament quotations are concerned, we have to distinguish between those 'quotations' which have simply become part of the text, where Old Testament phrases (often very brief) have been incorporated completely into the context and those quotations which Paul consciously uses as such. It is not always certain where the dividing line lies, and we cannot always be sure whether Paul is consciously using Old Testament phrases. It is possible that they are simply part of his vocabulary. When we apply this distinction we see that there is no uniformity in Paul's practice in his letters. There are frequent quotations in Gal., 1 and 2 Cor. and Rom., but hardly any or none at all in 1 Thess., Phil. and Phm., but there are 'incorporated' quotations in all the letters with the exception of Phm. It is not necessary to give examples here, as the quotations are indicated in the Nestle text by heavy print.

In the framework of New Testament Introduction this question of the way in which traditional material is used is by no means of interest only from the point of view of literary criticism, but can also be of great significance for exegesis. The more consciously an author uses a quotation, the greater care the exegete needs to take. All these quotations, whether from the Old Testament, the primitive Christian *kerygma* or some other source, already had of course their own particular meaning in their context, but we cannot simply carry this original meaning over and then take it to be a statement of Paul's views. We need to note carefully in connection with which line of thought the apostle alludes to or uses the quotation. Often only one aspect of the original meaning is taken over, and often the decisive factor is the way in which the earlier statement is modified or the context in which it appears.

It will be helpful if we draw a distinction in terminology here between explanation and exegesis. If we take exegesis to mean the repetition in my language of what an author wanted to say to his readers, then we can say that explanation is concerned with the understanding of the quotations in their original context. It can also be used as exegesis if it asks the question what the author of the tradition used by Paul wanted to say to his original readers. This earlier exegesis, however, is in the framework of the exegesis of Paul's letters 'explanation', a preliminary to the work of exegesis; for the exegesis of a Pauline letter is something quite different from the sum total of the various explanations. We meet the problem wherever editorial work is present or where ideas have merely been adopted by a scribe.

If we wish to understand correctly Paul's use of the Old Testament, we must bear in mind that his method of exegesis is different from ours today. He uses the so-called allegorical method, which has played a part in many religions with sacred texts. The purpose of this method is to adhere to the traditional texts, although their original meaning has very little significance for a later age. The literal meaning is therefore abandoned and an allegorical exegesis is applied, with the result that the text is made to say something different (ἄλλα ἀγορεύειν). This generally leads to a deeper, more fundamental meaning than the literal reading suggests. If we often think of this method today as arbitrary, we must remember that allegorical exegesis is an attempt to deal with a need to which later ages have given rise, and that this exegesis is often applied only to the passages which present difficulties. It is not surprising therefore that this kind of exegesis is often arbitrary.

As far as Paul is concerned we cannot really speak of pure allegorizing, for he tends to turn it in the direction of typology. This means that Paul draws upon the Old Testament in his argument when he sees in it a typological parallel to Christian statements. So, for example, in 1 Cor. x. 1 ff. he develops the problem of 'sacrament and ethics' by reference to Old Testament events. In Gal. iv. 21 ff. he expounds freedom from the Law by an allegorical exegesis (N.B. Gal. iv. 24)—given a typological bearing —of the story of Abraham and his wives and their children.

We need to bear in mind all the time that Paul is not concerned with the Old Testament story as such, as we read it today, but with its 'Christian' message. He does not use the Old Testament as a text from which he sets out and which he interprets; his 'text' is rather the particular Christian lesson which he seeks to clarify by reference to the Old Testament for his Jewish-thinking readers or those who at least are influenced by Jewish thought. This way of using the Old Testament is implicitly apologetic, to the extent that Paul shows that the Old Testament speaks in his support, or rather in support of his Christian convictions. This is precisely what he succeeds in doing by his form of exegesis.

Paul, however, is aware of the problems that this approach raises, for he knows that it is possible to draw an entirely different meaning from the same texts. Nevertheless he asserts that whoever arrives at a different result (which is the case with Jewish exegesis which also to some extent adopts the allegorical approach) is reading the Old Testament 'through the veil' (2 Cor. iii. 14). It is clear therefore that Pauline exegesis of the Old Testament is not really a method (which one might come to revise), but is really a confession of faith. It is also clear that the purpose of Paul's use of the Old Testament is not to attract Christians to the Old Testament, but the opposite of this—to use the Old Testament when writing to those who are familiar with it in support of his own argument. There is no indication that Paul introduced the Old Testament to purely Gentile

Christian churches (e.g. Thessalonica), but occasionally it was introduced later by others (Galatia) or it became known in some other way (Corinth and Rome). Then Paul has to come to terms with it or he can at least draw examples from it.

BIBLIOGRAPHY

R. Bultmann, *Der Stil der paulinischen Predigt und die kynisch-stoische Diatribe* (1910).

A. Deißmann, *Licht vom Osten* (4 ed., 1923). (E.T. *Light from the Ancient East*, Baker Book House, n.d.).

E. Fascher, 'Briefliteratur, urchristliche, formgeschichtlich' in *RGG*, I, cols. 1412 ff.

H. Thyen, *Der Stil der jüdisch-hellenistischen Homilie* (1955).

O. Roller, *Das Formular der paulinischen Briefe* (1933).

F. F. Bruce, 'The Epistles of Paul' in Peake's *Commentary on the Bible*, Ed. M. Black and H. H. Rowley (1962).

P. Carrington, *The Primitive Christian Catechism* (1940).

C. H. Dodd, *The Apostolic Preaching and its Developments* (1936) and *According to the Scriptures* (1952).

2. THE FIRST EPISTLE TO THE THESSALONIANS

During the second missionary journey Paul came from Philippi to Thessalonica (1 Thess. ii. 2) and established a church there (i. 5 f.). After his departure he several times planned a further visit, but was prevented from making it (ii. 17 f.). He sent Timothy from Athens to the Thessalonians (iii. 1 f.), and in the meantime he has returned to the apostle with good news (iii. 6).

(1) *Contents.* The introduction (i. 1), compared with that in Paul's later letters, is relatively short. Silvanus and Timothy are mentioned as being associated with Paul in the sending of the letter. The recipient is the church in Thessalonica, the capital of the Roman province of Macedonia.

The first part of the letter (i. 2–iii. 13) falls into four sections.

(a) The thanksgiving (i. 2–10) has a similar form to that in the other Pauline letters. The apostle gives the content of his prayer of thanksgiving. He mentions the founding of the church (v. 5), which received the word in affliction, but with joy (v. 6) and therefore became an example for all believers in Macedonia and Achaia (where Paul is staying at the time he is writing the letter—see below). The apostle describes the church as his 'imitator' (μιμηταί, v. 6). He indicates here a relationship of dependence: Paul—the Thessalonians—other churches: a line which goes back through Paul direct to the Lord (ἡμῶν . . . καὶ τοῦ κυρίου, v. 6). This is not simply a line of missionary activity repeating itself in events, but an expression of the fact that the proclamation takes place not only in words (v. 5) but also through the whole Christian life and witness of the preacher. As the content of the message Paul mentions turning away from idols and turning to the living God—'And to wait for his Son from heaven, whom he raised from the dead, even Jesus, which delivereth us from the wrath to come'.

(b) ii. 1–12. Paul turns again to the past, to things with which his readers are familiar. He reminds them that after the persecution he suffered in Philippi he still proclaimed the Gospel among them with a good heart. Then follows (or so it appears—see below) an apologia: the apostle did not speak to please men, he did not come with flattering words, and did not seek men's approval; in order to be a burden to nobody, he earned his own living.

(c) ii. 13–16. A further thanksgiving for the reception of the Word by the church. The persecutions suffered by the Christians in Thessalonica at the hands of their fellow-countrymen are placed alongside the persecution of the Jewish churches by the Jews. The Thessalonians have become μιμηταί (imitators) of these churches, which is shown by a few examples. The *tertium comparationis* is persecution by one's own compatriots, which is explained by the fact that the persecutors are not men who seek to please God.

(d) ii. 17–iii. 13. Paul now speaks of his relationship to the church after his departure from Thessalonica. He has not been able to carry out a visit which he has twice planned (ii. 17–20). Out of concern for the church the apostle then sent Timothy from Athens to the church in order to strengthen it (iii. 1–5). He came back with good news, which is a relief to Paul, but only increases his desire to see the people again (vv. 6–10a). He would like to put right what is still amiss in the church, and embodies his wish in a further prayer which turns into an intercession (vv. 10b–13).

The second part of the letter (iv. 1–v. 22) develops directly out of these verses. It represents in effect a substitute for the presence of the apostle in Thessalonica. In chs. i.–iii. Paul expressed his train of thought up to the present, and now he writes about what he would have actually said or done if he had been present in Thessalonica. He points out the right way for the church.

(a) Paul exhorts the members of the church to walk perfectly (iv. 1–12) by reminding them of what he proclaimed at the founding of the church and giving a few practical instructions, interrupted by the assurance that the church is nevertheless on the right road. The most important thing is to give no cause for reproach to their non-Christian neighbours.

(b) iv. 13–18. Paul addresses himself to an immediate problem in the church: the death of certain members in Thessalonica had raised the question of what would happen to the departed who had not lived to see the *parousia* which was expected soon. Paul sets out here (as far as we can tell, for the first time in the early Church) statements concerning the Christian hope of resurrection: those who have fallen asleep in Christ suffer no disadvantage over against those who will still be living at the *parousia* (among which the apostle includes himself and the members of the church).

(c) Although Paul has reassured the church in this way, it is not meant to undermine the expectation of the Day of the Lord (v. 1–11). The question of the End (the Day will come suddenly) is immediately given an ethical application: those who are looking for the Day ought now to live as children of the day.

(d) A series of general exhortations follows (v. 12–22). The church should pay regard to those who labour on its behalf, keep peace, correct the disorderly, encourage the faint-hearted, etc. The conclusion (v. 23–28) contains a further expression of the desire for peace, a request for inter-cession, an exhortation to read the letter aloud and a blessing.

(2) *Background*. The contents of the letter make clear to some extent the 'history' of Paul's dealings with the church: starting from its foundation, the departure of the apostle and on to the sending of Timothy, his return to the apostle and the writing of the letter. The document occupies a quite definite place in this story; it furthers the story and (at least by the expressed desire for another visit—iii. 10) looks to the future. When we come to examine this history a number of problems present themselves.

We will begin with a comparison with Acts xvii. 1–10. According to this account, the mission of Paul and Silas (Timothy is not mentioned in this connection in Acts) begins in the synagogue, where Paul preached on three sabbath days. The mission has greater success among the God-fearing Greeks than among the Jews, who become jealous, stir up the mob, and stage an uproar. A certain Jason, in whose house they seek in vain for Paul and Silas, and a few Christians are dragged before the rulers of the city, but after the payment of a security they are set free. Paul and Silas are sent away during the night and go to Beroea, where they go straight to the synagogue again. According to this account the church in Thessalonica contains both Jewish and Gentile Christians, and Paul had to make a secret escape from the city because of a plot instigated by Jews. The reference to Paul's preaching on three sabbath days could be taken to imply a brief stay of three weeks. But there are certain difficulties that arise.

The evidence of 1 Thess. suggests that we should think of a church of Gentile Christians (N.B. i. 9). Besides, there is no mention in the letter of difficulties stirred up by the Jews for Paul during his stay in Thessalonica. iii. 4 suggests the contrary, and i. 6 and ii. 2 do not support the idea. Strangely the apostle does not mention either that he had to leave the city against his will. ii. 14 refers to later persecutions, after Paul's depar-ture. The church experienced the same from its compatriots as the Christian communities in Judaea did from the Jews.

When we remember that it is one of the features of Luke's account to make Paul begin his mission in the synagogue (in Acts xvii. 10 Paul goes straight back into the synagogue in Beroea; cf. also Gal. ii. 7), and that Luke also represents the persecution of Christians as instigated by Jews for this reason, cf. section 15, 3) then we have good grounds here for treating the account in Acts with a certain scepticism. It is more than likely that the church in Thessalonica consisted only of Gentile Christians, therefore persecution of the apostle in Thessalonica must be considered improbable at least.

The question of the length of Paul's stay is also an open one. As on the one hand Paul earned his own living (ii. 9) and on the other hand left behind him a lively church, we have to assume a longer period than three or four weeks. This is confirmed by Phil. iv. 15 f., according to which the Philippians sent gifts to Thessalonica for Paul for his support on at least two occasions (a distance of about 150 km.). We cannot be sure of the exact length of his stay.

The fact that the apostle was troubled about the relatively well-established church after his departure (ii. 17; iii. 1, 5) does not need to have had any immediate cause. To leave behind a newly established church in a pagan environment is always a risk for a missionary, and Paul may have heard of persecutions in the church when he was staying at some other place (iii. 4).

We should not allow too long for the period between Paul's departure and the writing of the letter. We need to think in terms of several months (allowing for Timothy's visit to Thessalonica from Athens and his return), but there is no reason to assume that the letter was not written until after the second missionary journey. Such a late date has occasionally been suggested. This question has no direct bearing upon the exegesis of 1 Thess., but it has an indirect significance. The order of composition of Paul's letters would have to be revised, and this would have a bearing upon the tracing of the development of the apostle's theological thought. In the exegesis of a later letter we can therefore presuppose ideas which we have found in an earlier one. We need to be much more cautious, however, in the exegesis of an earlier letter in calling to our aid ideas from a later letter, which had not yet become part of the apostle's thinking at that earlier period. Michaelis suggests that 1 Thess. was written on the third missionary journey during the fairly long stay at Ephesus, but his arguments in support of this are hardly convincing. It is true that according to Acts xviii. 15 ff. Paul was in Athens without Timothy (so that the apostle cannot have sent him to Thessalonica from Athens) but it is a questionable procedure to base our argument on the accuracy of Luke's account, for Silvanus, who is mentioned in connection with the sending of the letter (i. 1), was not in Ephesus with Paul (cf. Acts xix. 1 ff.). Silvanus (Silas according to Acts) is mentioned there for the last time in Acts

D

xviii. 5. Acts makes no reference to a second visit to Athens by Paul. But we cannot on the one hand rely on the accuracy of Acts and on the other hand make allowance for two inconsistencies it contains, when we have based our argument on the historical reliability of the account. It does not follow that the deaths that have taken place (iv. 13 ff.) imply a late date. Nor do we need to think of the church as being made up of old people, for we have to remember on the one hand that the church has experienced a persecution and on the other hand there need have been only one death to give rise to the question of the future of the departed.

We have therefore to come back to the idea of an early date. The letter was probably written about the year 50 from Athens or Corinth. 1 Thess. is the earliest letter by Paul, but we cannot say for certain whether it was the earliest of all or merely the earliest of the letters that have been preserved.

(3) *Occasion and Purpose*. The occasion of the letter could have been the enquiry (conveyed evidently by Timothy) about the departed (iv. 13), but this is hardly an adequate explanation of the origin of the letter. In particular, it does not explain the breadth of the first part, nor why Paul goes into such detail about matters with which the church is familiar. We need to understand this reminder of the beginnings of the church in relation to the present situation.

The church has experienced a persecution by its compatriots. We are not told that it is now being persecuted, but we have to allow for the possibility of further intrigues. When Paul arrived in Thessalonica he came from a persecution in Philippi (ii. 1 f.), and at that time on his first visit he spoke to the Thessalonians of the troubles that awaited them (iii. 3 f.). The relationship of the church to its environment was therefore not without tension, and the members must take care that they give no cause for hostility (iv. 12). There is virtually a repetition in the church of what Paul experienced at its foundation, or shortly before. The Thessalonians have become 'imitators' of Paul (i. 6 f.), also 'imitators' of the churches in Judaea (ii. 14), and 'examples' to other churches (i. 7 f.). They have received their strength from what Paul delivered to them as the messenger of his Lord (ii. 2), and this is what they are to 'remember' as they now live their lives as Christians in a pagan environment. This detailed review of the past is therefore not for the sake of historical reminiscence, but it has a kerygmatic character, as it issues the summons to go on living by the call that was heard at the beginning. If we see the details in this light we avoid the danger in our exegesis of drawing from them historical reminiscences, and it also becomes clear that Paul is stating something familiar, but not obvious, that he is in fact stating the familiar with a kerygmatic emphasis.

In this light we can also understand the so-called apologia by the apostle (ii. 1–12), in which Paul declares his preaching to have been free from all impure motives. Many of the features here can no doubt be linked with later policies against Gnostics, but it is not to be assumed that we are concerned in 1 Thess. with a defence against such attacks. It is rather the general problem posed by the environment. Paul distinguishes himself from pagan miracle-mongers, charlatans who travelled through the country canvassing for their gods, performing miracles and living by their preaching. This apologia follows the reference to the fact that Paul was persecuted in Philippi. The persecution, however, has not made him doubt his mission—even when faced with the charlatans. The church also has now experienced a persecution, but it too must not doubt its message, even if faced with these impostors with their miracle-mongering and their trickery. The reminder of Paul's preaching once again has the purpose of bringing the church back to its beginnings, when it was turned by the apostolic preaching from idols to the living God.

What really matters therefore is not remembrance of the past, but going forward into the future, and this is where instruction and exhortation play their part. It seems remarkable that during his stay in Thessalonica Paul said nothing to the church about the resurrection of the dead, and even more remarkable that Timothy apparently could not answer their query. This is connected with the expectation of an early *parousia*, which Paul and the church shared (iv. 13 ff.; v. 1 ff.; cf. i. 10; ii. 19; iii. 13). The nearer the expectation of the *parousia*, the smaller is the part played by the question of what happens to the dead. We do not know whether Paul had been faced with the question before. It can hardly have played a major part, as Paul otherwise would have spoken about it in Thessalonica—as he often does in the later epistles (Phil. i. 21; 1 Cor. xv.; 2 Cor. v., etc.). In this passage therefore (iv. 13 ff.) we have the earliest testimony to the Christian hope of resurrection. Paul answers the question by pressing the faith of the Thessalonians to its logical conclusion: it is not only Christians who are alive who belong to Christ; death does not dissolve this union; the dead are 'dead in Christ' ($\nu\epsilon\kappa\rho o\grave{\iota}$ $\dot{\epsilon}\nu$ $X\rho\iota\sigma\tau\hat{\omega}$, iv. 16). This forward-looking faith is immediately (v. 1 ff.) given an ethical application. It is not possible for us to trace back the practical directions at the conclusion of the letter to actual difficulties in the church. The repeated reference to the fact that the church is on the right road (i. 7 f.; ii. 13, iii. 6 f.; iv. 1, 9 f.) should prevent us from seeing unexpected difficulties here. The message of the conclusion is rather that the church should continue (iii. 12; iv. 1) by brotherly, peaceful behaviour to offer no opportunity to those outside for evil slander (iv. 10–12).

The whole letter can therefore be understood as a unity in its historical setting: it is a pastoral letter to the church in Thessalonica addressed to the actual situation in which it finds itself, a situation where it is important to strengthen the first steps in the Christian life against attacks and against doubt (resurrection of the dead), so that the church, remembering its beginnings, can confidently continue on the road upon which it has set out.

The clear structure and inner consistency of the letter do not lend support to the idea which has been put forward that 1 Thess. is the work of an editor who divided two originally separate letters of Paul to Thessalonica into seven parts, expanded them with non-Pauline material and from this by a process of editorial compilation formed 1 Thess. as we know it.[5]

BIBLIOGRAPHY

M. Dibelius, *An die Thessalonicher I, II, an die Philipper* (Lietzmann, 3 ed., 1937).

E. von Dobschütz, Die *Thessalonicherbriefe* (Meyer, 7 ed., 1909).

E. Bammel, 'Judenverfolgung und Naherwartung. Zur Eschatologie des Ersten Thessalonicherbriefes', *ZThK* (1959), pp. 294 ff.

Commentaries: J. E. Frame, ICC (1912); W. Neil, Moffatt (1950).

C. E. Faw, 'On the Writing of First Thessalonians', *JBL* 71 (1952), pp. 217 ff.

[5] Contrast K. G. Eckard, 'Der zweite echte Brief des Apostels Paulus an die Thessalonicher', *ZThK* (1961), pp. 30 ff.; cf. W. G. Kümmel, 'Das Problem des ersten Thessalonicherbriefes' in *Neotestamentica et Patristica*, Essays presented to Oscar Cullmann (1962), pp. 213 ff.

3. THE SECOND EPISTLE TO THE THESSALONIANS

In the case of 1 Thess. we could begin with an approximate placing of the letter in the chronology of Paul's life and the story of his relationship with the church, but we cannot do that here. If it actually is the second letter to Thessalonica (which the letter itself does not claim, but the secondary heading), then it should be possible with the help of this letter to trace the story of the apostle's dealings with the church a stage beyond that of 1 Thess.

(1) *Contents.* The introduction (i. 1–2) is almost the same word for word as 1 Thess. i. 1, and only the conclusion has been expanded. We do not find such a close parallel in any other of Paul's letters.

The first section (i. 3–12) begins with a thanksgiving (3 f.) which, although many of its phrases are reminiscent of 1 Thess., is very much shorter. The church is spoken of as positively as in 1 Thess., but here Paul praises the Thessalonian church along with the other churches (according to 1 Thess. i. 9 others mention the Thessalonians with praise for their treatment of Paul). The apostle then goes on directly to the theme of the *parousia*, which will bring recompense (5–10). The persecution of the church, which is obviously thought of here as going on at the present time, is a sign of the righteous judgement of God, for at the *parousia* the oppression which the persecutors inflict upon the church will be repaid, and the church which is at present afflicted—together with the apostle—will receive its recompense. The *parousia* itself is described in the apocalyptic style in vivid colours. A prayer follows (11 f.), that God may make the church worthy of its calling, and fulfil all its works, so that the name of Jesus may be glorified. The striking feature in this first section is the strongly forward-looking character of the whole passage. In view of the present misery of persecution salvation is looked for exclusively in the future.

The second section (ii. 1–12) contains an apocalyptic prospect. The day of the Lord is not coming immediately (1 1.), and the church should not allow itself to be easily shaken when people come and say, claiming to appeal to Paul, that the day of the Lord has already come. The great man of sin, who sets himself up against God and puts himself in God's place has first to come (3–5). The church needs to remember what Paul said when he was with the church. This man of sin is still bound, and will not be revealed until the time (καιρός) appointed for him (6 f.). When this restraint is removed he will emerge from his hiding (8), but Jesus will destroy him with the breath of his mouth. The revelation of this man of sin will be linked with deceit and corruption (9 f.). God sends the power of corruption in order that men may believe the lie. All those who do not believe the truth will be judged (11 f.). It is clear that over against an extremely heightened expectation of the *parousia* Paul is outlining an apocalyptic 'time-table' which, by listing the events that have first to be awaited, has the effect of postponing the 'day'. The future nature of salvation is again set out here emphatically.

The third section (ii. 13–iii. 5) contains first a renewed thanksgiving for the church (ii. 13–17). God has chosen the members of the church as the first-fruits of a future salvation. This has taken place through Paul's preaching. The church should now stand fast and preserve the traditions which they have received from Paul by word of mouth or in writing. This is followed by a request for intercession (iii. 1 f.) that Paul too may be delivered from evil men. Finally Paul expresses his confidence that God will strengthen and preserve the church, and that it will hold faithfully to the apostolic instructions (iii. 3–5). Whereas the first and second sections look to the future, this one looks to the past insofar as the church is told that it will only survive in the future if it remains loyal to the apostolic message.

The fourth section (iii. 6–16) introduces a new theme. The church is to sever connections with those who lead a disorderly life. This is not the way to imitate Paul, for he did not lead an idle life among the Thessalonians but, although as an apostle he was not obliged to do it, he worked day and night. When he was with the Thessalonians he had declared that he who would not work should not eat either. But now he has heard that some are disorderly and idle. These people are warned; but the church is instructed to have no fellowship with those who are disobedient, although it will seek to admonish them in a brotherly spirit. The ('model and imitator') idea is not given an existential interpretation here, as in 1 Thess., but is just used in the ethical sense.

In the conclusion to the letter (iii. 17–18) the emphasis on Paul's signature in his own hand is to be noted.

(2) *The Situation of the Church.* The occasion of this letter is obviously quite different from that of 1 Thess. Something has happened in the church that makes an intervention necessary. Eschatological fanatics have announced that the day of the Lord has already come (ii. 2). This

passage presents difficulties from the point of view of exegesis. What is the meaning of ἐνέστηκεν ἡ ἡμέρα τοῦ κυρίου? The sense of the words is quite plain: 'The day of the Lord has come, is present', but is this really the meaning? 'The day of the Lord' is an apocalyptic idea, but if we interpret it along the lines of apocalyptic, this meaning is impossible as the day is expected to bring with it a series of cosmic events, so that there can be no doubt as to whether it has come or not. Sometimes the passage is therefore interpreted to mean that the day of the Lord has come near, is immediately at hand, but this is not really what it says. The difficulty disappears if we recognize that here a Gnostic idea is being expressed apocalyptically. Gnostics could readily speak of the resurrection as having already taken place (e.g. 2 Tim. ii. 18); and the Gnostic, if he is a spiritual man, is already risen in his spirit—by means of gnosis—and freed from bondage to this world. From this point of view we can understand the phrase. When the apocalyptic writer speaks of the fulfilment, he knows that it will not happen until the day of the Lord, but the Gnostic can say that the fulfilment has already come. If the apocalyptic writer expresses this Gnostic conviction in his own language, he will say: The day of the Lord has already come.

This provides us with a clue for understanding the whole situation. The church has been confused by eschatological fanatics of Gnostic origin with the assertion that the fulfilment has already come. Against this assertion Paul sets an apocalyptic 'time-table' which enumerates the events which have to take place before the End, in order to show that the fulfilment cannot possibly have taken place as some assert. The apocalyptic material that is used here has a long tradition behind it. In Dan. xi. 36 we find it applied to Antiochus Epiphanes, and later it is used against Caligula and Nero. We cannot tell who is envisaged in this passage. If we knew it would of course throw light on the question of the authorship of the letter and the time of its composition. On the other hand, these two questions determine the possible people to whom this ancient motif could apply here. In this connection, however, it is enough to see for what purpose the material is used, and this is quite plain. The lesson is that the End has not yet come, as the 'time-table' must first run its course.

Another feature which is in accord with the Gnostic heresy is the idle and disorderly way of life, which is attacked in iii. 6–16. There are two possible ethical consequences of the Gnostic way of thinking, both springing from the fact that the Gnostic who claims to be perfected in the spirit has no more concern with the σάρξ (the flesh). This leads either to rigorism or (more often, and no doubt also in this instance) to libertinism.

The situation in the church is now clear. It is true that it is commended —somewhat strangely—for being in good order and that Paul can glory in the church (i. 3 f.), in phrases which strongly echo those of 1 Thess.; but errors for which the support of Paul has evidently been claimed (ii. 2) must have had some effect, for the disorderly conduct is to be found within the church itself. The Gnostic heresy has therefore become a problem, and this situation is the occasion for the letter. This makes one fact quite clear: if we draw a comparison with 1 Thess., it becomes obvious that we are faced with two quite different situations as far as the church is concerned. In this sense the two letters are to two different churches, and have therefore to be interpreted as statements addressed to two different churches.

(3) *The Relationship between I and II Thessalonians.* We are now confronted with a new problem—the fact that both letters are addressed to Thessalonica. We have to ask whether one situation follows upon the other in the history of the church in Thessalonica, and whether it is possible for us to clarify this sequence.

If we could assume a fairly long period of time between the letters, the difficulties would not be too great. We would be able to interpret the change in the eschatological conceptions as follows: in 1 Thess. the church is troubled by the fact that the *parousia* has not yet come, and is disturbed by cases of death among its members. The church has to be consoled in view of the delay of the *parousia*, but without losing faith in its nearness. In 2 Thess., however, the situation is the reverse: in parts of the church at least the End is thought of as being present. Now the emphasis has to be laid on the fact that it has not yet come.

The attempt to explain the change along these lines raises certain problems, as the letters are so closely related from the literary standpoint that they can only have been written within a short period of one another (i.e. if they were written by Paul—and this has to be assumed for the time being even for 2 Thess.). Wrede[6] pointed out these literary links. We have already referred to the introductions. We need to compare also 2 Thess. i. 3–12, etc. and 1 Thess. i. 2–10, ii. 14 ff., iii. 12 f.; 2 Thess. ii. 13 f. and 1 Thess. ii. 12 f., 1, 2–4, iv. 7, v. 9, etc.[7] In these passages we can see parallels not only in themes but also in terminology and wording. We can therefore only assume either that Paul wrote the two letters so close together that in writing the second he still had in mind what he said

[6] *Die Echtheit des zweiten Thessalonicherbriefs* (1903).
[7] *Ibid.*, pp. 4 ff.

in the first letter, or that there is a literary dependence, and the first letter was used in the writing of the second. But is it conceivable that Paul wrote 2 Thess. soon after 1 Thess.?

Another possibility—that of reversing the order—was considered long ago by Hugo Grotius, and it would in fact remove certain difficulties. An intense expectation would then come at the beginning, to be rejected by 2 Thess. There is quite a long period to wait before the *parousia*, but there are deaths among the members, and then 1 Thess. is written. This assumption, however, only gives rise to fresh problems, which make this unacceptable as a solution. 1 Thess. is clearly the first letter that Paul wrote to the church. Everything that has happened from the foundation of the church to the writing of the letter is mentioned. Apart from the fact that there is no suggestion in 1 Thess. that the faith of the church has been endangered by eschatological fanaticism, an earlier letter would surely have been referred to in what we know as 1 Thess. In this respect alone 1 Thess. shows itself to be the first letter. Apart from this, there are elements in 2 Thess. which mark it clearly as the later letter. 2 Thess. ii. 15, for example, clearly presupposes at least one letter. Furthermore, those who would mislead the people appeal, according to ii. 2, to a letter from Paul which the author of our letter calls a falsification. We cannot go into the question here whether this means only a false interpretation of the (genuine) 1 Thess. If 2 Thess. itself were in fact written as the first letter, or thought to be such, it would have seemed the natural thing to do in the attack upon those who would mislead to point out expressly that they could not in fact possess any letter from Paul. Grotius' argument,[8] that the emphasis on the apostle's own signature in iii. 17 shows that his signature is not known and that this letter must therefore be his first one, does not undermine this argument. We can conclude that a reversal of the order of the letters does not remove the difficulties.

If the letters were written in a short space of time, however, we have to explain the sudden change in the church. The various attempts to do this have not really produced any convincing evidence. Harnack[9] suggested that 2 Thess. was addressed to a Jewish–Christian minority in the church and was sent at the same time as 1 Thess. He deduced the existence of this minority from Acts xvii. 1 ff. Dibelius[10] has presented a variation of this hypothesis, in which he envisages two different groups of recipients.

---

[8] *Annotationes in Novum Testamentum* (Editio nova 1756, ed. Windheim), vol. II, part I, p. 715.

[9] *Das Problem des zweiten Thessalonicherbriefes* (1910), pp. 560 ff.

[10] *An die Thessalonicher I, II* in Lietzmann (3 ed., 1937) on 2 Thess. iii. 18.

In both cases it is rightly seen that the difference of situation in which the recipients are addressed excludes the possibility that they are the same group of people. Apart from other difficulties, however, this does not explain how such different, indeed sharply opposed, eschatological conceptions can exist in the same place, or how Paul deals with both views without ever referring the one group to the other.

E. Schweizer[11] suggests that 2 Thess. was originally a letter to Philippi, that it was sent at the same time as 1 Thess., and that it was copied in Thessalonica and preserved there. The assumption that the actual recipient was the church at Philippi is supported, among other things, by a quotation from Polycarp's Epistle to the Philippians (according to xi. 3, Paul praises the Philippians to all the churches—which is in harmony with 2 Thess. i. 4). If this hypothesis is correct, Paul's letter to the Philippians (on this view, the first letter) must have been lost and only the copy kept, in which the reference to the recipients has been changed. But does this seem likely? There is another difficulty besides: if 2 Thess. does not harmonize with 1 Thess., then Phil. certainly does not harmonize with 2 Thess. (cf. Phil. i. 5). We cannot remove the difficulties along these lines, but simply have to accept them.

At this point we could break off with the conclusion that it is no longer possible for us to explain the change of situation from 1 to 2 Thess. We would then have to carry out the exegesis of the two letters separately, and suggest that faced with a Gnostic perfectionism Paul laid great emphasis in 2 Thess. on the 'not yet'. If we bear in mind the aim of this statement in the particular situation we can say that such a statement is not entirely un-Pauline. In spite of the obscurities that remain it would be possible to make a reasonable exegesis along these lines.

(4) *The Question of Authorship.* (a) In 2 Thess. ii. 5, in the middle of the apocalyptic 'time-table', we read: 'Remember ye not, that, when I was yet with you, I told you these things?' How does this fit in with 1 Thess. v. 1 ff., where the reference is to the sudden coming of the day of the Lord, about which the Thessalonians have also been instructed? What was it that Paul taught them when he was there—the immediate expectation (1 Thess. v. 1 ff.) of the apocalyptic plan (2 Thess. ii. 1 ff.)?
(b) Neither elsewhere nor in 1 Thess. is salvation for Paul an exclusively future reality, but is always related to the present. Those who wait for

---

[11] 'Der zweite Thessalonicherbrief ein Philipperbrief?' *ThZ* (1945), pp. 90 ff.; cf. Michaelis, 'Der zweite Thessalonicherbrief kein Philipperbrief', and Schweizer's reply, *ThZ* (1945), pp. 282 ff. and 286 ff.

the coming day are already children of the day and therefore they should live as children of the day (1 Thess. v. 5 f.). This application of eschatology to the present is missing in 2 Thess., where everything points to the future. The future will bring punishment for the persecutors, but reward for those who are oppressed (i. 9 f.). It could of course be argued that Paul is deliberately allowing the application to the present to fall into the background because it would be dangerous in view of the Gnostic heresy; but he does not only allow it to fall into the background, he excludes it completely.

(c) According to 2 Thess. ii. 15 the church is to stand fast in that which it has learned from Paul, whether by word of mouth or by letter. In view of the heretics, this is understandable, but it becomes problematic when we ask which letter is being referred to here. If Paul is the author of 2 Thess., then it must be 1 Thess. that is referred to; but this letter would not really be of any help in the changed situation. According to ii .2 the position is that the opponents are also using supposedly Pauline letters. ii. 15 is then obviously meant to turn the church—in a quite general sense—to Paul. But this emphasis on apostolic authority is a post-Pauline motif.

(d) The same applies to iii. 17, where the expression of greeting and the signature in Paul's own hand is given as evidence of the authenticity of this and other letters. Paul mentioned in other instances that he wrote the conclusion in his own hand (Gal. vi. 11, 1 Cor. xvi. 21), but not in order to underline the genuineness of the letter. 2 Thess. therefore not only presupposes that there are false Pauline letters in existence, but also that his opponents are making use of them. But we never hear of this in any of his later letters. Nor do we ever hear that—in Paul's lifetime—opponents quote the apostle as authority for their own position. In later times, however, this certainly did happen (2 Pet. iii. 15 f.).

We could go on to mention further points, and could refute, or attempt to refute each argument. There is a surprising number of such points that could be raised but we now have to face the question whether 2 Thess. is or is not a Pauline letter. In answering this question we need to bear in mind that in determining the situation of the recipients it makes little difference whether we suggest a time twenty-five years earlier or later for the letter, for its message would in any case be the same. But if it is easier—with regard to terminology, theological viewpoint and the material employed, etc.—to interpret the letter against a later background, then it is certainly helpful from the point of view of exegesis to claim pseudonymity for the letter. The commentators who consider

2 Thess. to be Pauline show this quite clearly—though against their will. If we try to interpret its teaching as the teaching of Paul, we have to explain step by step why Paul uses different arguments and themes here than elsewhere. As a Pauline letter 2 Thess. certainly presents more difficulties than as a non-Pauline. For this reason it is hard to understand the view expressed in Jülicher-Fascher,[12] that it would not make much difference if we could prove that the letter was not genuine. Precisely the opposite seems to be the case. A sounder understanding seems now to have prevailed, and we could go so far as to say that we can now 'receive' the letter correctly for the first time.

In the period after Paul an author tries to withstand Gnostic aberrations, when they make their way into a church (or churches) by an appeal to Paul. This means that a Pauline approach is adopted, but the manner in which it is set out is not Pauline.

The letter was probably written soon after A.D. 70.

BIBLIOGRAPHY

M. Dibelius, *An die Thessalonicher I, II, an die Philipper* (Lietzmann, 3 ed., 1937).

E. von Dobschütz, *Die Thessalonicherbriefe* (Meyer, 7 ed., 1909).

H. Braun, 'Zur nachpaulinischen Herkunft des zweiten Thessalonicherbriefes', *ZNW* (1952–3), pp. 152 ff.

A. von Harnack, *Das Problem des zweiten Thessalonicherbriefes* (1910).

W. Wrede, *Die Echtheit des zweiten Thessalonicherbriefes* (1903).

Commentaries: see on 1 Thessalonians.

P. Day, 'The Practical Purpose of Second Thessalonians', *ATR* 45 (1963), pp. 203 ff.

[12] *Einleitung in das Neue Testament* (7 ed., 1931), p. 65.

4. THE EPISTLE TO THE GALATIANS

(1) *Background.* We learn from iv. 13 that when the apostle wrote the letter he had probably been in Galatia twice before, but the exegesis of this passage is a matter of controversy. 'Ye know that because of an infirmity of the flesh I preached the gospel unto you τὸ πρότερον.' We can translate this as 'the first', or 'earlier' or 'once before'.[13] The context however suggests that it is meant to refer to a visit which was not the last one. In any case Paul would hardly speak of his 'earlier' visit or the visit he 'once' made if he had only made one visit previously. This would also contradict i. 6, where the apostle expresses his surprise that the Galatians have fallen away 'so quickly' from his gospel. Paul's last visit to Galatia cannot therefore have taken place long before. On this occasion he had confirmed that the churches 'were running well'. Distinct from this there is an earlier visit, when the churches were founded. At that time Paul was ill and was cared for by the Galatians with great devotion (iv. 14 f.).

At first sight it seems quite easy to fit these two stays in Galatia into the chronology of Paul's life with the help of two passages in Acts. There are two references to a journey by the apostle through the region of Galatia, once (xvi. 6) in connection with the second missionary journey which is then confined to Europe and also (xviii. 23) at the beginning of the third missionary journey, the early part of which is specifically described as a visitation journey. Doubts have sometimes been expressed about this arrangement, for the following reasons, among others: Acts xvi. 6 speaks only of passing through the region of Galatia, not of a mission there, and according to Acts xviii. 23 it is not the 'churches' that are visited, but we are merely told that Paul strengthened the 'disciples'. For this reason it has been questioned whether there were any churches there at all. It has also been pointed out that among the Celtic inhabitants of Galatia (see below) Paul would have had considerable difficulties as regards language. The suggestion has therefore been made that the Galatian churches should be thought of as situated not in the region of Galatia but to the south, in Pisidia and Lycaonia, where on the first missionary journey (according to Acts) Paul established churches. This is what is known as the 'South Galatian hypothesis', in contrast to the 'North Galatian hypo-

---

[13] Bauer, art. πρότερος.

thesis', according to which the churches are to be sought in Galatia itself. The South Galatian hypothesis is made possible by the fact that Galatia is the name of a region as well as (later) the name of a Roman province.

The name Galatia is a later form of Keltai, and signifies the inhabitants of the region around Ancyra (present-day Ankara) who came from Gaul, migrated as early as the fourth century B.C. and settled here shortly after 280 B.C. As they had already been settled in the area for more than 300 years, they naturally were involved in the process of Hellenization, nevertheless they preserved some of their native customs and peculiarities, including a dislike of living in towns. The last king of the Galatians extended his territory to the south, including the districts around Pisidia and Lycaonia. When he died in 25 B.C. the district became a Roman province, and the whole region—extended to the South—was then given the name 'Galatia'. If Paul meant by 'Galatia' the Roman province, he could have been in the southern part of the province even on the first missionary journey—although not in the 'region of Galatia', as Acts always calls it. In this case the letter would have been written after the second visit (that is, on the second missionary journey—Acts xvi. 1 ff.). The South Galatian hypothesis, however, is extremely improbable. The assertion that is often made, that Paul always uses the names of the Roman provinces, is not correct.[14] Besides, Paul would hardly have been able to say in i. 21, 'Then I came into the regions of Syria and Cilicia', for this is the Pauline parallel to the first missionary journey in Acts. According to the South Galatian hypothesis he must have founded the Galatian churches at that time, but there is no mention of this. Finally, it seems unlikely that Paul would address the inhabitants of Pisidia and Lycaonia as 'Galatians' (iii. 1: 'O foolish Galatians'). This can only be a racial term and cannot refer to the inhabitants of a Roman administrative district.

We shall therefore have to assume (along the lines of the North Galatian hypothesis) that Paul founded the churches (N.B. plural—i. 2), on the second missionary journey, made a visitation on the third missionary journey and was delighted to find them in such a good condition. Soon afterwards he received disturbing news and wrote the letter. It seems most reasonable to assume that the place of composition was Ephesus, where Paul stayed for three years. The fact that there is no

---

[14] E. Haenchen, *Die Apostelgeschichte* in Meyer (13 ed., 1961) on xvi. 6. (E.T. in preparation, Blackwell).

CONTENTS

47

direct reference to Ephesus in the letter—there are, for example, no greetings conveyed—could be connected with the nature of the letter. It is also possible, of course, that Paul wrote the letter at some stopping-place before he reached Ephesus.

(2) *Contents*. The Epistle to the Galatians is an extremely passionate piece of writing. Paul is in a state of great excitement. Angry passages alternate with calmer statements, and biting irony with affectionate pleas for renewed trust.

Even the Introduction (i. 1–5) has a very different character from that of the other Pauline letters. In particular, no co-author is mentioned. The name of the sender is given clearly and concisely: Paul. He then makes it perfectly clear that he is 'an apostle not from men, neither through man, but through Jesus Christ, and God the Father'. There is no introduction as in 1 Thess., no prayer of thanksgiving. The first word after the introduction is an expression of amazement.

This provides the introduction to the preamble to the letter (i. 6–9), in which the situation in Galatia is briefly outlined. Paul is torn between sorrow and anger to think that the Galatians have so quickly fallen away. They have turned to another Gospel, which is not really a Gospel at all. Certain people have come and confused the Galatians. Paul twice pronounces anathema upon them, and includes in his curse all those who would declare a different Gospel from the one he delivered to them, whoever they might be.

In the first main section (i. 10–ii. 21) there is a detailed development of what was already announced in i. 1: that Paul has received his apostolate and his Gospel direct from God, and is therefore independent of other authorities. It should be mentioned in passing that these first two chapters are very valuable for the biography of Paul (section 1, 1); but it needs to be remembered that Paul does not mention these facts for a biographical, but for an apologetic, purpose. In vv. 10–12 the theme is set out. Paul is bound exclusively to God, and is Christ's slave; therefore it is neither necessary for him to speak to please men, nor has he any interest in doing so. He mentions four grounds for the independence of his apostolate (i. 13–24). First he reminds his readers that he was originally a persecutor of the church. Then he says that God revealed His Son in him, which in view of what preceded happened not only without but against any presupposition. Then Paul emphasizes that he did not discuss this revelation with any man. He did not go to Jerusalem, but first to Arabia. It was not until about two years later that he went to

Jerusalem, where he wanted to meet Cephas. Apart from him he met only James the Lord's brother. He finally mentions his stay of thirteen years in Syria and Cilicia, during which time he again had no contact with the Jewish churches. He had persecuted them; they heard that the former persecutor was now proclaiming the Gospel, and they praised God for what had happened; but no permanent association was established. The purpose behind this is plain: Paul probably mixed with a great variety of people, but he refers only to his contact with Jerusalem. In emphasizing his independence therefore he is seeking to underline his autonomy over against Jerusalem.

The question now arises whether the independent Pauline Gospel has anything to do with the Jerusalem Gospel. The danger of Paul's over-emphasizing his independence is that under certain circumstances this could tell against the Gospel he preaches. This would be a matter of great concern to Paul himself, and therefore at the same time as he emphasizes his independence he has also to mention his positive relation-ship with Jerusalem. He does this in ii. 1–10, where we learn that the apostle was able to vindicate his Gospel even in Jerusalem. He went there again about thirteen years later, not because he received an invitation but on the basis of a revelation, in other words, by divine command (ii. 2). Paul himself wishes to submit the Gospel which he preaches among the Gentiles to the church in Jerusalem in order to be reassured as to his position. There must have been some difficulties at the Apostolic Council. Paul speaks of false brethren who surreptitiously opposed him, but he did not yield. Titus, who accompanied him, was not circumcised. The leaders of the Jerusalem church made no attempt to restrict Paul in the freedom of the Gospel. The Gospel of Paul for the Gentiles is recognized as having equal right as the Gospel of Peter for the Jews. But Paul agrees to support the collection for Jerusalem. We can see that even now the apostle has not made himself dependent upon Jerusalem, but has been able to stand his ground there. He does the same later when confronted with Peter (ii. 11–21). The latter had originally had table fellowship with Gentiles at Antioch but had given it up when 'certain came from James'. Paul rebuked him sharply for this before the assembled church.

The second main section (iii. 1–v. 12) contains the heart of the letter. Paul first turns (iii. 1–5) directly to those to whom the letter is addressed: 'O foolish Galatians'. He reminds them that their own calling came from the preaching of faith, not from the works of the law. But if they now succumb to the law, all that was in vain. This indicates the theme of this main section: the freedom of the Gospel, which has to be preserved against the danger of succumbing again to the law. The theme is developed along three lines:

(a) Paul shows (iii. 6–18) by the example of Abraham and from Scripture that faith works salvation, but the law the curse. The real descendant of Abraham and bearer of the promise, according to Scripture, is Christ.

(b) The question of the law is raised (iii. 19–iv. 7), and Paul expresses himself very definitely. The law was given by a mediator, and was therefore not from God (iii. 19 f.). Until the coming of Christ it was a gaoler, or a παιδαγωγός (tutor), but with the coming of Christ it was abolished by faith. Christians are no longer under a guardian, but have received adoption through Christ.

(c) Paul several times introduces personal factors into his argument (iv. 8–v. 12). He asks the Galatians whether they, who previously served gods who were not really gods at all, having been set free from these, want to be in bondage again to the στοιχεῖα τοῦ κόσμου (the 'elements'— Paul is thinking here of personal angelic beings connected with the planets). The Galatians observe days, months, feasts and years. Paul reminds them of the time when he was among them. In spite of his illness they received him and cared for him in an exemplary way. Suddenly the tone of the letter changes. The opponents in their zeal are not seeking what is good for the churches, they are trying to draw the Galatians away from Paul, so that they will follow them. Paul's anger then turns into sorrow. He addresses the Galatians as 'my little children' (iv. 19), and expresses the desire to be with them. 'I am perplexed about you' (iv. 20). He returns to his main theme, and shows (by an allegorical exegesis of the story of Abraham's two wives and their children, iv. 22 ff.) that the Old Testament itself is a witness to the freedom with which Christ has set men free, and in which the Galatians should now stand. They must not fall back under a yoke of bondage. Anyone who allows himself to be circumcised is obliged to obey the whole law (v. 3). There can be no compromise. Paul hopes that the Galatians, who were running so well, will come back to the right path. The section closes on a sarcastic note with the remark that those who preach circumcision and so confuse the Galatians ought to 'cut themselves off'.

The third main section (v. 13–vi. 10) is devoted to ethics. The theme is first announced (v. 13–15): freedom does not mean freedom for the flesh, but freedom for the service of love, which is the fulfilment of the law. Paul deals with this theme under two headings. First (v. 16–25) he

E

sets out the contrast between spirit and flesh. He who is ruled by the spirit is not under the law. A 'catalogue of vices' (the 'works' of the flesh) is contrasted with a 'catalogue of virtues' (the 'fruit' of the spirit). As Christians live in the spirit, they should also walk in the spirit. Then there follows (v. 26–vi. 6) a series of specific exhortations: to brotherliness, to the mutual bearing of burdens, to fellowship with their teachers. This third main section closes with a summary (vi. 7–10): as the seed, so will the harvest be.

Paul has evidently dictated the letter so far, for there now follows a conclusion in his own hand (vi. 11–18), in which the apostle returns to the theme of the second main section, and describes the adversaries as people who want to make a show in the flesh, and demand circumcision of the Galatians but do not keep the law themselves. Their sole aim is to be able to boast of their successes among the Galatians. Paul, on the other hand, sees his only glory in the cross of Christ. The letter closes very abruptly: 'From henceforth let no man trouble me: for I bear branded on my body the marks of Jesus. The grace of our Lord Jesus Christ be with your spirit, brethren. Amen.'

(3) *The Opponents.* The situation in Galatia is clear insofar as we can establish that errors have crept into the church which have evidently soon exerted their influence and turned the churches away from the Pauline Gospel to another (i. 6f.), but it is difficult to answer the question as to what these errors were and what the 'Gospel' was like which they had presented to the Galatians. However, it is of considerable importance for the exegesis of the letter to be able to answer this question. But we find ourselves in a vicious circle, for it is only by the exegesis of the letter itself that we can discover anything about the errors. The problem is that Paul does not reveal in what way he received information as to what was happening in Galatia. It is also possible—in theory at least—that the picture Paul has formed of his enemies on the basis of the information he has received does not correspond to the true picture of these people. We must bear this possibility in mind, because the apostle on several occasions later attacks errors which seem partly to resemble the heresy attacked in Gal., but not to be identical with it. It is not permissible from the point of view of method for us simply to assume the historical image of these enemies in our exegesis of Gal. And if we suppose that Paul's opponents were in all cases the same (Gal., Phil., 1 and 2 Cor.), then perhaps we could to some extent get a clear idea of the historical image of the heretics by considering the evidence of these letters together; but at

the same time we would have to remember that this image is not necessarily identical with the idea Paul had of his opponents when writing the different letters. If we can determine that Paul had only a rough idea, or an actually false idea, of his enemies, then this is important for the question whether the Galatians could understand his letter. But for the exegesis of what Paul says this is irrelevant, for this has to be guided by the picture that presents itself to Paul. For this same reason we need to be cautious in attempting to discover who the enemies were and what their attitudes were, and particularly in drawing parallels with other letters (cf. section 8, 3).

A better starting-point is provided by the fact that the Galatians were Gentiles (iv. 8). The fact that the Old Testament is extensively quoted does not call this in question. If Paul believes (whether rightly or wrongly) that his opponents were subjecting the Galatians to the law (and that means to the Old Testament), then he naturally assumes that the churches are familiar with the Old Testament. The purpose for which Paul uses the Old Testament becomes clear straightaway: he is attacking the new authority to which the Galatians have been subjected with that very authority itself, that is, the law of the Old Testament (cf. iv. 21).

Paul's estimate of what has been happening in Galatia can be discovered from the following passages. He says: 'So we also, when *we* (N.B.) were children, were held in bondage under the rudiments of the world' (iv. 3). Then: 'Howbeit at that time, not knowing God, *ye* (N.B.) were in bondage to them which by nature are no gods' (iv. 8). And finally: 'But now that ye have come to . . . be known of God, how turn ye back *again* to the weak and beggarly rudiments, whereunto ye desire to be in bondage over again?' (iv. 9).

In other words, Paul describes the falling away of the Galatians as a relapse. This of course has to be defined carefully. It is not simply a case of a relapse into paganism, for the Galatians have not just become polytheists again (which they were before—iv. 8), but after they had become Christians through Paul's influence they have now become worshippers of the 'world elements' (iv. 9). Paul now projects these new 'gods' into the past, as it were, and says that he also, Paul the Jew (who, before he became a Christian, was under the law) as well as the Galatians (who previously served not the world elements, but the gods) was formerly subject to the world elements.

The difficulty of this apparent contradiction disappears if it was the false teachers who introduced the 'world elements' to the Galatians and Paul who identifies the new bondage with the old. For a Jew, this is an extremely bold idea—Paul the Christian sees that there is no real differ-ence between the bondage to the world elements on the one hand and the bondage to the law or to idols on the other. Although the Galatians have not actually fallen back into their old paganism, nevertheless there has been a relapse. This is the theme of the whole of the second main section of Gal.

We can already see that in considering who Paul's opponents were we are faced with two motifs, a Jewish one and a Gnostic one. This is the real problem: what is the connection between these two motifs? The attempt at a solution follows three main lines.

(a) Lütgert[15] assumes that Paul is fighting in Gal. on two fronts: against Judaists and against spiritual enthusiasts who incline to libertin-ism. The Judaists seek to introduce circumcision, and wish to subject the Galatians to the law. The enthusiasts, on the other hand, make it necessary to include the detailed ethical section of the letter, which appears superfluous for people who are wanting to adopt the law. This theory has not found much acceptance, but we shall have to consider whether it is entirely mistaken. In any case it is to be noted that Paul nowhere suggests in Gal. that he believes he is dealing with two different opponents.

(b) The traditional explanation is that the opponents are Judaists, although it is difficult to define more closely who they are. Two different possibilities are sometimes suggested. They certainly cannot be Judaists of a Pharisaic turn of mind, for they would not have introduced the Galatians to the world elements, or to the calendar of feasts (iv. 10). Nor can they have been the Jewish Christians of Jerusalem (Lietzmann[16] suggested a Petrine agitation against Paul). Against this there are not only the reasons we have already mentioned but also the fact that Paul in no way indicates that his adversaries at the Apostolic Council (ii. 7–10) had failed to keep the agreements they had made. Peter is rebuked not for a breach of the agreement but for inconsistency of behaviour (ii. 11–21). What kind of Judaists were they then? Schlier[17] holds that the opponents did not belong to the correct rabbinical school of Judaism but rather were representatives of a type of apocryphal Judaism. Stählin[18] speaks of a sectarian Jewish–Christian movement which had a 'Gnostic colouring, but was principally legalistic'. In other words, the most widely held view

[15] *Gesetz und Geist* (1919).
[16] *Geschichte der alten Kirche*, I (3 ed., 1953), pp. 108 ff. (E.T. *The Beginnings of the Christian Church*, 3 ed., Lutterworth Press, 1953, pp. 109 ff.).
[17] *Der Brief an die Galater* in Meyer (11 ed., 1952), p. 204.
[18] 'Galaterbrief' in *RGG*, II, cols. 1188 ff.

is that the opponents were a syncretistic group in which legal elements from Judaism (including circumcision), Gnostic and also Christian elements were combined; the difference of view is as regards the relative proportions of these separate elements.

(c) Schmithals[19] has set out a third hypothesis, which differs from these latter interpretations, but links up with Lütgert's suggestions. He discovers an abundance of anti-Gnostic expressions in the letter—far more than had been noticed before—and describes the opponents as Jewish–Christian Gnostics. The emphasis here (although the syncretist nature of the group remains) is clearly on 'Gnostics', who, for example, no longer think of circumcision in the Jewish way but have re-interpreted it and can also renounce it. Schmithals suggests that Paul met these same people again in Corinth, and points out a number of parallels. In Corinth they have given up circumcision, but this is not their essential characteristic, which is libertinism. The advantage of this solution is that it helps us to recognize the opposition confronting Paul much more distinctly. The treatment of chs. iii. and iv., however, is unsatisfactory, for Schmithals takes them to be a midrash type of excursus without any deeper connection with the actual situation.

We can proceed now from this last suggested solution and take for granted the points that have already been made. If the opponents introduced the Galatians to the world elements and the calendar of feasts, there is a considerable parallel to the heretics who are attacked in Col. There also there was worship of the elements, the calendar of feasts and a cult of angels (Col. ii. 8, 16, 18, 20). But we need to be careful here. We evidently have the same heresy in both cases, but—for the reasons mentioned above—it is questionable whether Paul fully understood his opponents. He does not really enter into a direct encounter with this heresy (as he does elsewhere, e.g. in 2 Cor.), but he discusses it in relation to the law; and he does it in such a way as he might have done if his opponents had been Pharisaic Judaists, which they obviously were not.

The best approach in order to determine who the opponents were (as seen by Paul) would seem to be to consider the practice of circumcision which these people brought to Galatia. It is not at all clear what this practice meant to them. It is surprising that Paul has to write to the Galatians: 'Yea, I testify again to every man that receiveth circumcision, that he is a debtor to do the whole law.' If circumcision is practised strictly according to Jewish observance, such a statement would really be unnecessary. The question that now arises is whether the Galatians were

[19] 'Die Häretiker in Galatien', _ZNW_ (1956), pp. 25 ff.

not aware of this, and whether the heretics had not introduced a circumcision which did not correspond to strict Jewish observance, or whether it was just a case of laxity. However, there is something more that we learn about circumcision. In the conclusion to the letter written in his own hand Paul writes: 'As many as desire to make a fair show in the flesh, they compel you to be circumcised; only that they may not be persecuted for the cross of Christ' (vi. 12).

Can one escape persecution by being circumcised? In a Jewish environment this can certainly be the case, but it can hardly be assumed for Galatia, as there were not many Jews there; and in any case it would be difficult to imagine Jews persecuting Gentile Christians simply because they would not be circumcised. But if we forget about Galatia for a moment, then we can say that it is possible that the motif of escaping persecution by the practice of circumcision played a part in Jerusalem. The question therefore arises whether Paul is speaking here in the light of his knowledge of circumstances in Jerusalem. The fact that circumcision was practised in a Jewish–Christian community could arise simply from adherence to custom, more or less unconsciously. Paul did not demand at the Apostolic Council that the Jewish Christians should break with their practice. Why not? Is it going too far to assume that the practice of circumcision in the Jewish–Christian community was almost a prerequisite if this community was to exist in Jerusalem at all? We shall return to this point in a moment.

First, however, we need to consider v. 11. This verse offers direct evidence for the correctness of the assumption that Paul had the situation in Jerusalem in mind in vi. 12. He writes: 'But I, brethren, if I still preach circumcision, why am I still persecuted? then hath the stumblingblock of the cross been done away.' According to this, Paul is supposed still to preach circumcision. As he does not do so (as the Galatians know) this can only mean that he is accused of tolerating circumcision, which could well be correct, at least as far as the Jewish–Christians in Jerusalem were concerned. But still Paul did not preach circumcision—and for this reason he is persecuted (by the Jews in Jerusalem).

Circumcision can therefore in fact save one from persecution. He who preaches against circumcision can expect persecution. But this could not have been the case in Galatia. The Galatians at least did not need to fear persecution for being uncircumcised. We can see therefore that here Paul is interpreting circumcision in the light of his earlier experiences. We therefore cannot say that the heretics introduced circumcision in Galatia with the argument that the churches would then escape persecution.

They simply introduced the practice of circumcision. Paul, however, knows that it is an important motive for circumcision in Jewish–Christian circles that one can thereby escape persecution, and in this way he explains to himself the practice that has been introduced.

The basis for this hypothesis would be very slender if we did not have other evidence besides. If we turn to vi. 12 again we see that those who demand circumcision do so because they wish to win esteem. Circumcision is linked, in other words, with a further motive: the 'circumcizers' wish to gain esteem. We meet the same motive elsewhere quite apart from the reference to circumcision. The opponents wish to glory in the flesh of the Galatians (vi. 13), they do not seek the good of the churches but rather desire to 'shut them out' so that the Galatians will seek them (iv. 17). What is common to these statements is that men—the opponents—are putting themselves in the centre. The Galatians are meant to be bound to these men. This is something of which Paul must have heard, and it points fairly clearly to Gnostic motifs, but originally it has no direct connection with circumcision.

We can therefore say that Paul mentions a motive of the opponents three times: they want to have glory, to win esteem and to be sought after. This is what Paul has heard. He has also heard that the Galatians are to be circumcised. On one occasion he combines the two ideas (vi. 12), then he uses one of the motives (glory) to interpret the practice that has been introduced (vi. 13). This interpretative combination obviously originates with Paul again. In other words, the apostle is trying to discern some meaning in circumcision in Galatia, because to all appearances he is unable to understand it. For this purpose he draws on the idea of the avoidance of persecution and the motive of glory.

Once we recognize Gnostic features among the opponents, we cannot interpret the circumcision they introduced in a Jewish or Pharisaic sense. There was no reason why Galatian circumcision should involve subjection to the law; but for Paul as a former Pharisee circumcision does subject one to the law (v. 3), and for this reason he cannot but interpret the action of the opponents as a relapse. Seen in this light his line of argument becomes intelligible.

The various difficulties are best solved by assuming that Paul did not fully understand the position of his opponents. His information was probably not exact. He hears of the emergence of these people, who are evidently lax ethically, and he also hears that they are introducing circumcision. Then came the experience of the Apostolic Council, where he won the concession that the Gentiles should not be circumcised. For the sake of the freedom of the Gospel circumcision cannot be demanded of the Gentiles. Now that it has been introduced into Galatia, his reaction is quite understandable. The freedom of the Gospel is in danger, and the Galatians are falling away. They have fallen under the world elements. Paul has heard of these, but he equates them with the law. In other words, his polemic against subjection to the law is linked with the fact that he goes too far in interpreting the practice of circumcision in Galatia. Paul is well aware of the fact that his interpretation is not really in keeping with the general behaviour of the heretics, with their ethical laxity, and perhaps even with their libertinism. He is simply perplexed about them (iv. 20).

We have come to these conclusions mainly in the light of the second and third sections of the letter. It is noticeable that in the whole of the second section there is not a single reference to any concrete events in Galatia apart from a mere mention of the world elements and circumcision. It is different in the third (ethical) section. This again supports the view put forward that the freedom of the Gospel—the main theme of the letter—was not a theme that sprang from concrete evidence but was one constructed by Paul, on the basis of the information he had received. Paul deduces from his scanty information that the opponents have caused the churches to fall away. In fact they were introducing something new: a Christian–Jewish–Gnostic syncretism.

If this assumption is correct, it helps to explain how Lütgert hit on his theory that Paul was fighting on two fronts, and also how so many different attempts have been made to bring together the Gnostic and Judaistic elements. The uncertainty springs not so much from the exegesis as from Paul's inadequate knowledge.

Let us look once again at the first two chapters. Paul is obviously developing here what he has announced in the introduction: 'an apostle, not from men, neither through man' (i. 1). Underlying this is probably a reproach from his opponents that he is not a real apostle but received his apostolate through human mediation. This was meant to undermine Paul's apostolic authority among the Galatians. There is a Gnostic idea at work here, for the Gnostic apostle receives a direct call.

However, Paul does not engage here in anti-Gnostic polemics (as in 2 Cor.) by including in his reputation the ideas underlying his opponents' assertion, but he merely addresses himself to the assertion they have made. In 2 Cor. he has evidently recognized the Gnostic element in the reproach, but in Gal. he hears only the reproach itself. Nevertheless his method of argument is similar. Paul has to prove his independence of human authorities (Jerusalem), but at the same time he has to show that this acknowledged centre of the Christian community is in entire agreement with him, even—and this is of decisive importance—in those issues which in his opinion are the cardinal points of the controversy: circumcision and the question of the law.

If we set out from this standpoint, we can understand the two chapters quite easily. Paul cannot have become an apostle through men, for he was a persecutor of the church. When he became a Christian he had no connection with those people through whom he might have become an apostle. Therefore he did not confer with flesh and blood but went to Arabia. When he came to Jerusalem two years later he met Cephas and James. Then he went on missionary journeys in Syria and Cilicia. It was not until he had been active independently as an apostle for thirteen years that he went to the Apostolic Council. Here—in spite of certain opposition—his Gospel was accepted; as a result Paul was in a position to rebuke even Peter. In this way he succeeded in asserting his view of the freedom of the Gospel from the law. From this point there is a direct transition to the main section of the letter.

(4) *Points of Exegesis.* We have to admit, in summing up the position, that Lütgert was not far wrong when he spoke of two fronts; however, it was not a case of two actual fronts against which Paul had to fight but only one, which Paul fails to understand properly as a whole. By going too far in his interpretation of the practice of circumcision he cannot clearly distinguish the Gnostic features. In fact he is fighting against a Pharisaically interpreted legalism, which he fills out with Gnostic features (equating the world elements with the law), and then goes on in the ethical section to speak of the conduct of the church, which does not really fit in with the legalism that he has been attacking.

There are certain consequences of this as far as exegesis is concerned. We need to consider in each instance the views of the opponents as Paul envisages them. But as these are not uniform we have to be ready to ask the question in each case: to which group of his opponents is Paul addressing himself here?

In iii. 6–iv. 7 and iv. 21–v. 1 he is attacking the view that Christians are still subject to the law, and engages in a sharp anti-legalist polemic which must have sounded quite blasphemous to Jewish ears (cf. esp. iii. 19 f.). Of course these statements are one-sided, but it would be a dangerous procedure to attempt to smooth over the sharp edges by pointing to what Paul says about the law in other letters. Exegesis has to have the courage to let one-sided statements stand, as they are called forth by the situation, and any attempt to whittle them down and fit them into the general pattern would make a historical understanding difficult or quite impossible. In the third section Paul attacks an abuse of freedom as a cover for evil, a problem that repeatedly arises when dealing with Gnostics of all kinds. As far as exegesis is concerned, therefore, there are two opponents, although historically there was only one. If this is correct, then the problem of the various suggested solutions becomes understandable and is at the same time removed.

There is one further point to be added. It is very strange that we meet for the first time in this letter what was later called the Pauline doctrine of justification (although it would be better to speak of the Pauline message of justification). Justification by faith and not by works is met here (in an abstract form) for the first time. The Galatians' relapse—as Paul sees it—made the apostle creative in a way which was later to make history. The strange thing is that Paul develops his terminology in face of a situation which he in fact misconceived, but of course this does not affect in any way the theological legitimacy of what he says. When Paul again develops these ideas later (Rom.) he really is faced with the problem (section 9).

BIBLIOGRAPHY

A. Oepke, *Der Brief des Paulus an die Galater* (Handkommentar, 2 ed., 1957).

H. Schlier, *Der Brief an die Galater* (Meyer, 12 ed., 1962).

W. Lütgert, *Gesetz und Geist* (1919).

W. Schmithals, 'Die Häretiker in Galatien', *ZNW* (1956), pp. 25 ff.

Commentaries: E. DeW. Burton, ICC (1921); G. S. Duncan, Moffatt (1934); J. B. Lightfoot (7 ed., 1881).

C. H. Buck, 'The Date of Galatians', *JBL* 70 (1951), pp. 113 ff.

F. C. Crownfield, 'The Singular Problem of the Dual Galatians', *JBL* 64 (1945), pp. 491 ff.

B. Orchard, 'A New Solution of the Galatians Problem', *BJRL* 28(1944), pp. 154 ff.

5. THE EPISTLE TO THE PHILIPPIANS

Paul founded the church in Philippi on the second missionary journey (Acts xvi. 12 ff.). He had to leave the city on account of a persecution (1 Thess. ii. 2), but the church remained loyal to him and on at least two occasions sent him gifts to Thessalonica (Phil. iv. 16). This suggests that Paul had a particularly cordial relationship with the church, for otherwise he was always very careful to provide for his own maintenance (Phil. iv. 15; 1 Thess. ii. 9; 2 Cor. xi. 8 f.).

(1) *Contents*. In the Introduction (i. 1–2) Timothy is mentioned as associated with Paul in the sending of the letter. The recipients are 'the saints in Christ Jesus which are at Philippi, with the bishops and deacons'. It is to be noted that this is the first time bishops are mentioned within the church, and that this is also the first time that we find bishops and deacons referred to together. We cannot say whether this is connected with the fact that the letter as we have it is the result of an editorial process (see below) or whether this is a later interpolation deriving from a period during which the letters were collected and became authoritative within the Church as a whole. Even if the phrase does come from Paul himself, we certainly cannot interpret these bishops (=overseers) and servants as officials in the later ecclesiastical sense. Here we find only the concepts, and there is no hint of the functions; but we should not deduce these from later times and read them into the text here. Paul does not refer to bishops on any other occasion. Furthermore, overseers and deacons are not uncommon descriptions for those who carried out administrative tasks in societies, cultic groups and such like.

The first section extends from i. 3 to iii. 1. We learn in the preface (i. 3–11), which as usual contains thanks and intercession for the church, that Paul is in prison (v. 7), but he is confident as far as the faith of the Philippians is concerned. i. 12–26 gives us a good insight into the position in which the apostle finds himself. It is known in the whole praetorium that he bears his bonds for the sake of Christ (v. 13), and this has given confidence to the brethren in proclaiming their faith. The motives for proclamation in some cases, however, are less pure, for there are those who would like to create trouble for Paul. The apostle has to reckon with the possibility of his death. He is ready to die (i. 21), but feels it is more needful for him to 'abide in the flesh' for the church's sake. His fate is therefore uncertain. If he is set free, it is his wish to visit the church. In view of Paul's belief in the nearness of the *parousia* expressed elsewhere (cf. iv. 5–6) this declaration is to be noted. It is clear that it is closely connected with his present situation.

There follow (i. 27–ii. 18) exhortations to harmony and to worthy behaviour. In i. 28 opponents are mentioned, of whom the church is not to be afraid. It must be prepared to suffer for Christ's sake in the same conflict in which it sees Paul engaged, or of which it hears. It is characteristic that here—as often—Paul does not simply give information about matters which concern him personally, but he goes on directly to an address to his readers.

Paul weaves into his exhortations to humble love, to unity and to readiness to suffer, the Christ-hymn (ii. 5–11), which is traditional but has been expanded by way of commentary and this is followed by a summons to strive for salvation. Then come further personal remarks (ii. 19–iii. 1). As soon as he knows what is to happen to himself Paul intends to send Timothy to the church, whom he recommends as particularly reliable, but he hopes he will also be able to go himself. In addition he intends to send Epaphroditus, who—as a messenger from the church in Philippi—was ill when he was with Paul, but has now recovered.

After the summons 'Rejoice' (iii. 1) we expect the conclusion of the letter; instead, iii. 2 opens a second section of the letter (iii. 2–iv. 3). It begins with a sharp attack: 'Beware of the dogs, beware of the evil workers, beware of the concision' (iii. 2), and then proceeds to a kind of apologia. The apostle speaks of his Jewish past, of which—as a Jew—he could be proud, and was proud, but which he has counted as refuse in view of the righteousness that is of faith. Paul then obviously turns to attack perfectionist notions (iii. 12–21), and emphasizes that he himself is still on the way and would not presume to claim that he is already perfect. But there are evidently other views in the church about being perfect. Paul demands that whatever degree of perfection has been attained must show itself in conduct. This is where many of the members are lacking, as Paul sadly confirms. At the end of this section of the letter there are further personal admonitions (iv. 1–3). Two women are exhorted to be of the same mind, a loyal σύζυγος (fellow-labourer?) is suddenly addressed without being mentioned by name, and Clement and other workers are mentioned.

Again we expect the close of the letter, but there now begins a third section (iv. 4–20), which opens with a renewed summons to rejoice (iv. 4–7), thus echoing the close of the first section of the letter (iii. 1). After a few general exhortations Paul expresses thanks for the gift the Philippians have sent to him (iv. 10–20). Again we see the personal message leads on into an address. The giving by the Philippians is interpreted, and this interpretation takes the form of a proclamation to the church.

In the conclusion (iv. 21–23) οἱ ἐκ τῆς Καίσαρος οἰκίας ('they that are of Caesar's household') are particularly mentioned among those who join in sending greetings.

(2) *The Question of the Literary Unity of the Letter.* The somewhat disjointed train of thought in the letter has raised the question of its original unity.[20] It seems probable in fact that the second section of the letter (iii. 2–iv. 3) is an insertion, possibly a separate letter to Philippi—or part of one—in which Paul deals with opponents who have arisen there. As adversaries are mentioned already in i. 28 without being described in any detail, but iii. 2–4 gives us a much clearer idea of the opponents, the interpolated letter (or section) is probably earlier. It seems therefore that there are at least two letters to the Philippians.

In all probability, however, we have to take into account a still further letter. It seems very strange that it is not until the end of the letter (iv. 10 ff.) that Paul refers to the gift that the Philippians have sent him. We might have expected it to be mentioned in connection with i. 5 ff. Epaphroditus is mentioned in iv. 18 as the bearer of the gift. We are told that he was seriously ill while he was with Paul (ii. 27). Not only have the Philippians learned this in the meantime, but Paul and Epaphroditus also already know that the Philippians are concerned about his illness, and therefore Paul sends the messenger back (ii. 25). There was therefore not only a fairly long period between the time when Epaphroditus reached Paul and the writing of ii. 25 ff., but there was also regular contact between Philippi and Paul's place of imprisonment. Is it likely that the apostle would not have expressed his thanks until now—and, what is more, not until the end of the letter, almost as though he had forgotten to do so previously? If we assume that Paul wrote iv. 10 ff. soon after the arrival of the messenger and that the events mentioned in ii. 25 ff. did not take place until later, then the difficulties disappear. The text of

[20] Cf. W. Schmithals, 'Die Irrlehrer des Philipperbriefes', *ZThK* (1957), pp. 297 ff.; G. Bornkamm, 'Der Philipperbrief als paulinische Briefsammlung', in *Neotestamentica et Patristica*, Essays presented to Oscar Cullmann (1962), pp. 192 ff.

Philippians as it has come down to us could then be divided into the following three letters, or parts of letters: A: iv. 10–20; B: i.1–iii. 1; iv. 4–7, 21–23; C: iii. 2–4; ♯,8–9.

It seems quite plain that iv. 4 follows directly upon iii. 1, and it seems reasonable to link iv. 21–23 with letter B, as those 'of Caesar's household' who send greetings in iv. 22 could well be connected with the praetorium mentioned in i. 13. We cannot say for certain where iv. 8–9 originally belonged, but these verses could well stand as the conclusion to letter C. We cannot be sure whether the introduction as we now have it comes in its entirety from letter B. It could have been expanded from the introduction to letter A, because it is very probable that the gift was sent to Paul on the initiative of the 'officials' of the church ('bishops and deacons'). In view of the difficulties in determining the extent of the different sections, the question arises—as a task for literary critical analysis—whether the three letters can be understood in sequence as the correspondence of the apostle with the church in Philippi.

(3) *The Situation.* In considering the situation in Philippi we shall have to differentiate between the situation in the first, second and third letters.

In the first letter (iv. 10–20) we learn nothing about the position in Philippi. Paul merely expresses thanks for the gift, and we cannot say for certain whether he is already a prisoner. He does speak in iv. 14 of his θλῖψις (grief, affliction), but does not tell us what this is. We cannot conclude simply from the sending of the gift that Paul was in prison, for according to iv. 16 the Philippians had already sent him money to Thessalonica on two previous occasions, although he was not in prison there.

In the second letter (i. 1–iii. 1; iv. 4–7, 21–23) the situation is not entirely clear. It has sometimes been concluded in the light of i. 29 f. that the church was suffering persecution, in other words, that there were difficulties external in origin. Paul does not go into details. Perhaps he has no concrete information, or maybe the external pressure does not seem to him of any great importance. If it did, there would be a much stronger expression in the letter of comfort and encouragement. In Paul's view difficulties within the church are no doubt of greater importance. The Philippians are exhorted to preserve unanimity (i. 27), and they are to practise obedience not only in his presence, but also in his absence (ii. 12). We cannot tell, however, how these difficulties arose or what the reason for them was. Paul has evidently heard of opponents who have made their way into the church and had some influence there. The

Philippians are not to be afraid of them (i. 28). The desire for glory is possibly linked with these impostors (ii. 3), a desire which is countered by Paul with his summons to unanimity and humility (ii. 1–4, leading into the Christ-hymn). We can assume therefore that by means of the various links between Philippi and his place of imprisonment after the arrival of Epaphroditus (ii. 25 ff.) Paul learned something about the church. During this time 'adversaries' have no doubt come to Philippi, of whose ideas and activities the apostle has so far received only very vague indications. He does not seem to see any serious danger yet.

He is anxious, however (in the second letter) to point out these early signs of a split within the church. He does this by reminding his readers of the particularly cordial relationship that he has had with the church hitherto: and he underlines this by pointing to his own fate in prison. All this is addressed to the Philippians by way of proclamation. The characteristically cordial tone of the letter therefore serves to express Paul's pastoral concern for the church.

After writing this letter Paul must have learned more details about the adversaries, and this gave rise to the third letter (iii. 2–iv. 3, 8–9). Here—to the extent that the letter has been preserved—we can see two main themes: a sharp rejection of the false teaching (iii. 2) and a loving concern for the Philippians (iii. 17). The opponents are representatives of a perfectionist ideal which has marked Gnostic features. It is possible that they rejected a future *parousia* (iii. 20 f.) and maybe also a resurrection in the future (iii. 10). They do this because to their way of thinking the future is already here. At the same time, however, they seem to lack ethical seriousness, for their perfectionism does not manifest itself in their conduct (iii. 15 f.), and iii. 19 suggests libertinist features.

It is significant that circumcision was practised by the Gnostics in Philippi, just as in Galatia. In other words, they are from a Jewish background, but again it is not altogether clear what meaning they attach to circumcision. The fact that Paul contrasts the righteousness that is of the law with the righteousness that is of faith in Christ in iii. 9 might lead us to suppose that the heretics represent a righteousness of works; but this is not in keeping with the ethical conduct of these people. Here again, therefore, we can assume that Paul reads too much into the circumcision practised by these intruders (cf. section 4). In Paul's discussion of circumcision the theme of glory is much more prominent, a theme that is related to the Gnostic theme of perfection. We can probably assume that Paul believes he is dealing here with the same group of people as those who caused confusion in the Galatian churches. At least he sees them against the background of his earlier experiences (cf. section 9, 3). The difference from Gal. is simply that Paul recognizes more clearly the Gnostic aspect of these opponents than he did when he wrote Gal. His argument makes this clear. In his third letter to the Philippians he seizes upon the Jewish element and the specifically Gnostic element in the heretics as regards one point—glory and a supposed perfection; and now he turns in argument against the superiority to which the opponents lay claim. Paul himself could with even greater justice claim pride as regards the past (iii. 4 ff.), but for Christ's sake he regards all this as nothing. He also asserts the present nature of salvation to the extent that he has been apprehended by Christ (iii. 12), but he refuses to think of himself as therefore perfect, because he is still travelling towards the goal (iii. 12, 14).

It is difficult to give a definite answer as to whether Paul was still in prison when he wrote the third letter. This was probably not so, as he does not refer to his imprisonment any more. One could deduce a willingness for martyrdom from iii. 10 ff., but the exegesis of this passage is too uncertain for us to be able to draw any conclusions from it.

(4) *Place and Time of Composition.* We can only conjecture what the temporal relationship is in which the three Philippian letters stand. In view of ii. 25 ff. we have to allow a few months between the first and second letters, but we can say nothing at all about the time that elapsed between the second and third. The question of the place of imprisonment cannot be answered with complete certainty either. From the information in Acts there are only two places to be considered: Caesarea (Acts xxiii. 35) and Rome (Acts xxviii. 30). But as Paul himself says that he was often in prison (2 Cor. vi. 5; xi. 23) it is conceivable that the letters were written in any of the places Paul visited where there was a prison. We have therefore to be guided by the information given in the letter itself, which is none too clear. Unfortunately Paul does not say where the praetorium mentioned in i. 13 was situated. 'Praetorium' really means the tent in which the praetor and his people live when in camp. The word later also meant the 'official residence of the governor'. Acts xxiii. 35 mentions (in Caesarea) 'Herod's praetorium' (in other words Herod's palace was used as the praetorium; according to Acts Paul was held prisoner there). This piece of information seems to point to Caesarea as the place of writing, although this does give rise to further difficulties, for there is no evidence of a church in Caesarea. In addition—at least in the second letter—Paul is awaiting an early trial; in any case he expects an early decision concerning his fate. According to Acts xxv. 11, however,

in Caesarea Paul made his appeal to the Emperor; the judgement could not therefore be given at this place. Praetorium, however, can also mean praetorian barracks, and the phrase 'in the whole praetorium' can be interpreted as 'in the whole imperial guard'. However, as these were to be found everywhere in the imperial provinces, the whole question still has to be left open.

iv. 22, where 'they that are of Caesar's household' are mentioned among those who send greetings, does not throw much more light on the subject. It seems at first sight to point to Rome, but the difficulty is simply that we have no evidence for the description of the imperial palace as a praetorium. Besides, the reference here is not to members of the imperial household, but to the emancipated imperial slaves who were to be found in Rome and in many other places as well.

The direct information we are given does not take us very far, and so we have to turn to what we can deduce indirectly. The second letter in particular, but also the sequence of the three letters, shows that there was a lively intercourse between Paul's place of imprisonment and Philippi. The Philippians learn where the apostle is being held, and they send Epaphroditus to him with a gift. Paul writes his first letter, then he receives news of adversaries in the church. In the meantime the church has heard of the illness of Epaphroditus, whilst at the same time Paul learns that the Philippians are concerned about their messenger. He writes a second letter, but before writing the third letter he must have received further news from Philippi. This suggests that Paul is being held somewhere that is not as far from Philippi as Caesarea or Rome. It has often been assumed that Ephesus was the place, and in fact—so far as we can still ascertain the facts—this seems to be the most acceptable solution.

i. 13 (praetorium) and iv. 22 (imperial slaves) do not rule out Ephesus. It is true that Acts contains no reference to an Ephesian imprisonment of Paul, but in view of the incompleteness of the account in Acts this is not of great significance. The statement in 1 Cor. xv. 32 could be of decisive importance here. According to this the apostle fought at Ephesus with wild animals. We must either interpret this statement conditionally ('If I had endured a fight with wild beasts at Ephesus'—as a result of a negative outcome of his trial) but this raises problems, because as a Roman citizen Paul could have been condemned to wild beasts only after being deprived of his citizenship. Besides, wild beasts are not mentioned in the detailed list in 2 Cor. xi. 23 ff. The alternative is to take the statement in a figurative sense as referring to an imprisonment in Ephesus.

F

In addition we have to remember the closeness of the second and third letters to Gal. on the one hand and to 1 and 2 Cor. on the other. As Gal. was written from Ephesus, and also 1 Cor. and parts of 2 Cor., we can assume that Phil. was also written there, and that the letters were written on the third missionary journey during Paul's three-year stay in Ephesus.

(5) *The Question of Editorial Treatment.* The disjointed train of thought in Phil., which presented difficulties for exegesis when the attempt was made to understand the letter as a unity, has led us to this finding from the standpoint of literary criticism: it can be assumed that Phil. grew out of a redaction of three Pauline letters. These can be interpreted—as we have shown—in sequence as the apostle's correspondence with the church. The difficulties which presented themselves to exegesis previously now disappear. We are given an insight into a living conversation that Paul is holding with the church, in which he addresses himself to each new situation as it arises and says just what is necessary for this situation. We can leave open the question whether the picture Paul has of the situation changes—or, indeed, the situation itself.

The question now arises, how an editor could bring together into a unity these three separate letters which make such good sense in themselves. It appears that he did not simply ignore all that we need for a historical understanding, but at the same time destroyed the possibility of any such understanding. But is this really conceivable? It would mean imputing to this man, who shows such obvious skill in his editorial work, lack of comprehension to a high degree. (The same applies to the redaction of 2 Cor.—cf. section 8, 4.)

We need to remember, of course, that we cannot presuppose in the editor the same interest in historical understanding that we have. The concern of the early church in the post-apostolic period was to keep in line with the apostolic witness. We shall meet this problem particularly when we come to the pseudo-Pauline letters. Although there are differences of attitude to Paul—or, more precisely, to the apostle Paul—even within the New Testament (for Luke, who restricts the concept of the apostle to the circle of the Twelve, Paul was not an apostle), the Church cannot—and does not wish to—abandon him, because his historical significance is well known and beyond question and because in the post-Pauline period heretics appealed to Paul's authority (2 Pet. iii, 15 f.; cf. 2 Thess. ii. 2). The important thing, therefore, is for the Church to 'claim' Paul's writings officially so that they will not be lost. This marks the beginning of the conflict concerning tradition, which now becomes a basic problem. It is striking that as early as the so-called Apostolic Fathers and in other writings we find quotations from Paul occurring repeatedly. This means that the apostolic writings are on the way to becoming 'Holy Scripture', and we can see the first signs of the developing Canon. In all this, however, the original circumstances in which the documents appeared are no longer of any significance, and the need to preserve the letters as items of correspondence addressed to a particular situation disappears. What is of interest is no longer the fact that Paul wanted to say something to earlier readers, nor what he wanted to say to them in particular, but his letters are now interpreted as an apostolic legacy to the whole Church.

In these circumstances it is easy to understand how the shorter Pauline letters in particular, or even fragments of letters, which survived have been preserved and handed down together. In different instances of course the redaction follows a different course. In Rom. xvi. the redaction takes the form of a simple addition (cf. section 9, 4), whereas in 2 Cor. it is obviously very carefully thought out (cf. section 8, 4); and as regards the editorial process in Phil. we have to ask whether the editor (apart from the general considerations we have already mentioned, which make such editorial work possible at a later period) reveals any other deliberate intention.

We cannot decide this question with any certainty. Nevertheless we can assume that Phil. as we have it includes all the letters that were subsequently sent to the church in Philippi. If the redaction was made in Philippi we can understand why the editor did not maintain the sequence of the correspondence (assuming he was aware of it or had found it out). The final letter contains a pointed statement of Paul's views—in other words, the correspondence closes on a discordant note. If we assume— and there is nothing to contradict the assumption—that this final letter to Philippi was 'successful', and that the church did not succumb to the heresies, then to place this letter at the end in the redaction would cast not only an unfavourable but also a false light upon the church. But if the impression was gained that Paul had a particularly cordial relationship with the Philippians (cf. iv. 15) then the emergence of the heresies appears as a mere episode. This is expressed in the redaction by the fact that the attack on the heresies is put in the middle of the letter. It is surrounded by the much less severe second letter, which is placed first, and the specially cordial first letter, which comes at the end. In this way the editor brings together the letters which Paul once sent to this church —and by his manner of editing sets out the apostle's successful ministry to the church. At the same time he leaves behind the general impression of the cordial relationship that Paul had with the Philippians.

In this connection it is worth noting a passage in Polycarp's Epistle to the Philippians, which was written around the middle of the second century. 'For neither can I, nor any other such as I am, come up to the wisdom of the blessed and renowned Paul, who, being himself in person with those who then lived, did with all exactness and soundness teach the word of truth, and, being gone from you, wrote an epistle to you; into which, if you look, you will be able to edify yourselves in the faith that has been delivered unto you' (iii. 2). We can see here on the one hand what was mentioned earlier, the significance attaching to the Pauline letters in a later period; on the other hand the plural 'letters' is striking, and possibly shows that Polycarp either was familiar with the separate letters or was aware of the fact that the letters had been assembled.

In the exegesis of Phil. we have to distinguish therefore between two 'settings in life'. We can expound the three letters along the lines of literary criticism in their sequence as statements addressed to three distinct situations; or—taking Phil. as a unity—we can expound the edited work, by asking what the editor was seeking to say to a later age in the way he used the Pauline letters.

BIBLIOGRAPHY

M. Dibelius, *An die Thessalonicher I, II, an die Philipper* (Lietzmann, 3 ed., 1937).

G. Friedrich, *Der Philipperbrief* (NTD, vol. 8, 9 ed., 1962).

G. Bornkamm, 'Der Philipperbrief als paulinische Briefsammlung' in *Neotestamentica et Patristica*, Essays presented to Oscar Cullmann (1962), pp. 192 ff.

G. Delling, 'Phillipperbrief', *RGG*, V, cols. 333 ff.

W. Schmithals, 'Die Irrlehrer des Philipperbriefes', *ZThK* (1957), pp. 297 ff.

Commentaries: F. W. Beare, Black (1959); J. B. Lightfoot (4 ed. 1878); J. H. Michael, Moffatt (1928).

G. S. Duncan, *St. Paul's Ephesian Ministry* (1929); 'Were Paul's Imprisonment Epistles written from Ephesus?', *ET* 67 (1955–6), pp. 163 ff.

T. E. Pollard, 'The Integrity of Philippians', *NTS* 13 (1966–7), pp. 57 ff.

B. D. Rahtjen, 'The Three Letters of Paul to the Philippians', *NTS* 6 (1959–60), pp. 167 ff.

6. THE EPISTLE TO PHILEMON

This shortest of Paul's letters gives the impression—on account of its strictly limited circle of recipients—of being obviously a private letter, but it is at the same time an 'apostolic' letter. A slave called Onesimus ('profitable') has run away from his master Philemon, who, we have reason to believe, is a wealthy man. He has presumably taken with him money or something of value, for Paul offers to make good the loss (18 f.): but at the same time the apostle points out that Philemon (figuratively speaking) is really his debtor. Indirectly, therefore, Paul is asking that he should renounce any claim for compensation. Paul is now sending back Onesimus, who had found him out somewhere and had been converted by him (cf. 10: 'my son, whom I have begotten in my bonds') with the request that Philemon should now receive the runaway slave as a brother and, if possible, send him back to Paul as he had proved to be very useful to him (cf. 13 f.). Paul pleads in a very moving way for the fugitive; but the outstanding feature of the letter is not so much this personal element, but the way in which Paul uses it for setting out his message.

In those times it was a serious crime for a slave to run away. There were soldiers specially appointed to pursue the fugitives. If a slave did not succeed in finding shelter in a sanctuary he usually—if he was not caught—went underground among the populace of a large city. It is significant that Paul accepts the legal situation. He neither extenuates the wrong that Onesimus has done, nor does he attack slavery like a social revolutionary. This does not mean, of course, that Paul approves of slavery: he accepts it as a fact. (In any case, what would have been the point of trying to alter social institutions shortly before the *parousia*?) The important thing to notice is what Paul makes out of the given situation. The central idea in his message is the new factor that has come into being in Christ. As far as slavery is concerned, this means that slave masters are now slaves themselves, slaves of Christ; the slaves, on the other hand, although they are still slaves, are free men in Christ. Viewed in this light, it is possible for masters and slaves to be brethren, although from the social point of view they are still masters and slaves. This of course is bound to have consequences for the relationship of masters and slaves, but it does not overthrow the legal position.

Paul writes this letter from prison (1), but he does not mention the place. He is counting on being released soon (22) and intends to visit Philemon, who is to prepare accommodation for him. Caesarea and Rome have therefore probably to be excluded as places where the letter could have been written, but Ephesus is a possibility. The temple of Artemis at Ephesus was one of the places of refuge for runaway slaves.

We are faced with a similar difficulty when we turn to the question of where Philemon lived. In Col. a certain Onesimus is mentioned who lives in Colossae (iv. 9), but in view of the widespread occurrence of the name we cannot be certain whether the bearers of this name in Phm. and Col. are the same person. Therefore we cannot assume simply on the basis of the similarity of name that Philemon, as Onesimus' master, lived in Colossae. Paul probably never visited Colossae (this is expressly pointed out in Col.—cf. section 16), but this is not a compelling argument, as Paul could have met Philemon anywhere. Although five of the names mentioned in Col. and Phm. correspond, this does not provide any final proof in view of our lack of information as to the situation prevailing in the two instances. It has sometimes been assumed that Phm. is the 'epistle from Laodicea' referred to in Col. iv. 16, but this is unlikely, as the Laodicean letter was meant to be read publicly and Phm. as we know it does not seem suitable for this. We can only leave these questions open.

We have dealt with this letter at this point on account of the presumed imprisonment at Ephesus. When he wrote his second letter to the Philippians the apostle was still in prison, and when he wrote Phm. his imprisonment was coming to an end. Paul then probably wrote his third letter to the Philippians—and 1 Cor. certainly—after his release.

In his letter to Ephesus Ignatius mentions (i. 3; ii. 1; vi. 2) a bishop Onesimus of Ephesus. To identify this man with the former slave, particularly in view of the frequent occurrence of the name, is mere speculation.

BIBLIOGRAPHY

M. Dibelius, *An die Kolosser, Epheser, an Philemon*, edited by H. Greeven (Lietzmann, 3 ed., 1953).

E. Lohmeyer, *Die Briefe an die Kolosser und an Philemon* (Meyer, 12 ed., 1961).

Commentaries: J. B. Lightfoot (with Colossians), (6 ed., 1882); C. F. D. Moule (with Colossians), CGTC (1957).

P. N. Harrison, 'Onesimus and Philemon', *ATR* 32 (1950), pp. 268 ff.

J. Knox, *Philemon among the Letters of Paul* (2 ed., 1959).

7. THE FIRST EPISTLE TO THE CORINTHIANS

(1) *Background*. Paul founded the church at Corinth on the second missionary journey. 1 Cor. as we know it was written from Ephesus or from the neighbourhood of Ephesus (1 Cor. xvi. 8), in other words, during the third missionary journey. This gives us two definite points of reference. According to v. 9, however, Paul had already written at least once before to Corinth: 'I wrote unto you in my epistle to have no company with fornicators.' We have no way of finding out what the occasion of this first letter was, but it gave rise to a misunderstanding, which Paul now clears up. We might mention in passing the question whether this earlier letter from Paul to Corinth was just lost or whether it has become part of 1 Cor. Bornkamm[21] suggests that the letter referred to in v. 9 might possibly have been incorporated in 1 Cor. vi. 1–11 or 1 Cor. vi. 12–20, but this seems improbable.

A letter was also sent by the Corinthians to Paul (vii. 1). In vii. 25, viii. 1 and xii. 1 Paul seems to be dealing with questions raised by this letter. This means that some uncertainty prevails in the church, although it is not clear at the moment what the cause of it was. At the same time we can see that Paul's advice is being sought, which means that he is recognized as the authority by the church—or at least by the sections of the church that wrote the letter. In view of later events this fact is not without significance.

Paul also received news about disputes in the church, conveyed to him by 'them which are of the household of Chloe' (i. 11), a woman otherwise unknown to us. Several people are mentioned besides, who maintain the link between him and the church. A certain Stephanas, whose 'household' Paul had baptized at Corinth (i. 16), is together with Fortunatus and Achaius in Ephesus (xvi. 17). Finally we learn that Paul has sent Timothy to Corinth (iv. 17). As the church is exhorted in the same letter to receive Timothy with kindness (xvi. 10 f.), we can assume that he has taken the land route via Macedonia, whilst Paul is sending the letter direct, that is, by the sea route, to Corinth. The letter will therefore arrive before Timothy. There were obviously various links between Paul and the church at Corinth.

[21] *Die Vorgeschichte des sogenannten zweiten Korintherbriefes* (1961), pp. 34 ff., n. 131.

(2) *Contents*. The introduction (i. 1–3) mentions as associated with the sending of the letter 'Sosthenes our brother'. The church in Corinth is the recipient, but this is followed by a broader generalization, which includes 'all that call upon the name of our Lord Jesus Christ in every place'. It seems possible that this is a secondary amplification of the circle of people to whom the letter is addressed, introduced at a time when the Pauline letters were being assembled for the use of the churches.

After the usual thanksgiving (i. 4–9) there follows the first main section (i. 10–iv. 21) in which Paul turns his attention to the divisions within the church. These involve the names of individuals. One group attaches itself to Paul, another to Cephas, another to Christ (i. 12). These names raise a number of questions. It is significant that the absent apostle himself is looked upon as the leader of a group. Apollos similarly is at the time not in Corinth, but with Paul in Ephesus (xvi. 12). The apostle speaks of him as 'the brother', which hardly suggests that there is any rivalry. Paul has asked Apollos to return to Corinth, but for reasons which are not altogether clear he has refused for the time being to do so. It is an open question whether Peter was ever in Corinth. If we assume that he was, we certainly cannot assume that he was—even in part—the originator of the split. But what does the 'Christ party' stand for? This can hardly be an interpolation by a copyist, as Michaelis suggests. Perhaps we can find the answer by considering the subsequent course of the letter, for after listing the various parties Paul seems to go on to other themes. He speaks of the preaching of the cross in contrast to the wisdom of the world and sets out the contrast of 'wisdom and foolishness' with the characteristic inversion that the divine foolishness is wisdom and the human wisdom foolishness, and he also goes on to deal in the same way with the theme of 'weakness and strength' (i. 18–ii. 16). He then goes on to speak of himself (iii. 1–2), who has fed the Corinthians with milk, not with solid food, because they would not have been able to take it, and are still not able. Then he returns (iii. 4 ff.) to the theme of the divisions and asks who in fact are Apollos and Paul. He answers that they are servants, through whom the Corinthians have come to believe, and then proceeds to set out the position and function of such servants (iii. 15–iv. 5). One cannot and ought not to boast of these servants, but take them for what they are—servants of Christ and stewards of God's mysteries.

From all this one thing becomes clear—that this is a polemic against Gnosticism. A 'party' is therefore to be taken in the Gnostic sense, as we shall see more clearly later, and this is what the 'Christ-people' probably are. It follows, therefore, that there are not really four parties in Corinth, but two, the Gnostics and the Christians, who wish to remain attached to their teachers. The Gnostics, who wish to be attached directly to Christ, look down on those whose link is only indirect—that is, through their teachers—and try to lord it over them. It is for this reason that Paul sets over against this overweening attitude that has arisen in Corinth his own picture and speaks of weakness, lowliness, hunger and thirst (iv. 6–13), in order by means of this picture to bring the Corinthians back to his Gospel; he writes as the 'father' of the church and exhorts his children to become once again his 'imitators', and expresses his intention of visiting the church soon, when he will take matters firmly in hand (iv. 14–21).

At this point we can raise the question whether Paul is really thinking in terms of four (or more) groups in Corinth, in other words, whether he has not yet got an exact idea of the situation. The mention of the four groups could be taken to suggest this, but the way in which he carries out his reprimand shows that he understands at least the main cause of the disturbance of Corinth. In 1 Cor. he is dealing all the time with matters of 'principle', but later in 2 Cor. he turns much more to the persons involved, the mischief-makers. If they are the representatives of the 'Christ-party', then it is very likely that they were in Corinth at the time of the writing of 1 Cor. Paul is dealing here with the heresy they have introduced and its consequences in the church, and later takes up the cudgels with the people themselves. This sharpening of the attack, which we shall discuss in greater detail later, is no doubt linked with the fact that Paul did not meet the opponents until after he had written 1 Cor. and only then realized the threat they represented.

In the second main section (v. 1–vii. 20) Paul deals with various scandals in the church, in the course of which he touches on the following problems: a case of gross immorality in Corinth (v. 1–13), instituting lawsuits before pagan courts (vi. 1–11), and a warning against intercourse with prostitutes (vi. 12–20). All these things are probably connected for the most part with the heresy that has been introduced.

In the third main section (vii. 1–xii) Paul answers questions that have been raised by the church. The Corinthians are uncertain as to the question of marriage or celibacy (ch. vii) and the question of meat offered to idols (ch. viii). As a matter of principle Paul advocates freedom, but a freedom which has regard for the weaker brother—for not all men have the same knowledge (viii. 7). In the great ch. ix. Paul applies the problem that has arisen here in the form of a paradigm to himself. Obviously he has the right to use his freedom: he could, for example, take around with him a member as his wife, as some of the other apostles such as the Lord's brethren and Cephas do (ix. 5). But Paul, as a free man, has made himself a slave for the sake of all men.

Paul now goes on to the theme of sacraments and ethics (ch. x). By a typological use of the Old Testament he shows that the sacraments do not guarantee salvation (x. 1–13); they do not make ethics superfluous but require them. It is therefore important to avoid idol worship, for the Lord's Supper and a sacrifice offered to idols are mutually exclusive (x. 14–22). This does not mean that freedom is undermined (x. 23 ff.), for in principle a Christian can eat anything. We need to remember in this connection that practically all the meat available in the markets came from animals killed for cultic purposes. But Paul again limits freedom by stressing the importance of love and regard for others.

The fourth main section (xi. 2–xiv. 40) deals with special problems concerning worship: xi. 2–16 with the question of the veiling of women, and xi. 17–34 with the worthy celebration of the Lord's Supper. Paul closes this section with the remark that he will set the rest in order when he comes to Corinth. Ch. xii possibly arose from another enquiry (N.B. verse 2) requesting information either about those who claim to be filled with the Spirit or about the gifts of the Spirit. (The translation allows for both possibilities.) It is conceivable that Paul goes on from the question of those filled with the Spirit to that of the gifts of the Spirit (xii. 4 ff.); the two may be different, but they are both the working of the same Spirit. The unity of the church is then set out by means of the idea of the many limbs of the one body (xii. 12–31). After the great hymn in praise of love (ch. xiii), in ch. xiv the theme is again that of the gifts of the Spirit, in particular glossolalia and its significance in worship. The guiding principle is that everything should be done εὐσχημόνως καὶ κατὰ τάξιν ('decently and in order'—xiv. 40).

In the fifth main section (ch. xv) Paul deals with the theme of the resurrection and in the sixth (ch. xvi) with the plan for a collection; this is followed by further plans for Paul's journeys, exhortations and greetings.

(3) *The Situation in Corinth.* In spite of the variety of themes the letter presents a considerable unity. We are given the picture of a church which lives anything but a ghetto existence. We hear of lawsuits before pagan courts (vi. 1), and the question of relations with non-Christians is touched upon (v. 10); the reference to the question of eating meat offered to idols (x. 25 ff.) is probably also connected with the fact that Christians came into contact socially with non-Christians. In this connection we should

also note that this church was set in a great port with all the problems that that presented. There are temples for every possible deity, some of them thronged with prostitutes. The immorality of the place was proverbial (κορινθιάζεσθαι meant 'to live an immoral life').

Yet it is clearly not the case that the insecurity of the church in so many matters arose from its environment. It was rather that people had appeared—within the church—who were the cause of this insecurity. They have evidently exerted some influence, for the Corinthian Christians have been torn to and fro and divided, even though only in their views and practises. There is no evidence of an actual schism, for in spite of the differences they still continue to meet together (xi. 17 ff.).

The opponents can certainly—though indirectly, by the kind of inquiry that is made and the scandals that have arisen—be identified as Gnostics. There are several characteristic features to be noted. These people esteem most highly *gnosis* and the possession of the Spirit, and from this they derive their freedom, which they use in a great variety of directions: they have intercourse with prostitutes (vi. 13 ff.), take part in sacrificial offerings to idols (viii. 1 ff.; x. 23 ff.) and have no regard for the scruples of the weaker brethren. The fact that they claim to possess the Spirit in the present leads them to deny a future resurrection (ch. xv). They value the sacraments very highly, not so much as feasts in which the fellowship of the church is expressed, but rather as means whereby the gifts of salvation are guaranteed and at the same time ethics are made superfluous (x. 1 ff.; xi. 17 ff.). The earthly Jesus is anathema to them, and only the spiritual Christ means anything to them (xii. 3). The preaching of the cross is foolishness to them (i. 18 ff.); they can see no sense in such weakness. On the other hand, they attach great importance to demonstrations such as speaking with tongues (xiv. 1 ff.), and in this way they assert their superiority over those who are not possessed by the Spirit.

The very varied problems that Paul deals with in 1 Cor. can therefore be interpreted in the light of this one underlying aim—to repel the Gnostic influence that has penetrated the church in Corinth. The significant thing is that Paul takes up question after question, problem after problem, and yet throughout argues along the same lines against the abuses and errors. We must bear in mind that the Gnostic standpoint agrees with the Christian (Pauline) standpoint in one matter at least. The Christian has the spirit and is therefore free. He has this gift and this freedom, however, not for himself, to misuse selfishly in a reckless and arbitrary way, but in order that he may put it to service for the benefit of his brother and for building up the church in love. Paul is therefore seeking by means of this letter to bring the church back to its original unity.

(4) *Integrity and Composition.* Attempts have been made by means of literary critical analysis to divide 1 Cor. into several letters or parts of letters, but these attempts cannot really be said to have succeeded. We can therefore still regard the letter as a unity.

1 Cor. was written from Ephesus during the third missionary journey (xvi. 8).

BIBLIOGRAPHY

H. Lietzmann–W. G. Kümmel, *An die Korinther I, II* (Lietzmann, 4 ed., 1949).

H. D. Wendland, *Die Briefe an die Korinther* (NTD, vol. 7, 7–8 ed., 1956).

E. Dinkler, 'Korintherbrief' in *RGG*, IV, cols. 17 ff.

W. Schmithals, *Die Gnosis in Korinth* (1956).

Commentaries: J. Moffatt, Moffatt (1938); A. Robertson and A. Plummer, ICC (2 ed., 1914).

J. T. Dean, *St. Paul and Corinth* (1947).

K. Lake, *The Earlier Epistles of Paul* (1911).

J. R. Richards, 'Romans and I Corinthians: their chronological relationship and comparative dates', *NTS* 13 (1966–7), pp. 14 ff.

8. THE SECOND EPISTLE TO THE CORINTHIANS

According to 1 Cor. xvi. 11 it is Paul's intention to wait at Ephesus until Timothy returns from Corinth. He is probably counting on the fact that his messenger and his letter will remove the difficulties in the church. As Timothy is mentioned in 2 Cor. i. 1 as the co-sender of the letter, he must have returned to Paul in the meantime. It is strange, however, that 2 Cor. bears no obvious relation to 1 Cor. The most we can say generally speaking is that there have been further considerable tensions between Paul and the church. The events that have taken place between the writing of the two letters can be reconstructed only very vaguely from the few scattered remarks in the letter. This is to a considerable extent the result of the fact that 2 Cor. contains statements which it is hard to reconcile. As we can see alongside abrupt transitions (e.g. ix. 15–x. 1) also evidence of joinings which indicate editorial work, it is improbable that 2 Cor. as we have it represents an original unity; but if it is the result of an editorial process we must first try to determine the separate parts which the editor had to work with, and then try to arrange them in chronological order. If we succeed in bringing to light the course of Paul's correspondence with the church we shall have a better understanding of the course of events. This in turn will give us a clearer understanding of the different sections of the letter, when we can place them in their historical context.

(1) *The Literary Problem.*[22] Doubts have been expressed for a long time that 2 Cor. as we know it represents an original unity. Attention was first drawn to the break between chs. i–ix and x–xiii. After Paul had spoken in the first part of the letter of reconciliation between himself and the church (vii. 5 ff., esp. v. 16. 'I rejoice that in everything I am of good courage concerning you'), the sharp, indeed violent, attack upon his opponents in chs. x–xiii is very surprising. A. Hausrath[23]—drawing on the suggestions of other writers—was the first to set out the so-called 'four-chapter hypothesis'. He assumed that chs. x–xiii were written earlier than the other parts of the letter and suggested that what we have here is a fragment of the so-called 'tearful letter' mentioned in ii. 4.

[22] Cf. W. Schmithals, *Die Gnosis in Korinth* (1956), pp. 18–22, and Bornkamm, *op.cit.*
[23] *Der Vierkapitelbrief des Paulus an die Korinther* (1870).

Whether this is in fact the case is a question we must leave open for the moment. But as there is really no satisfactory way of explaining how Paul wrote chs. x–xiii in the same letter following upon chs. i–ix, we must start from the assumption that these four chapters were originally independent.

Immediately before this sharp polemic the theme of the collection for Jerusalem is dealt with in chs. viii and ix, but the treatment is different in the two chapters. Ch. viii is a letter of recommendation for Titus and his companions who are to carry to its completion this collection in Corinth (viii. 6, 16–19, 22 f.). The churches of Macedonia are held up to the Corinthians as an example. In ix. 1 the theme is introduced afresh without any obvious connection with what has been said in ch. viii. Again, in ch. ix there is no mention of the exemplary zeal of the Macedonians, but on the contrary the eagerness of the Achaians for the collection is held up as an example before the Macedonians. The two chapters therefore presuppose different situations, and therefore cannot originally have belonged together.

Chs. i–vii do not form a unity either. It has been recognized for a long time that ii. 13 is continued in vii. 5. Paul writes in ii. 12 f. that when he came to Troas, in spite of the good opportunities for preaching which presented themselves there, he was not content because he did not find Titus there. He took leave of the people there and went to Macedonia. vii. 5 f. then speaks of Paul's arrival in Macedonia and his continuing unhappiness which was resolved by the arrival of Titus. We cannot say that in vii. 5 Paul is merely taking up again a thread that he left behind, for the section in between (ii. 14–vii. 4) is noticeably different from the passages which surround it (i. 3–ii. 13 and vii. 5–16). It contains a clearly constructed apologia for the apostolic office, 'theologically without doubt the most significant passage in the whole letter' (Bornkamm), but it is surrounded by arguments which clearly allude to the reconciliation that has been effected in the meantime between Paul and the church.

Finally it should be noted that within the apologia (ii. 14–vii. 4) there is a short section (vi. 14–vii. 1) containing an apocalyptic exhortation expressed in un-Pauline terminology, which breaks the continuity between vi. 13 and vii. 2.

The pattern that emerges is as follows:

i. 3 – ii.13 ‖ ii.14 ——————— vii.4 ‖ vii.5 – vii.16‖viii‖ix‖ x –xiii
vi.13 ‖ vi.14 —— vii.1 ‖ vii.2

We can distinguish the following elements:

a conciliatory letter: i. 3–ii. 13 and vii. 5–16;

an apologia: ii. 14–vi. 13 and vii. 2–4;

a violent attack: x–xiii;

two letters concerning the collection: viii and ix;

an apocalyptic exhortation (probably non-Pauline): vi. 14–vii. 1.

(2) *The Sequence of the Letters*. In order to arrange the correspondence chronologically we shall need to note any allusions in the various sections which point to concrete events.

There are two passages in the polemical letter of four chapters (x–xiii) which provide the first indication. In connection with his immediate plans Paul says in xii. 14: 'Behold, this is the third time (τρίτον) I am ready to come to you,' and repeats this in xiii. 1: 'This is the third time I am coming to you.' When he wrote these four chapters, therefore, Paul must have been in Corinth twice already. The first stay was at the founding of the church during the second missionary journey. This visit was before the writing of 1 Cor. But when did Paul pay his second visit? We can say for certain that it was not only before the composition of the 'four-chapter letter', but also before the composition of the conciliatory letter. Paul writes in ii. 1 that he did not want to come to the church again in sorrow. This cannot refer to the occasion of the founding of the Church, but only to the so-called 'in-between visit', when there had been a violent quarrel. This is also mentioned in the conciliatory letter. In ii. 5 ff. Paul asks the church not to punish too severely the man who did him an injury, but to forgive him (cf. also vii. 12). As there are a number of allusions in connection with this 'sorrowful stay' to the 'tearful letter' that was subsequently written (ii. 4, 9; vii. 12), we can suggest tentatively the following picture of the course of events.

In the course of what was no doubt only a very short visit to Corinth Paul was evidently not able to deal with the situation he found there, so he departed and then wrote the 'tearful letter'. It was not until later that he wrote the conciliatory letter. As the 'four-chapter letter' must have been written after this visit (on account of xii. 14 and xiii. 1), it is possible that it is the same size as this 'tearful letter'. This suggestion by Hausrath has often been disputed by scholars, however, because there is no mention in the 'four-chapter letter' of the incident of the wrongdoer and because in the conciliatory letter the opponents attacked in the 'four-chapter letter' are passed over in silence. Bornkamm[24] has shown, however, that

[24] *Op. cit.*, p. 19.

the objections are not conclusive, although it is possible that chs. x–xiii do not give us the 'tearful letter' in full. Besides, the incident probably arose from the agitation of the opponents. Paul attacks these people in the 'tearful letter', and therefore to this extent the incident is dealt with here also. However, even if the 'tearful letter' had gone into this matter expressly, the later editor of the different letters could have left this section out, because the incident has already been mentioned before as being settled (ii. 5 ff.; vii. 7, etc.). In the conciliatory letter, on the other hand, the church is no longer under the direct influence of the opponents. Paul's aim here is, without referring again to the agitators, to put a stop to their after-effects in the church (reproach of unreliability, i. 12 ff.). It is here also that we find the reconciliation with the trouble-maker (ii. 5 ff.) who came from within the church, but not from among the opponents. On the basis of these internal arguments we can assume therefore that Paul wrote his 'tearful letter' after the intermediate visit, and the conciliatory letter later still.

Before we go into the further events we need to consider where the apologia (ii. 14–vi. 13 and vii. 2–4) should be fitted in. It has sometimes been held (by Bultmann[25] and others) that it belongs to the last four chapters. This is questionable, as the situation in the two cases is different. In the apologia Paul obviously feels quite sure of his position. The activities of his opponents are presupposed, but Paul believes he can convince them by sound argument. He is very confident and hopes that he has won the Corinthians back. The position in the 'tearful letter' is quite different. Paul bitterly reproaches the church for having not only been taken in by the activities of his opponents, but also for having obviously gladly associated themselves with them (xi. 20 f.); with bitter irony he delivers a mock speech of glorying (xi. 21–xii. 11) and threatens that on his next visit he will take stern measures (xiii. 2, 10).

These differences show that the apologia must have been written earlier, at a period, that is, when Paul still felt that he could overcome the difficulties by rational argument. This can only have been before the intermediate visit. The following argument emerges, therefore, for the three main constituents of 2 Cor.: letter A (apologia: ii. 14–vii. 4)— intermediate visit—letter B ('tearful letter': x–xiii), letter C (conciliatory letter: i. 3–ii. 13 and vii. 5–16).

Ch. viii is probably closely connected with letter C. The request for the collection to be completed presupposes that Paul has been reconciled with the church again. The joyful tone of the conciliatory letter can still

[25] *Exegetische Probleme des zweiten Korintherbriefes* (1947).

be heard here. On an earlier visit Paul had to persuade Titus (vii. 14), but now he can speak of Titus' warm affection for the Corinthians. He did not need any encouragement, but went on a visit to the church on his own initiative (viii. 16 f.). Paul sends him together with several brethren from Macedonia. He points to the example of the Macedonians as far as the collection is concerned. It is possible that ch. viii which concerns the collection is the conclusion of the conciliatory letter, but it is also possible that the conciliatory letter was sent first (also from Macedonia—cf. vii. 5 f.). The letter about the collection then followed—but very soon afterwards.

This geographical evidence helps us to determine the place of composition of the other letters, or parts of letters. As Paul did not stay long in Troas on the journey from Ephesus to Macedonia (ii. 12 f.; vii. 5), it seems very reasonable to assume that letters A and B were written from Ephesus. The intermediate visit must have been a direct visit (Ephesus—Corinth—Ephesus) by sea.

We cannot be certain how often Titus was in Corinth. What is certain is that he was there between the 'tearful letter' and the conciliatory letter. The reconciliation between Paul and the church could be the result of his work. But had Titus been in Corinth previously? xii. 18 seems to indicate this with a fair degree of certainty. There is an allusion to an earlier visit in the 'tearful letter' also, but in this connection the question of the collection is mentioned. Paul has to defend himself against false accusations (xii. 14 ff.). This first stay by Titus in Corinth may have served the purpose of a preparation for the collection. This is in fact mentioned in viii. 6—in connection with viii. 10. Titus had therefore been in Corinth the year before.

But when was this? We do not know how much time elapsed between the events in Corinth. After Paul's intermediate visit to Corinth with its quarrel the work of collecting can hardly have started, and therefore we have to assume that this visit by Titus took place at the beginning of the collection, between the writing of 1 Cor. and letter A (in 1 Cor. xvi. 1 ff. the collection is in fact announced). In this case Paul's whole correspondence with Corinth lasts about a year.

Possibly—but this cannot be anything more than a guess—Titus passed on to Paul the news which led the latter to write his apologia. If this was what happened it explains why Titus had no great desire to go to Corinth a second time—to make an attempt at reconciliation.

The picture of the various events that took place can be summed up as follows. After writing 1 Cor. Paul sends Titus to Corinth to carry out the

G

collection. Through him (or in some other way) Paul receives the news that his letter to the church (1 Cor.) has not established order as was desired and that the uncertainty of the church did not spring in the first place (as he had previously assumed—cf. 1 Cor.) from actual misunderstandings or simple ignorance, but that the difficulties at Corinth arose rather from a questioning of his apostolate instigated by the Gnostics. Paul replies with his own apologia (letter A). When he receives further news he decides to pay a visit to Corinth himself, and then the conflict comes out into the open. Paul has to depart and writes his 'tearful letter', which gives us a clearer picture of the opponents, because now Paul has met them for the first time. He then persuades Titus to make a second visit to Corinth. He awaits him on his way back by land and sets off sooner than he anticipated to Troas. The disturbances force him to go on further to Macedonia. Here he finally meets Titus, who now has good news, which causes Paul to write letter C. If ch. viii is an originally independent letter, then it was probably written soon afterwards. Titus then goes once again to Corinth.

We have not yet considered the position of ch. ix. This letter—or part of a letter—was written in Macedonia (ix. 2). As Paul praises the collection in Achaia to the Macedonians—which is the opposite of what he does in ch. viii—and as he refers to the brethren who have been sent in advance (ix. 5), it is possible that this chapter was not written until some time after ch. viii. It is the last letter that Paul wrote to Corinth. (Achaia here no doubt refers mainly to Corinth.) It was written shortly before Paul's arrival in Corinth and is meant to provide further encouragement for the collection, which Paul wishes to take to Jerusalem.

(3) *The Contents of the Letters. The Opponents.* Before we go into the question of how the separate letters came to be brought together in this way, we need to examine Paul's correspondence with the Corinthians once again and try by setting out the contents of the letters to gain an insight into the position and views of the opponents.

In letter A (ii. 14–vii. 4 with the exception of vi. 14–vii. 1) Paul sets out an apologetic argument for his apostolate. The trouble-makers at Corinth came with letters of recommendation from other churches. Paul's objection is that he does not need such letters, for the Corinthian church itself is his letter of recommendation (iii. 1–3). The opponents assert that they are 'sufficient'. Paul also claims sufficiency himself, but he does not have it of himself, as the opponents no doubt claim to have, for his sufficiency derives exclusively from God (iii. 4–6). He thus proves himself to be a 'servant', and goes on to speak of his 'service' (διακονία) in a fairly long section (iii. 7–18); it is a service of glory (δόξα) in contrast to the service of Moses which was not glorified (N.B. v. 10).

The apostle again finds in his opponents Gnostic ideas (the emphasis on 'sufficiency') and Jewish ideas (the appeal to Moses); he no doubt saw them therefore once again as Jewish Christians with a Gnostic flavour, similar to those we have already met in Gal., Phil. and 1 Cor. It is difficult to say with any degree of historical accuracy who these opponents are. Neither Schmithals' theory that the opponents were always the same people, who moved from east to west with the apostle, nor the opposite approach represented by Bornkamm[26] and others, which tries to sketch a different picture of each of the various groups, can be shown to be historically accurate. Bornkamm is no doubt right when he points out that 'one must treat with great suspicion any theory of uniformity . . . in the sphere of contemporary and primitive Christian syncretism, with the manifestations of which Paul had to come to terms'. We need to adopt the same caution also as regards any attempt to distinguish specific groups within this syncretism in the light of what are after all mostly polemical statements by Paul. We need to remember that Paul most probably first made contact personally with his opponents or with a particular group of them only on his intermediate visit before the 'tearful letter', and that in general he was dependent on news the reliability of which we have no means of proving. As Paul himself had only a more or less indirect knowledge of the opponents, so we also have literary access only to the picture that Paul formed of these people—and even this only in a polemical context. We need to bear in mind these various sources of error and maintain great caution towards them. We can see certain constantly recurring features in the conception that Paul forms of his opponents in the various letters. Whereas in Gal. he allows himself to be drawn into lengthy anti-Jewish passages on the subject of the Jewish practice of circumcision as adopted by the Gnostic heretics, in the later letter he gives greater prominence to the Gnostic element in his opponents. And even if he was not dealing all the time with the same group of opponents, as Schmithals suggests, his conception of his opponents was built up from the varied experiences that he had with them in different places. It is quite understandable psychologically that in each new conflict the experience of previous encounters played a part, and this is borne out clearly by the evidence of the letters. We can therefore go so far as to say that it is not so much the opponents themselves but rather

[26] *Op. cit.*, pp. 16 ff., n. 66.

the picture that Paul has formed of them that goes with him as he travels from east to west, and is supplemented or modified in each new conflict by the particular situation and the problems it presents. As far as exegesis is concerned we can only deal with the opponents as Paul conceives them.

It is significant that in this apologia Paul does not attack the position of the opponents as a whole, but accepts it in part, although he gives it a different orientation. Although his opponents' claims are ultimately based upon themselves, Paul accepts their claims and self-assertions, but always from the standpoint that he has received everything as a gift through Christ from God, which means that he himself is paradoxically always one who is not really important in himself but who can nevertheless as a servant of his Lord advance his claim. He speaks of the purity of motive underlying his ministry. He does not proclaim himself (as his opponents obviously do), but Jesus Christ as Lord—and for Jesus' sake he is the servant of the church (iv. 1–6).

This leads him on to a detailed account of his sufferings (iv. 7–18). These sufferings are an expression of the dying of Jesus, which the opponents have pronounced anathema because they can make no sense of it (cf. 1 Cor. xii. 3); but this 'dying' of the apostle works life in the church and for the church. One has to be able to 'see through' such apostolic, such Christian existence, for only then can one see the glory in lowliness. What is seen by the natural eye is transient; what is not seen is permanent (iv. 18). The reference to the final fulfilment (v. 1–10) is again, as in Phil. iii. 11, 20 f. and 1 Cor. xv, an indirect polemic against the assertion of the opponents that the future fulfilment is already a present possession.

In what sense, however, can we speak of a present salvation? It is to be seen precisely in the lowliness of which Paul has been speaking (vii. 13). Here Paul is giving the church grounds for glorying in the apostle in contrast to those who 'glory in appearance, and not in heart' (v. 12). In all this he is ruled by the love of Christ (v. 14–21). Because one died for all, all have died; they live no more themselves, know nobody any longer 'after the flesh', and are a new creature. All these are implicitly polemical phrases directed against those who wish to prove that they have been made new by mighty manifestations, but who in fact do so in the 'flesh', to which the Christian is meant to have died.

There follow exhortations which point to the way in which Paul has fulfilled his ministry; he has given offence in nothing and to nobody, but has persevered in his ministry, through persecution and every kind of trial (vi. 1–10). The lowliness of Paul therefore is the paradoxical proof of the validity of his activity as a servant of Christ.

Paul now concludes his letter (vi. 11–13 and vii. 2–4). He has interpreted his apostolic existence to the Corinthians in opposition to those who have misled the church by their external impressions. He is convinced that the church will recognize and also admit that Paul accepted for the sake of the church that which his opponents despise.

In this letter A, therefore, we have a document in which Paul goes to the root of the troubles and uncertainties in Corinth which he had touched upon in 1 Cor. He has realized that all the difficulties spring from the activities of these opponents. He expounds his apostolic function by way of an apologia in opposition to their viewpoint. He interprets himself and his activity and seeks by his interpretation to show that what he does is authentically Christian. He does not proclaim himself, but himself as the servant of Christ, and as such he stands as a paradigm of Christian existence.

But this objective account was obviously no longer adequate in view of the influence the opponents had already achieved. The letter does not seem to have met with success, but rather to have called forth ridicule among the opponents (cf. 2 Cor. x. 10). The situation is clearly coming to a head. The intermediate visit becomes necessary, and leads to the clash of Paul with the church—in particular with one of its members. Paul brings this stay to an end in sorrow, and then writes his 'tearful letter' (letter B, chs. x–xiii), full of anger and grief, yet deeply concerned about the church. Here he deals with his opponents very severely.

He begins (x. 1–11) with the most recent events, his (intermediate) visit and the letters, and refers to the reaction that they have provoked in Corinth (mainly under the influence of the opponents). It has been said that Paul is humble face to face, and forceful only from a distance (x. 1). It has been said that his letters are weighty, but his personal presence feeble and his speech worthless (x. 10). This characterization of Paul is not without interest; and although we cannot conclude for certain that it is strictly correct, it is quite likely in fact that Paul was not a gifted speaker and that he did not have a very impressive appearance. Paul now asks that they should not compel him to be forceful when the time comes for him to visit them. Against those who think that he walks 'according to the flesh', i.e. that they can identify his external appearance with the great potentiality of what he is undertaking, he intends to act very resolutely. It is true that he walks in the flesh, but his weapons are powerful, and he is prepared to use them against any sophistry, against any arrogance. And if anyone claims to belong to Christ (cf. 1 Cor. i. 12), let him remember that Paul makes the same claim for himself.

Paul now deals with the theme of glory, first by contrasting his own legitimate self-glorying with the presumptuous self-glorying of his opponents (x. 12–18). He says ironically that he would not dare to compare himself with certain people, who commend themselves. Such people only reassure themselves by themselves. The measure of his glorying, however, is the church, for it was he who founded the church in Corinth, not his opponents, who have forced their way in as impostors. But even as the founder of the church, he glories only in God. 'For not he that commendeth himself is approved, but whom the Lord commendeth' (x. 18).

Paul now begins his great address on the 'foolishness' of glory (xi. 1– xii. 13). He asks the church to put up with a little foolishness from him. It has already put up with a lot from his opponents: the preaching of a different Jesus, a different Spirit, a different Gospel (xi. 1–4). Paul does not believe that he is in any way inferior to these 'chief apostles'. He may be ill-equipped in speech, but not in knowledge (xi. 5–6). He asks whether he committed a sin in humiliating himself and proclaiming the Gospel for no reward. No one shall take this glory from him, that he will go on doing the same for no reward. This is aimed directly at his opponents, who gladly allow themselves to be supported by the church and would be only too pleased if Paul did the same. But they are 'false apostles, deceitful workers, fashioning themselves into apostles of Christ' (xi. 13).

Once again Paul asks the church to put up with his self-glorying (xi. 16–21a). As everyone else glories, he will do the same. If the Corinthians have endured being brought into bondage, taken advantage of, lorded over, struck in the face, they will surely endure a little foolishness on the part of Paul. He now launches upon his self-glorying (xi. 21b–xii), reminds his readers of his descent to show that he is a minister of Christ to a far greater extent than his opponents, and lists the many sufferings he has endured in his apostolic ministry. He can point to miraculous revelations that he has experienced—and he even glories in his weaknesses, which find expression in his sickness. Because the Lord has said to him, that his grace is sufficient for him, and that his power is made perfect in weakness, Paul knows that 'when I am weak, then am I strong' (xii. 10). He closes this self-glorying (xii. 11–13) with the remark that he was forced to speak in this foolish way. He is not inferior to the chief apostles, although he himself is nothing. The signs of an apostle were manifested among the Corinthians at the founding of the church, but Paul did not accept any payment. With bitter irony he says: 'Forgive me this wrong.'

In the final section of the letter (xii. 14–xiii. 10) Paul first announces what will be his third visit, when once again he will not be a burden to the Corinthians (xii. 14–18). This is not to be interpreted—as his opponents obviously do—as hypocrisy; those whom Paul has sent, including Titus (no doubt in connection with the plan for a collection), did not wish to involve the church in any expense. 'I seek not yours, but you' (xii. 14). With these statements, however, Paul is not seeking to defend himself (xii. 19–21); he makes them with the aim of building up the church, for he is afraid that when he comes he will not find the church as he would like to find it. Once again he announces his visit, and says that he will not spare anyone (xiii. 1–10). In this way the church will be able to prove to itself whether it stands firm in the faith. Paul is writing before he goes so that he will not need to use too much severity. The final exhortations, greetings and blessings (xiii. 11–13) breathe the spirit of reconciliation.

In no letter is the danger represented by Paul's opponents made as clear as it is here. They claim to be Christians (x. 7; xi. 23), boast of their Jewish past (xi. 22) and thus put themselves right in the centre of their preaching. They have probably asserted that Christ really speaks through them (xiii. 3)—in contrast to Paul—and think they need only point to their mighty deeds and miracles. They no doubt also claim to have a plentiful share of revelations (cf. xii. 1). This leads to an exaggerated self-glorying, in which, however, they only measure themselves by themselves (x. 12).

These 'Christ-apostles' claim the right to be supported by the church (xii. 13 ff.). In order to denigrate Paul in the church they accuse him of taking money from it under the disguise of a collection (xii. 16 ff.). In other words, they impute to him dishonesty. At the same time they point the finger of scorn at his weak appearance and his ineffective speech (x. 1, 10). Such people certainly represent a danger to the church, for 'according to the flesh' (i.e. visibly and demonstrably) Paul has no answer. But Paul goes on to interpret his very weakness as his glory in the service of Christ (xii. 9 f.). If he wished he could enumerate more things as justification for his glorying than these 'chief apostles', but would only give the impression that he now stood at the centre. According to Paul's understanding of his apostolate as service, this must never happen. Paradoxically, therefore, lowliness becomes the sign of real authority, which is able to exert a powerful influence.

It is a matter of argument whether we should call these opponents Gnostics or not. There is certainly no evidence here of the mythological or speculative soteriology that is a feature of many Gnostic systems, but on the other hand there are Gnostic phenomena to be noted. The self-glorifying of the opponents indicates perfection. The man filled with the Spirit has an impressive appearance and can display powerful manifestations—features which are present among the opponents. We cannot call them pure Gnostics, but rather representatives of a syncretism in which Christian, Jewish and Gnostic elements are combined. Such syncretism—with other combinations as well—was nothing unusual at that time.

We do not know how Paul dispatched the letter. He must have either trusted in its effectiveness or received news of its effect, for otherwise it is difficult to understand why he should encourage Titus to make the journey and even praises the Corinthians to him when he hesitates (vii. 14). We must also allow for the possibility that his opponents went elsewhere, and that Paul had heard of this. Nevertheless he waits impatiently for the return of his messenger, goes to meet him, and so great is his unrest that he forgoes the possibility of doing missionary work in Troas (ii. 12 f.) and meets Titus in Macedonia.

Letter C (i. 3–ii. 13; vii. 5–16) is on the one hand an expression of happy relief, and on the other hand it seeks at the same time to remove the last remaining difficulties and re-establish harmony in and with the church. The letter begins with a particularly cordial expression of thanks for the comfort he has experienced (i. 3–7), which Paul goes on to promise to his readers. He mentions troubles that he experienced in Asia Minor (i. 8–11), and then deals with the charge of insincerity, which has evidently not been completely dismissed in Corinth (i. 12–ii. 4). The apostle is quite confident that this will happen. He has been accused of promising a visit and of not having kept his promise. This promised visit could be the one announced in the 'tearful letter' (xii. 14; xiii. 1), but not the one mentioned in 1 Cor. xvi. 5 ff. If we adopt this view, the often discussed problem of the route of the journey presents no further problems.

According to 1 Cor. xvi. 5 ff. Paul's intention is to travel from Ephesus via Macedonia to Corinth. In the conciliatory letter he states that he had intended to go from Ephesus to Corinth, and then to go on from there to Macedonia. But when he writes the conciliatory letter he is in Macedonia —in other words, on the journey mentioned in 1 Cor. xvi. 5 ff., but he has not yet been to Corinth. The adoption of this route which corresponds to his original plan, was made necessary by the premature sending of Titus, whom Paul is going to meet. The complaint, therefore, does not concern the route, but the fact that the visit announced in the 'tearful letter' has not yet taken place. Paul admits that when he wrote the 'tearful letter' he was thinking of an early journey (i. 15); but on reflection he changed his mind, because he wanted to be sure that it would not become another sorrowful visit. He wished to spare the church. What might look like unreliability therefore sprang in fact from a loving concern for the church. The third visit should really bring a δευτέρα χάρις (i. 15); in other words, the church should now—following upon the visit when it was founded—receive 'grace' for the second time.

In the next section (ii. 5–11) Paul asks the church to forgive the man who wronged him on his intermediate visit. This is followed (ii. 12–13 and vii. 5–7) by the news of Paul's waiting for Titus in Troas and Macedonia and of his joy at the latter's report. In the final section (vii. 8–16) the apostle can now give a positive evaluation of the past which has brought so much sadness: for if Paul troubled the church with his letter, he can now rejoice in the fact that this sorrow has led to repentance. The letter ends therefore on a note of exuberant joy.

Paul can now give instructions concerning the collection (ch. viii). What the Corinthians began a year ago (viii. 10) they should now complete. He does not wish to command that the collection should be made, for it should arise spontaneously as the fruit of love. The purpose of sending Titus and the messengers is to prevent a wrong interpretation of the collection being made again (viii. 20 f.).

Ch. ix was probably written a little later, immediately before Paul's arrival in Corinth.

(4) *The Editorial Process.* In considering this aspect we need to bear in mind the general considerations we set out in connection with the redaction of Phil. (cf. section 5, 5). In addition we need to examine the problems that arise in connection with the editing of 2 Cor. in particular.

First of all we need to note that for the most part the editor simply added one item to another. The letters about the collection and the 'tearful letter' were joined to the conciliatory letter. The apologia was then inserted, and the whole rounded off by the very caustic 'tearful letter' which leaves a rather surprising final impression. These are the two main points that we have to try and explain. On both of them Bornkamm[27] has some valuable suggestions to make.

The apologia, which breaks the continuity between ii. 13 and vii. 5, opens with a hymn. This is not very appropriate at this point, because

[27] *Op. cit.*, pp. 24 ff.

here Paul is speaking of his hasty and anxious journey from Ephesus via Troas to Macedonia. The hymn goes as follows: 'But thanks be unto God, which always leadeth us in triumph in Christ, and maketh manifest through us the savour of his knowledge in every place'. Paul's journey, however, as a matter of historical fact, was by no means a triumphal procession—but it is *we* who see it in this light. The editor, on the other hand was not expounding his material from the historical point of view. The picture that he and his period had of the apostle was that of a triumphant evangelist—and in the end the news that Titus brought when Paul met him in Macedonia did in fact mean a victory for the apostle. This insertion therefore is quite understandable: what it achieves is that it gives us—together with what Paul has written—a further illustration of his activities, although, it is true, from a later standpoint.

If we take seriously the editor's aim to make a whole out of the separate parts, then the rounding off with the sharp polemic no longer seems strange. It is part of the style of a whole series of documents of that period, which conclude with a warning concerning errors. These are to appear before the End, the prelude to which is apocalyptic confusion. For this reason these admonitory warnings—and also documents concerned with Church discipline such as the Didache—often conclude with a summons not to allow oneself to be led astray in the last times. In other words, the editor is following, as far as the structure of the letter is concerned, what was the common practice of his time.

In the opening address (i. 1 f.) the phrase 'with all the saints which are in the whole of Achaia' was probably added later by the editor (on account of ix. 2). The conciliatory final verses (xiii. 11–13) are probably the original conclusion to the conciliatory letter, but could just possibly be read as the conclusion to the 'tearful letter'. We cannot really say when the passage vi. 14–vii. 1 (probably non-Pauline) was inserted. It is possible that the final editor found it already linked with the apologia.

In connection with the editorial problem it is worth noting that in the letters of Ignatius and Polycarp 1 Cor. is often quoted, but 2 Cor. probably not at all. The few passages where one might assume that 2 Cor. had been used can easily be explained in other ways. This raises the question, therefore, whether the letters that have been assembled in what we know as 2 Cor. were known at that time. This suspicion is indirectly confirmed by 1 Clem. xlvii. 1, where all that is mentioned is *the* letter of the blessed apostle Paul to Corinth. The first definite evidence of 2 Cor. is Marcion's Canon. In this case the editing could have been carried out at the beginning of the second century. We can assume fairly certainly that it took place in Corinth.

In the exegesis of 2 Cor., therefore, we have to distinguish again between two 'settings in life'. The various letters are statements conditioned by the situation in which they arose; but 2 Cor. as a whole has to be expounded from the standpoint of the post-apostolic period, in which reference was made back to the words of the apostle and at the same time the attempt was made to idealize the picture of him.

BIBLIOGRAPHY

H. Lietzmann-W. G. Kümmel, *An die Korinther I, II* (Lietzmann, 4 ed., 1949).

H. D. Wendland, *Die Briefe an die Korinther* (NTD, vol. 7, 7–8 ed., 1956).

G. Bornkamm, *Die Vorgeschichte des sogenannten zweiten Korintherbriefes* (1962).

R. Bultmann, *Exegetische Probleme des zweiten Korintherbriefes* (1947).

E. Dinkler, 'Korintherbriefe' in *RGG*, IV, cols. 17 ff.

E. Käsemann, 'Die Legitimität des Apostels', *ZNW* (1942), pp. 13 ff.

W. Schmithals, *Die Gnosis in Korinth* (1956).

Commentaries: A. Plummer, ICC (1925); R. H. Strachan, Moffatt (1935). See Bibliography on 1 Corinthians.

G. C. Campbell, *The Corinthian Letters of Paul* (1947).

J. H. Kennedy, *The Second and Third Epistles of St. Paul to the Corinthians* (1900).

L. P. Phenigo, 'Paul and the Corinthian Church', *JBL* 68 (1949), pp. 341 ff.

A. M. G. Stephenson, 'Partition Theories on II Corinthians', *Studia Evangelica* II, TU 87 (1964), pp. 639 ff.

9. THE LETTER TO THE ROMANS

(1) *Its Literary Character.* Paul sends this letter to a church which he neither founded nor has yet visited. It is not surprising, therefore, that this document is different in character from all the apostle's other letters. He cannot refer either to his visit to the church or to events that have taken place after his departure; nor does he pursue in this letter his 'dealings with the church'. The question that arises in the first place, therefore, is why he wrote the letter at all.

One reason—although only an immediate one—can be mentioned straightaway: that Paul intends at last, in fulfilment of a long cherished wish (cf. i. 13) to pay a visit to the church (xv. 22 ff.). This would provide the occasion for the writing of a letter. The strange thing, however, is that Paul speaks of his plans to make the journey only incidentally, and we certainly cannot say that they are the theme of the letter. This letter in fact gives the impression of being a treatise. This raises the question whether Paul, on the occasion of his intended visit, sent such a treatise only to the Romans.

If this were the case this document would represent from the purely literary point of view something entirely different from what we have seen in all Pauline letters we have discussed so far, in which the contents of the letter have always had a direct bearing upon the situation of the church. We would still have a 'letter' according to Deißmann's definition,[28] but one which has gone a considerable way towards becoming an 'epistle'. As far as exegesis is concerned, this would mean that we would not need to pay any attention to the situation in Rome. If the letter were a treatise, then in principle it could have been sent anywhere, and we would have had to take a 'situation' into consideration only insofar as it touched upon the general situation of the Pauline churches, as the apostle saw it at the time. The question of the literary nature of this document is therefore an introductory question of considerable importance. If we answer it wrongly, we shall be led inevitably into a misunderstanding of the whole document.

We will examine the question step by step. In xv. 22–26 Paul writes: 'Wherefore also I was hindered these many times from coming to you:

[28] *Bibelstudien*, pp. 189 ff. (E.T. *Bible Studies*, pp. 3 ff.); *Licht vom Osten*, pp. 194 ff. (E.T. *Light from the Ancient East*, pp. 228 ff.).

but now, having no more any τόπος (sphere of activity) in these regions (i.e. in the East), and having these many years a longing to come unto you, whensoever I go into Spain (for I hope to see you on my journey, and to be brought on my way thitherward by you . . .)—but now, I say, I go unto Jerusalem, ministering unto the saints. For it hath been the good pleasure of Macedonia and Achaia to make a certain contribution for the poor among the saints that are at Jerusalem.'

This statement amplifies what we already know from Paul's previous plans (cf. sections 7 and 8). The journey for the purpose of the collection that is just mentioned in 1 Cor. xvi. 4 is now actually taking place. Achaia is taking part, which means that Paul's relations with the Corinthians have evidently been restored. As Paul is writing the letter shortly before leaving for Jerusalem, Corinth could be the place of composition. The remark that Paul no longer has any τόπος (sphere of activity) is also interesting. He evidently thinks that his work in the East is in a sense completed. This is characteristic of the way in which he understands his missionary task. He founds here and there a church, which then has to continue the work; he himself intends to travel westwards, via Rome to Spain. But why should he write to the Romans this kind of letter, which Melanchthon in his *Loci* calls 'doctrinae christianae compendium', and which to a large extent has been used as such in dogmatic theology? This is the problem we have to consider. We cannot just regard this letter as Paul's dogmatics, although attempts have been made to interpret it in this sense.

According to Feine-Behm,[29] Paul intends to use the church at Rome as a campaign base for his further work and is aiming in this letter to introduce himself to the church. The need for such an introduction provided the occasion for Paul to give an account of his theological ideas at this turning point in his missionary work. 'What the apostle is here setting down are his *confessiones*.' These are connected, according to Feine-Behm, with his Jewish past in particular, with which he is here coming to terms. 'For this reason the letter gives the impression more of being a monologue than something written for others.' The turning-point at which Paul was standing led him to an act of self-examination and clarification, to draw up a balance sheet of his activities so far. These suggestions are of considerable importance for the question of the literary category to which the letter belongs, for these *confessiones* could—in theory at least—have been sent anywhere by Paul. But can we really describe

---

[29] *Einleitung in das Neue Testament* (11 ed., 1956), p. 173. (E.T. *Introduction to the New Testament* (from 14 ed.), SCM; Abingdon Press, 1966, p. 220).

this letter accurately as a monologue? And if we look at the matter from
the psychological point of view and say that it was the right moment for
Paul to review his ministry so far, would it not be equally understandable
or even more so, if it had taken the form of a farewell letter to the
churches he had founded? Why does Paul address these *confessiones* to
Rome in particular? We have to try and find a reason for this.

Michel[30] has a further suggestion to make. He thinks that in this
'didactic letter' Paul is setting out an apologia. 'The real question that
raised repeated opposition to the apostle is the relationship between
Judaism and paganism, or Jewish Christianity and Gentile Christianity
in his preaching.' Paul's preaching roused the synagogue to anger time
after time, and Paul must be afraid that the Roman church will believe
the evil reports about him. Michel therefore specifically rejects the
description of the letter as a *confessio*. 'What we have in the letter to the
Romans is the exegetical demonstration that Paul's preaching confronts
both Judaism and paganism in the proper way with the truth of the
Gospel.'

This seems in fact to be a more accurate description of the letter, insofar as the question of the relationship of Jewish and Gentile Christianity
really does arise, but is it true to say that 'the real question that raised
repeated opposition to the apostle' was the relationship of Jewish and
Gentile Christianity? This certainly could be said as far as Gal. is concerned—and this is the letter most often referred to in support of such
theories. At least Paul was aware of the problem there (cf. section 4) and
if we simply put Gal. alongside Rom.—as far as Protestant theology is
concerned they are usually accepted without question as the main letters
—we can be misled into thinking that this is *the* problem facing Paul.
But this is to take a quite unhistorical view of the facts, for this was by no
means the central problem that Paul had to deal with.

The opposition to the apostle did not arise in connection with the
problem of Jewish and Gentile Christianity, but with that of Christianity
and Gnosticism (although it is true the letter took a Jewish–Christian
form). There is only one exception to this—Jerusalem. Looking back to
the Apostolic Council, Paul could well have said there was a problem
here. Fuchs,[31] therefore, has suggested that Jerusalem was the church for
which Rom. was secretly intended. This, however, in no way solves the
problem, for Rom. is not a secret letter to Jerusalem, but obviously a
letter to Rome. Even though these problems did exist for Paul in Jeru-

[30] *Der Brief an die Römer* in Meyer (11 ed., 1957), p. 4.
[31] *Hermeneutik* (1954), p. 191.

salem (and this certainly was the case), this does not explain why he sent the letter—as we would be forced to say—to a 'false address'. It is quite possible, of course, that in writing this letter Paul has in certain respects the problems at Jerusalem in mind—a matter to which we shall return— but to speak of a 'secret address' is not really helpful, because the letter is quite clearly and openly addressed.

The address may in fact be quite correct. The fact that the letter deals with problems that arose at Jerusalem does not exclude the possibility that the same problems were present at Rome as well. We must now consider this possibility.

(2) *The Situation of the Church at Rome.* We can deduce this fairly clearly from chs. xii–xv. xii. 1–2 (in effect a heading) clearly marks the transition from the discussion of fundamental principles to that of ethics, which can be divided into three sections (a: xii. 3–21; b: xiii; c: xiv. 1–xv. 13). Paul exhorts the members of the church to give their bodies as a living sacrifice, holy and pleasing to God, for this is their λογικὴ λατρεία (not 'their reasonable worship', but rather 'their relevant worship'). They are to be transformed through the renewing of their minds, so that they can prove what the will of God is.

(a) xii. 3–21 contains general exhortations concerning the life of the church. The beginning evokes interest straightaway: I say on the basis of the grace that has been given to me to everyone among you, that none of you should think more highly of himself than he ought to think, but he should think of himself soberly, according to the gifts of grace he has received. Was this then the situation in the church at Rome, that one thought more highly of himself than of others? When we remember that the theme of 'the weak and the strong' comes later, we can see that in this passage the same theme is being dealt with, but in more general terms. In vv. 4–8 Paul turns to charismatic gifts, and the emphasis here is to be noted: different gifts should not lead to different evaluations. Everyone should exercise his gift but not seek to exalt himself above the rest. This is logically followed by the commandment of love (vv. 9–21); for if men who esteem themselves more highly than others are made to see that the distinctions between them are connected with different gifts of *grace*, they are turned towards one another again in love. This theme is developed at some length.

(b) In ch. xiii the exhortations are now directed outwards. Love must rule not only among the brethren, but the church must also accommodate itself to external institutions. Paul begins with the section about the authorities, which has often been misinterpreted. vv. 1–7: everyone should submit himself to the powers that be. The authorities have the power of life and death, and Christians should pay their taxes (see below). In conclusion (vv. 8–14) Paul contrasts the fulfilment of the laws of the State with that of the *nomos*, which is fulfilled in love. He goes on to give an eschatological basis to ethics: the night is far spent, the day is at hand; therefore Christians should live as children of the coming day, which is now nearer than at the time when they first believed. Even in this last of Paul's letters, therefore, there is a reference to the nearness of the *parousia*.

(c) xiv. 1–xv. 13 deals with the strong and the weak. This passage can be divided again into three sections.

(*a*) xiv. 1–12. They who are weak in faith should be received into the fellowship, and one should not dispute with such people about differences of opinion. What are the points of disagreement? The one believes he can eat anything, the other eats only vegetables. The one draws a distinction between different days, the other considers all days the same. (Later— xiv. 21—a further problem is mentioned: the one drinks wine, the other does not.) This throws light on xii. 3, which we have already considered —no one should think more highly of himself. In the context of the letter it is clearly the strong who are being addressed; it is those who eat meat, drink wine and observe no special days who mark themselves out as the strong ones. They are exhorted to accept the weak, not out of pity, but because strong and weak have to obey their own conscience and because they have the same Lord, although they are led to make different decisions. Strong and weak are really not theological descriptions at all, but distinctions according to the flesh. Here, then, is one problem that faced Paul at Rome, for the whole context rules out the possibility that Paul is setting out his ethical views here merely in the form of a paradigm (there might be weak . . . there might be strong. . . .). Later (xv. 1) he actually says: 'Now we that are strong. . . .'

(*β*) xiv. 13–23: Paul turns again specially to those who are strong. It is no doubt true basically that nothing in itself is unclean and that everything therefore can be enjoyed; but if a man considers something to be unclean, he cannot enjoy it. Therefore one cannot demand that a weak man should live in the same way as a strong one, but out of love and for the sake of peace a strong man can practise renunciation. 'For if because of meat thy brother is grieved, thou walkest no longer in love' (v. 15); and 'Overthrow not for meat's sake the work of God' (v. 20). In other words, he who considers himself strong, has the greater opportunities for showing love. This problem has evidently led to a conflict in Rome, and Paul is now trying to settle the dispute.

(γ) xv. 1–13: 'Now we that are strong ought to bear the infirmities of the weak, and not to please ourselves. . . .' This theme is then developed christologically—'for Christ also pleased not himself'. From v. 8 onwards it becomes quite clear what the two groups are: 'For I say that Christ hath been made a minister of the circumcision for the truth of God . . . that the Gentiles might glorify God for his mercy.' 'Strong' and 'weak' are therefore connected with Jews and Gentiles. As it is a question of food regulations and the observance of special days, the weak ones are the Jews and the strong the Gentiles. In the first place it is the Gentiles who are addressed—but not they alone. The peculiar feature of this letter is that its main message comes at the end. We have already seen this in the section we have considered. In ch. xii the general theme is that of 'not thinking more highly of oneself than of others', which is developed in detail. And all this is by way of preparation for what is set out at the end—the practical implications of it all. This preparation does not begin in ch. xii, but earlier.

First of all (i–viii) Paul deals generally with the question of Jews and Gentiles, and then (ix–xi) he turns specially to the Gentiles, who—as we now know—consider themselves to be the strong ones; in chs. xii ff. Paul goes on to deal in greater detail with the practical problems. This pattern in the train of thought should be noted. It is only at the end that the letter really discloses itself as a 'letter'. This circumstantial approach arises from the fact that Paul is not acquainted with the church and therefore has to set out his argument very cautiously.

We will now try to develop a little further the observations we made at the beginning. In particular we need to look more carefully at the suggestion that 'weak' and 'strong' refer to Jews and Gentiles. It would be more exact to say Jewish and Gentile Christians, but even this is not exact enough. We are familiar with the type of the Gentile Christian from our knowledge of the Pauline churches (or, to be more accurate, the churches founded by Paul). A Gentile Christian is one who has become a Christian directly from paganism without first being circumcised. Although we are very familiar with this, precisely on account of the Pauline churches, it would be by no means obvious to everyone at the time. After years of missionary work Paul still had to fight at the Apostolic Council for the principle that the Gentile Titus should not be circumcised. Gentiles had obviously been allowed to become Christians only after first becoming Jews. We have to assume this was the practice at Jerusalem at

H

least, but the same is probably true also for those churches that were formed in connection with a synagogue. At that time therefore there were alongside each other Jewish Christians, proselyte Christians and (Pauline) Gentile Christians.

To which group did these proselyte Christians really belong? Were they Gentile Christians, or—as they had in fact become Jews—had they to be counted among the Jewish Christians? In any case 'narrow' Jewish Christians would very easily quarrel with them when questions of food arose, more easily than with Gentile Christians. Seen in this light the disputes in the church at Rome become understandable, for—as becomes clear from the statements in the letter—the 'strong' naturally turn to the man from whom they can expect most support, i.e. Paul. This seems to be the most satisfactory explanation, although we must not overlook the fact that there are not such clear references here to an inquiry from the church as there are, for example, in 1 Cor. The strong ones have heard that Paul has founded Gentile Christian churches, and remembering that they were formerly Gentiles, they see that the 'fetters' they bear are connected with the proselyte status which they once adopted—and so they turn against the 'weak' ones.

We must remember that this is only an attempt to explain these disputes, and that all we actually know is that there were such disputes. However, the attempt to explain how the differences arose can help us to understand them better, but we have to draw a clear distinction between what is hypothesis and what can be definitely ascertained. The situation could of course have been quite different: it might have been that pure Gentile Christians had come to Rome, where there was a Jewish Christian community, and this gave rise to the tensions. But the other explanation seems more probable, because it is much less likely that new arrivals would have been able to exercise influence in a church than a group that was already there and had been a special group from the beginning.

We have very little information about the beginnings of the church in Rome. So far we have touched on only the more general considerations, but there is one more significant piece of evidence to be considered. In the year 49 or 50 the Emperor Claudius published an edict which expelled the Jews from Rome. The Roman historian Suetonius wrote in his *Vita Claudii* (round about the year 120) that the Emperor drove from Rome the Jews who had constantly caused disturbances at the instigation of a certain 'Chrestos'. This piece of information is not very clear, as it is not absolutely certain, though very likely, that Chrestos is the same as Christ.

If this is the case, Suetonius assumed that Chrestos himself was in Rome and caused the disturbance there. In any case, his statement was probably based on the knowledge that it was the Gospel of Christ that had called forth the ferment among the Jews of Rome.

This edict of Claudius is mentioned also in Acts xviii. 1–2. On the second missionary journey Paul travelled from Athens to Corinth, 'and he found a certain Jew (N.B.) named Aquila, a man of Pontus by race, lately come from Italy, with his wife Priscilla, because Claudius had commanded all the Jews to depart from Rome'. Paul stays with them. The couple were probably well-to-do. We meet them once again later: in 1 Cor., which was written during the third missionary journey, Paul sends greetings to the Corinthians from Aquila and Priscilla and their household—from Ephesus. In other words, after being expelled from Rome they went to Corinth and then on to Ephesus.

The statement seems plain enough, but there are certain difficulties. Were Aquila and Priscilla already Christians when they came to Corinth? If they were not, they would hardly have given hospitality to a Christian missionary, when they had been expelled from Rome on account of Christian–Jewish disturbances. But if this were the case, there must have been Christians in Corinth before Paul's arrival. The statement in 1 Cor. i. 16 according to which Paul himself baptized the household of Stephanus (in Corinth) which he describes in 1 Cor. xvi. 15 as the ἀπαρχὴ τῆς Ἀχαίας (the first fruits of Achaia), then presents certain difficulties. The statement cannot be correct if Aquila and Priscilla were already Christians at the time of Paul's arrival in Corinth. Or does Paul describe the household of Stephanus as 'the first fruits' because they were the first Achaian Christians?

In any case, the edict was certainly published, and if we combine the statement of Suetonius with the information in Acts we can conclude that the expulsion was connected with disturbances which arose in the Jewish synagogue, evidently as a result of the intrusion of Christian elements. We do not know, of course, whether the statement that 'all the Jews' had to leave Rome is to be taken literally. Haenchen[32] suggests that the edict applied only to the 'leaders and activists', but in view of the two pieces of evidence (Suetonius and Acts, which are independent of one another) this is only a supposition. But if the Jews had to leave the city, the Gentile Christian (or proselyte Christian) community would remain behind. However, this community would then almost certainly develop along different lines from what would have been possible within the synagogue.

[32] *Die Apostelgeschichte*, p. 475.

Claudius died in the year 54, and this brought about a relaxation of the edict, particularly as Nero was influenced by his wife who was favourably disposed towards the Jews. They soon attained greater importance again and even succeeded in winning special privileges. Rom. was written during the time when the Jews were allowed to return to Rome—but this also meant the Jewish Christians, who now find a Christian community very different from the one they had left. This goes a long way towards explaining the whole problem. It also helps to explain the passage xiii. 1 ff. What we have here is not a dogmatic treatise on the government and the State, but a demand for loyal conduct in order to avoid a fresh edict. In view of the imminence of the *parousia* a doctrine of the State was as out of place as any kind of social reform (cf. Phm. and 1 Cor. vii. 20 ff.).

Although we cannot say for certain just how this conflict arose in Rome, our suggestions concerning the composition of the church and also the sources (although incomplete) do show clearly enough that there were many occasions for the emergence of this very problem. And the problem is in fact the old 'Jerusalem' problem, which has now become an acute and genuinely Roman problem. Paul now takes his stand as regards this in view of his journey to Jerusalem, the outcome of which is completely uncertain and which evidently greatly concerns him. He writes: 'Now I beseech you, brethren, by our Lord Jesus Christ, and by the love of the Spirit, that ye strive together with me in your prayers to God for me; that I may be delivered from them that are disobedient in Judaea, and that my ministration which I have for Jerusalem may be acceptable to the saints; that I may come unto you in joy through the will of God, and together with you find rest' (xv. 30–32). We can see here the personal interest that Paul took in the problem he deals with in Rom. Originally he had not completely made up his mind to go to Jerusalem. In 1 Cor. xvi. 4 he merely hinted at the possibility that he himself might deliver the collection, together with a few people from Corinth. After this initial hesitation he now sees, immediately before setting out on his journey, what may possibly be awaiting him—persecution by the unbelieving Jews. This is understandable, for the method Paul adopted in his mission to the Gentiles—in contrast to the activities of the Jewish Christian church in Jerusalem—was difficult for the non-believing Jews to accept. Besides, Rom. xv. 30–32 still contains an echo of the anxious question as to how he will be welcomed by the church there.

Against this background we can understand why there are such detailed arguments as regards principles in Rom. The letter is concerned with a genuinely Roman problem—it is important to see this—but it is the same problem with which Paul finds himself faced now. In this sense one could almost speak of two 'recipients'. Of course this is not true from the literary point of view: the letter is still a letter to Rome and it seeks to say something to the Romans in their situation. But at the same time it has to be noted that the situation at Jerusalem, which Paul knows from previous experience, provides him at least with the illustrative material which he uses here. For this reason we can use chs. i–xi only with great caution for clarifying the situation. We need to be very cautious about assuming that all the elements we find here were actually present in Rome. To this extent there is a parallel with Gal. Once again Paul knows only by hearsay what the situation in Rome is and we have therefore to make allowance for the possibility that—drawing upon his experiences at Jerusalem—he to some extent exaggerates the situation.

What can we say then about this 'indirect' situation, of which we cannot be certain that it actually did obtain in Rome, but which Paul nevertheless envisaged on the basis of his experiences at Jerusalem?[33] As we saw when considering chs. xii–xv, the problem at Rome centred on the question whether first being a Jew meant anything for the Christian, as expressed in the observance of special days, food laws, etc. To what extent is the Jewish Christian still a Jew? Has Judaism still any significance for him? If we put the question in this form, we have to distinguish between the self-awareness of the Jew before he became a Christian and his self-awareness as a Jew after he has become a Christian. Between the two there lies (in Paul's terminology) the change from the old to the new aeon. For this reason Paul almost always argues dialectically, and if we do not take note of this fact our interpretation will inevitably be mistaken. We always need to ascertain in the first place the aeon Paul is thinking of in any particular statement.

In chs. i–xi by means of a discussion of the principles involved Paul is preparing his solution of the Roman problem, which he does not set out until the end of the letter after he has completed his detailed arguments. Time after time we hear the contrast: circumcision—uncircumcision. Paul leaves no doubt that one must first speak of the Jew and then of the Gentile—but since Christ there is no longer any first or second. 'Or is God the God of the Jews only? Is he not the God of Gentiles also? Yea, of Gentiles also: if so be that God is one, and he shall justify the circumcision by faith, and the uncircumcision through faith' (iii. 29 f.). Basically

[33] Cf. G. Harder, 'Der konkrete Anlaß des Römerbriefes', *Theologia Viatorum* 8 (1954), pp. 13 ff.

this is the same idea that Paul expressed in Gal. iii. 23 ff. After speaking of Abraham's justification by faith Paul asks 'Is this blessing then pronounced upon the circumcision, or upon the uncircumcision also?' and then goes on to argue (10–12) that Abraham received the blessing in uncircumcision. This means that he is the father of all those believers who are uncircumcised. Finally Paul says that Christ has become a minister of the circumcision as well as of the Gentiles (xv. 8–9).

It is quite clear that Paul's aim is to place Jews and Gentiles side by side as believers, for there is no difference between them. But why does Paul say this? The reason becomes obvious as soon as we note the surprising frequency of the word πάντες (all). Jews and Greeks, *all* are under sin (iii. 9). This word 'all' makes the two groups, whose relationship to God from the Jewish standpoint is a fundamentally different one, into a unity. The righteousness of God comes upon *all*. *All* have sinned, and *all* are freely pronounced just. God is the same Lord, rich in mercy to all who call upon him. But it must be remembered that there are people who want to be something special and who live as though they were something that others are not. This can only apply to Jews, who can in fact point to their 'outward' peculiarity, particularly in view of the fact that by contrast Paul emphasizes along the lines of Hellenistic Jewish thought the hidden, inward Jew who is circumcised in the heart and in the spirit, and not in the letter of the law (ii. 29).[34]

Paul is obviously arguing here in the light of his Jerusalem experiences. His arguments are directed against those who even as Christians still see their real guarantee of salvation in their having been Jews, in their circumcision. The same could have been said as regards Jerusalem at least until the Apostolic Council took place, although perhaps not thought out to the same extent, as circumcision was still taken for granted there. However, the whole question became a problem for Peter at Antioch. And the very same argument about circumcision that Paul had at Jerusalem, is involved in the dispute at Rome between the strong and the weak, for the weak expect the strong to behave like Jews even as Christians in the sense that they should adopt all that goes along with circumcision: the observance of the sabbath, food regulations, etc.

We have already seen that Paul in no way demands that the weak should live like the strong. They cannot do this for conscience's sake—although Paul can. This means that as far as Paul is concerned it is possible in principle for a Jewish Christian to renounce circumcision and the consequences that follow from it, but this is not demanded of him:

[34] Cf. *ibid.*, pp. 20 ff.

the point is that it is not permissible for Jewish Christians for their part to demand of the strong that they should adopt circumcision. It will not do for them to think that they are the only real Christians. It is for this reason that Paul emphasizes so strongly their equality: it is not circumcision or uncircumcision that matters most, but faith. This is an anti-Jewish polemic insofar as it is directed against the special claims made by the Jewish Christians, but at the same time Paul is very careful not to give the Gentiles any excuse for boasting on their part. They are confirmed as the strong—but this does not by any means imply a disqualification of the weak. Paul deals with these possible misunderstandings in chs. ix–xi particularly. He does not give the Jews up, for they are his compatriots; and the Gentile Christians for their part have no ground for exalting themselves above the Jews; for they must not and cannot, forget, that—as John put it—salvation is of the Jews.

In Rom. Paul expresses his argument in both directions—much more frequently than in other letters—in the form of the Cynic–Stoic diatribe. Time after time a possible objection is stated, taken up, dismissed and then the argument proceeds. If we take note of these different emphases in Rom. it becomes quite clear what Paul's aim really is. Taken out of context, several passages could be interpreted in an anti-Jewish sense; but taken out of context chs. ix–xi could also be interpreted in a pro-Jewish sense. But Paul's concern is with neither the one nor the other, but with peace in the new aeon. His aim is to bring about peace in a church in which there is tension between the weak and the strong because they are divided over the Jewish question, and it is to this situation that he addresses himself. What we find in Rom. therefore is not the problem as to what the attitude of Christianity to Judaism ought to be, as a matter of principle, nor do we find a dogmatic treatment of the 'problem of Israel' as it affects the Church.

This is not to say, of course, that this problem does not exist; but we cannot clarify this problem by an exegesis of Rom., because this general problem is not the same as the particular difficulty that has arisen in Rome. If this had been the case the arguments Paul puts forward for solving this difficulty could also be taken as the answer to the general problem. The subject of chs. ix–xi is not the general one of 'Church and Israel', for these chapters are addressed to Gentile Christians who find themselves together in the same church with Jewish Christians. Paul has supported these Gentile Christians in their stand against Jewish–Christian claims, but he tells them now that they for their part should not lord it over the Jews. What Paul says is therefore determined by the situation, and for this reason we cannot take these chapters as giving direct dogmatic guidance.

Only once does Paul go beyond this problem of Jewish and Gentile Christians, and that is in ch. xi, where he speaks of the conversion of Israel. But even here he does not use apocalyptic arguments and gives no 'time-table': first there comes the mission to the Gentiles, and when that is completed—in several centuries—Israel will be converted. Paul says all this in the light of the imminence of the *parousia* (cf. xiii. 11–14). This is connected with his understanding of the mission—or, conversely, his understanding of the mission is connected with his expectation of an early *parousia*. The East is by no means Christian after the founding of a few churches, but Paul no longer has a τόπος there and so must go elsewhere.

It is worth considering the possibility that Paul saw a connection between his intended visit to Jerusalem and the conversion of Israel. Will not the Gentile Christian church which is now in existence and is growing inevitably prove an attraction to Israel? We know that this did not happen, nor did the imminently expected *parousia* take place. For this reason the passages in Rom. that seem so important from the point of view of dogma can be used as material for a systematic theology only with the greatest caution, and much more 'piece-meal' than has often been done in the past.

(3) *A Survey of Chapters i–xi.* At the beginning there is a lengthy introduction (i. 1–7). In i. 8–17 the theme is introduced. After a thanksgiving for the faith of the Romans, which is known in the whole world and after an apology that he has not yet been to Rome, Paul says 'I am debtor both to Greeks and to barbarians, both to the wise and to the foolish. So, as much as in me is, I am ready to preach the gospel to you also that are in Rome. For I am not ashamed of the gospel: for it is the power of God unto salvation to every one that believeth; to the Jew first, and also to the Greek. For therein is revealed a righteousness of God by faith unto faith: as it is written, But the righteous shall live by faith.' We can already hear the main theme: Paul is the apostle to the Gentiles; the Gospel is in the first place for the Jews and then for the Gentiles. But this apparent distinction of rank is immediately removed, for the supreme importance attaches to faith. The just shall live by faith. We now come to the real substance of the letter, which has a very clear structure.

Section One: Gentiles and Jews in the old aeon (i. 18–iii. 20). It should be noted that Paul is speaking here of 'earlier' times. As one who lives in the new aeon, he looks back and asks: What was it like then? He considers the Gentiles first.

(a) The Gentiles in the former aeon (i. 18–32). They were under the wrath of God. They could have known the will of God by the aid of reason, but they did not act in accordance with God's will, and God therefore gave them up to immorality, greed, envy, etc.

(b) The Jews in the former aeon (ii. 1–iii. 20). The Jew also is without excuse, for neither the law nor circumcision provide protection from the wrath of God. What Paul is attacking here, therefore, is a false security. If an uncircumcised man keeps the law, he is regarded as a circumcised man (ii. 26). He is not a Jew who claims to be one outwardly, for the true Jew is the one who is a Jew inwardly.

The conclusion of the first section, in which the former aeon is considered from the standpoint of the new, is as follows: Jews and Gentiles stand under the same accusation, under the same guilt, before God. Paul asks (iii. 9)—very directly: 'What then? are we in worse case than they? No, in no wise: for we before laid to the charge both of Jews and Greeks, that they are all under sin; as it is written, There is none righteous, no, not one.' From the standpoint of the new aeon the Jew (in the former aeon) has no advantage over the Gentile (in the former aeon).

Section Two now turns to the new aeon (iii. 21–viii. 39), and Paul deals with (a) man in the new aeon (iii. 21–iv. 25) and (b) life in the new aeon (v–viii).

(a) The new righteousness has been manifested through Christ. It comes not from works, but from faith. This is illustrated by reference to Abraham, who received the promise before he was circumcised (i.e. apart from the law). Therefore the promised inheritance is linked with faith, in other words, it is a gift. In conclusion (iv. 22–25) Paul shows what the example of Abraham means: 'Wherefore also it was reckoned unto him for righteousness. Now it was not written for his sake alone, that it was reckoned unto him; but for our sake also, unto whom it shall be reckoned, who believe on him that raised Jesus our Lord from the dead.' This passage is very significant: the Scripture was written for Abraham—and for us. The fact is that in Scripture something is revealed in the case of Abraham, but Paul draws a distinction between Abraham and Scripture. The important thing is not that something happened to Abraham, but that something happened to Abraham that was set down. And as it is true for Christians as well, that they should live by faith, Abraham is now seen as a type of the believer. Those who try to show that there is a *Heilsgeschichte* in Paul (as there is, for example in Luke) overlook the special way in which he uses Scripture. Paul says in fact that if Scripture is read correctly we can learn from it that righteousness comes from faith. Abraham is seen to be on our side.

The new aeon is therefore marked by the fact that man lives by that new thing that has been given, by faith.

(b) Nygren[35] divides this section about life in the new aeon (v–viii) very suggestively:

> v: free from wrath
> vi: free from sin
> vii: free from the law
> viii: free from death.

The last chapter closes with the hymn: 'Nothing can separate us from the love of God.'

If the Gentile Christians stand side by side with the Jewish Christians and the claim of the Jewish Christians to be something special cannot be upheld, and if their Judaism is of no avail, does this mean that one can despise Israel?

Paul deals with this question in *Section Three* (ix–xi). He places Judaism—the Judaism of the Jewish Christians—which is the immediate problem, in its right relation to Gentile Christianity. Even if God promises something, he does not thereby forfeit his sovereignty. The promise is made to the 'true' Israel, which is the 'believing' Israel. 'For they are not all Israel, which are of Israel' (ix. 6). The Israel of the flesh has in fact offended by striving after its own righteousness instead of submitting to God's righteousness. Paul admits that the people of Israel have a zeal for God, but their zeal is without understanding, for Christ is the end of the law (x. 2–4). This has to be said and made known to Israel, and this is where the mission of the Gentile Christian to Israel lies. 'How then shall they call on him in whom they have not believed? and how shall they believe in him whom they have not heard? and how shall they hear without a preacher? and how shall they preach, except they be sent?' (x. 14 ff.) But Paul has to go on immediately and ask: But have they not in fact heard?—Of course they have. The sound of the Word has gone out into all the world. But who responded? Those who had not sought God—in other words, the Gentiles. They should now make Israel envious.

In the parable of the olive tree (xii. 17–24) Paul pleads with the Gentile Christians not to claim superiority over Israel. They have a task

---

[35] *Der Römerbrief* (3 ed., 1959). (E.T. *Commentary on Romans* (from the 1944 ed.), SCM; Fortress Press, 1952).

to perform for Israel, which they will carry out best by showing to Israel what the church is. God will then put Israel also on the right path. 'For God hath shut up all unto disobedience, that he might have mercy upon all' (xi. 32).

This section also ends with a hymn: 'O the depth of the riches both of the wisdom and the knowledge of God! how unsearchable are his judgements, and his ways past tracing out!'

This leads directly to the fourth section, which we have already considered.

(4) *Chapter xvi.* It is strange that at the end of ch. xv, after discussing his plans for his travels, Paul uses a phrase he regularly employs for concluding a letter (v. 33): 'Now the God of peace be with you all. Amen.' Then there follows:

xvi. 1–2:   A commendation of Phoebe, a servant of the church at Cenchreae, the eastern harbour of Corinth. He asks the Romans to receive her and help her.

xvi. 3–16:   A list of the names of twenty-six people to whom Paul sends his greetings. This list of greetings again closes with its own conclusion: 'Salute one another with a holy kiss. All the churches of Christ salute you.'

xvi. 17–20: A warning about errors. They cause scandal and division, for their god is the belly. Again there follows a separate conclusion: 'The grace of our Lord Jesus Christ be with you.'

xvi. 21–24: A further list of greetings, but this time greetings from fellow-workers with Paul, followed once again by its own conclusion: 'The grace of our Lord Jesus Christ be with you all.'

xvi. 25–27: A doxology.

The various conclusions are in some cases lacking in the manuscripts—for the obvious reason that so many conclusions following upon one another must have seemed excessive to a scribe.

How can we explain this strange chapter? We could of course say that Paul concluded the letter with ch. xv, but then met Phoebe who was on the way to Rome and wished to take the letter with her, and therefore he wrote the commendation for her and also added some other greetings. It then occurred to him that the heresies might be wreaking havoc in Rome also, and so he added a prophylactic warning against them. It then also occurred to him that he might send greetings to some of his fellow-workers, and to this he went on to add a doxology. Such an explanation, however, can hardly be taken seriously.

There are certain difficulties, however, not only as regards the psychology of the writer but also as regards the contents. The doxology at the end is completely out of keeping with Paul's terminology, and it is generally agreed nowadays that what we have here is a liturgical formula from the post-apostolic period. The doxology therefore is certainly secondary. Besides, it is found in different positions in several manuscripts. In P[46] the order is: i–xv; xvi. 25–27; xvi. 1–23. The *Koine* text puts the doxology after xiv. 23, and occasionally it is found twice (after xiv. 23 and after xvi. 23). In other words, it was repeated in the course of the transmission of the text.

Is it possible that Paul knew twenty-six people in Rome whom he mentions in his list of greetings in vv. 3–16? It is conceivable, of course, that as a result of the relaxation of Claudius' edict members of the church who came from Rome and whom Paul had got to know in the East while the edict was in force, have now returned to Rome. But those to whom Paul sends greetings—apart from a few exceptions—do not have Jewish names. In addition, greetings are sent to Aquila and Priscilla; they had in fact fled from Rome, but at the time of the founding of the Corinthian church they were (according to Acts) in Corinth, and at the time when 1 Cor. was written they were in Ephesus (for in 1 Cor. xvi. 19 Paul conveys greetings from them—in Ephesus—to Corinth). We could of course say that they were now in Rome once again; but at the same time greetings are sent to Epaenetus (Rom. xvi. 5), who is described as ἀπαρχὴ τῆς Ἀσίας (the first-fruits of Asia), and was therefore the first converted Christian of Asia (i.e. from the district of Ephesus). Is it just by chance that he also happens to be in Rome?

The most probable explanation therefore seems to be that this list of greetings is a fragment from a letter to Ephesus. This is the explanation generally accepted nowadays. The remaining parts of Rom. xvi appear to be sections of letters which have otherwise disappeared. It is possible that some of the sections come from the same source, but it is impossible to demonstrate that this is the case. As one section has simply been added to another, we cannot really speak of a process of editing. As far as the exegesis of Rom. is concerned we cannot really find much to help us in ch. xvi.

BIBLIOGRAPHY

E. Gaugler, *Der Römerbrief* (Prophezei, 2 vols., 1945 and 1952).
O. Kuß, *Der Römerbrief* (1957 ff.—Catholic).
O. Michel, *Der Brief an die Römer* (Meyer, 12 ed., 1962).
G. Friedrich, 'Römerbrief' in *RGG*, V, cols. 1137 ff.
G. Harder, 'Der konkrete Anlaß des Römerbriefes', *Theologia Viatorum* 8 (1954), pp. 13 ff.

Commentaries: C. K. Barrett, Black (1957); C. H. Dodd, Moffat (1932); W. Sanday and A. C. Headlam, ICC (5 ed., 1902).
F. F. Bruce, 'St. Paul in Rome', *BJRL* 46 (1963-4), pp. 326 ff.
E. J. Goodspeed, 'Phoebe's Letter of Introduction,' *HTR* 44 (1951), pp. 55 ff.
T. M. Taylor, 'The Place of Origin of Romans', *JBL* 67 (1948), pp. 281 ff.

II. The Synoptic Gospels and the Acts of the Apostles

The four books that come first in the present sequence of the Canon bear the title 'Gospels'. These, however, are not the titles provided by the books themselves (the only exception to some extent is Mark), but are headings that derive from the second century. This is the outcome of a later process of levelling which raises a number of problems, as a result of which—regardless of the specific character of the various works—all writings which contained stories of Jesus were included under the concept of 'Gospel'.

The four 'Gospels' do in fact give the impression at first sight of presenting the course of Jesus' life, but if we compare them from this point of view alone, we can see immediately far-reaching differences, particularly between the first three Gospels and the fourth. According to the first three Gospels Jesus begins his public ministry after John the Baptist has been imprisoned (Mk. i. 14, et parr.), but according to John Jesus and John the Baptist work alongside each other for a time (Jn. iii. 22–24). According to Mt., Mk. and Lk. Jesus makes only one journey to Jerusalem, but according to Jn. he visited the capital several times during his public ministry (Jn. ii. 13; v. 1; vii. 10; xii. 12). Whereas according to Mk. xiv. 12 ff. et parr. Jesus holds his last supper as a Passover meal, from which it follows that he dies on the 15th Nisan, Jn. gives a different date, according to which Jesus was crucified on the 14th (cf. Jn. xviii. 28; xix. 14).

The mere mention of these differences—and there are many more—makes it clear that to consider the Gospels from the historical point of view raises many problems. If we were to adopt this course, we should find ourselves faced all the time with a variety of alternatives, for such differences cannot be harmonized. As there are other distinctions among the four Gospels (Jn., for example, uses to a large extent quite different traditions and makes Jesus speak in a quite different style), and the main contrast is always between the first three Gospels and Jn., the usual approach is to take the Gospels according to Matthew, Mark and Luke as a group and consider them together.

10. THE SYNOPTIC PROBLEM

The extensive parallels in the structure of the Gospels according to Matthew, Mark and Luke make it possible to set them out alongside each other in such a way that the corresponding sections in the three Gospels stand opposite each other. On account of the possibility of such a synoptic view these works have been called the 'Synoptics' since the end of the eighteenth century. If we take this synoptic view of them, the points of similarity stand out clearly. This is particularly true as regards their construction, where it is noticeable that there are quite similar compilations of material (e.g. the chapter of parables in Mt. xiii, Mk. iv and Lk. viii). The affinity, however, goes far beyond this, often to details of language and style, and quite frequently there are passages which correspond almost word for word (cf. Mt. xxi. 23–27 = Mk. xi. 27–33 = Lk. xx. 1–8; or Mt. xxiv. 4–8 = Mk. xiii. 5–8 = Lk. xxi, 8–11).

On the other hand, in spite of these striking similarities there are also noticeable differences. At the beginning and the end Mt. and Lk. go into greater detail than Mk., but they are not in agreement with one another (cf. the genealogy of Jesus in Mt. i. 1 ff. and Lk. iii. 23 ff. According to Mt. xxviii. 9, 16 the Risen Lord appears in Jerusalem and in Galilee, but according to Lk. xxiv only in and around Jerusalem). In other passages Mt. and Lk. use material which corresponds almost word for word, to which there is no parallel in Mk. (e.g. Mt. vi. 25–34 = Lk. xii. 22–31; Mt. xii. 43–45 = Lk. xi. 24–26). On the other hand, each of the three Gospels contains material that is found in none of the others (Mt. xxvii. 62–66; Mk. iv. 26–29; Lk. xix. 1–10).

The Synoptic Problem can therefore be expressed as follows: How can we explain the considerable similarity of the three works to one another, and how can we explain the differences that exist in spite of the extensive agreement?

(1) *Earlier Attempts to solve the Problem.* It was not until the beginning of the study of New Testament Introduction—in other words, not until about the middle of the eighteenth century—that the Synoptic Problem was really recognized and the attempt made to find a solution to it. Four different theories were developed, some of them at the same time, others successively, of which we shall give a brief outline. It should be noted that these theories were varied in a number of directions and were sometimes

I

blended with elements from other theories with the result that to some extent we have only a very confused picture of earlier research. The following basic types, however, can be distinguished.

(a) The 'original Gospel' theory assumes that there was an original Gospel—of which no trace remains—that was written in Aramaic. The Gospels as we know them would then have to be taken as independent translations of this original Gospel. After Lessing[1] proposed this theory it was taken up by Eichhorn,[2] who developed it to the extent that he assumed there were several revisions which formed intermediate stages between the original Gospel and the Synoptic Gospels.

This theory, however, breaks down because an independent translation would not explain what is often a word for word agreement, and because what we find is not just translation, but far-reaching revision. Although Eichhorn made allowance for this, he had to introduce too many unknown factors. Nevertheless this theory was based on the realization that the Synoptic Gospels were the outcome of a fairly long process of development.

(b) The 'narrative theory'—also known as the 'fragment theory'—followed an entirely different line. It assumed that many different individual stories (narratives, or fragments) were in circulation, which were brought together by the Gospel writers in different selections and sequences (Schleiermacher[3]). This approach does not explain the extensive resemblance in the structure of the Gospels, but on the other hand it does rightly see that the emergence of the works can at least be traced back to a process of compilation.

(c) The 'tradition theory' envisages a pre-literary oral tradition. It assumes that a uniform oral Gospel was developed among the apostles at Jerusalem at an early stage. According to the missionary requirements it was then translated, modified and later committed to writing. In Matthew and Mark—but even here considerably Hellenized—it was given a Palestinian form: Luke, on the other hand, wrote a Pauline Gospel. Herder[4] first suggested this theory, and Gieseler[5] developed it a

---

[1] G. E. Lessing, *Theses aus der Kirchengeschichte* (1776); *Neue Hypothesen über die Evangelisten als bloß menschliche Geschichtsschreiber betrachtet* (1778).

[2] J. G. Eichhorn, *Über die drey ersten Evangelien* (1794); *Einleitung in das Neue Testament*, I (1804).

[3] F. Schleiermacher, *Über die Schriften des Lukas. Ein kritischer Versuch*, I (1817).

[4] J. G. Herder, *Christliche Schriften*, 3. Sammlung: 'Von Gottes Sohn, der Welt Heiland. Nach Johannes Evangelium. Nebst einer Regel der Zusammenstimmung unserer Evangelien aus ihrer Entstehung und Ordnung' (1797).

[5] J. C. L. Gieseler, *Historisch-kritischer Versuch über die Entstehung und die frühesten Schicksale der schriftlichen Evangelien* (1818).

few years later. This theory certainly takes into account the part played by oral transmission in the development of tradition, but the relationship of the Synoptic Gospels to one another cannot be adequately explained unless one assumes that there was a literary dependence.

(d) The 'interdependence theory' does assume a literary dependence and thus follows a basically different line from the other theories. The fact is now seriously faced that the relationship of the three Gospels to one another is not based on a common dependence upon a fourth factor, but arose as a result of direct use. Again, there are various possibilities here. Griesbach,[6] for example, assumed that Mk. was an extract from Mt. and Lk., but this does not explain why Mark should have omitted so much material and therefore we have to adopt a different approach. It was Lachmann[7] who made the decisive and far-reaching observation that Mt. and Lk. are in agreement only when they are in agreement with Mk.; but on the other hand, where they introduce material that is not present in Mk. they introduce it in different places. This can be explained however only on the assumption that Mk. formed the basis for the pattern of the two other accounts. This observation was then developed and led eventually to the two-sources theory which is generally accepted nowadays (H. J. Holtzmann[8] and B. Weiß[9]).

(2) *The Two-Sources Theory.* As the name implies, it is assumed that two sources formed the literary origin of the Synoptic Gospels. The first source (and to this extent the Two-Sources theory is a form of the 'interdependence' theory) is one of the Gospels themselves, i.e. Mk. We have to ask straightaway whether the other two longer Gospels had as their model the canonical Mk. or whether they used an earlier form of it, the so-called 'original Mark' (*Urmarkus*). It is noticeable that a number of the traditions in Mk. as we know it are to be found in only one of the other Gospels, for example Mk. vi. 17–19 = Mt. xiv. 3–12; Mk. viii. 1–10 = Mt. xv. 32–39, with no parallels in Lk.; on the other hand, Mk. i. 21–28 = Lk. iv. 31–37; Mk. ix. 38–41 = Lk. ix. 49–50; Mk. vii. 41–44 = Lk. xxi. 1–4, with no parallels in Mt. There are also some

---

[6] J. J. Griesbach, *Commentatio qua Marci euangelium totum e Matthaei et Lucae commentariis decerptum esse monstratur* (1789–90).

[7] C. Lachmann, 'De ordine narrationum in evangeliis synopticis', *ThStKr* 8 (1835), pp. 570 ff.

[8] H. J. Holtzmann, *Die synoptischen Evangelien, ihr Ursprung und ihr geschichtlicher Charakter* (1863).

[9] B. Weiß, *Lehrbuch der Einleitung in das Neue Testament* (1886). (E.T. *A Manual of Introduction to the New Testament*, 2 vols., 1887–8).

passages in Mk. that are missing in both the other Gospels (Mk. iv. 26–29; vii. 32–36; viii. 22–26). The suggestion has therefore sometimes been made that Matthew and Luke used as their model a shorter Mk. than the one we know today, and that perhaps the versions the two used were different.

This assumption, however, is not only unnecessary, but at the same time it also raises fresh difficulties. The fact that one of the later Gospels does not contain a particular pericope found in Mk. does not necessarily mean that it was not present in the model that was used. In many instances it is possible to suggest good reasons for making an abbreviation. And we cannot ignore the cases where both Mt. and Lk. omit the same sections. Are we to take these as accidental? This would not be to assume any more than if we postulate an *Urmarkus*. In fact there is no trace of such an original Mk. It would be possible to suggest that it had been subsequently lost, but this would imply a very strange course in the transmission of Mk. As Matthew and Luke did not use the same copy of Mk. and as they also lived in different places, we should have to allow for a widespread distribution of the *Urmarkus*. Somewhere a copy of this *Urmarkus* was then expanded into the Mk. that we know—and we would have to assume that this was the starting-point for all the subsequent history of the transmission of Mk. The widespread *Urmarkus*, on the other hand, was no longer copied, and (accidentally?) all existing copies were lost. This seems so improbable that it is better to abandon the *Urmarkus* theory.

We also need to note that the Two-Sources theory looks at the connections between Mk. and the other Synoptics merely from the angle of literary dependence. But we now know that in their writing Matthew and Luke were influenced by definite theological concepts, which often resulted in a very independent treatment of their models (cf. sections 13 and 14). The absence of Marcan passages from the other two Gospels cannot therefore be explained by the questionable assumption of a source in which these passages were already missing, but it can point to a deliberate omission by the evangelists as a result of the viewpoint they adopted. We can therefore regard Mk. as the one source of the other two Synoptic Gospels.

We have also to note that Mt. and Lk. contain a considerable amount of common material not present in Mk. that is either identical word for word or evidently derived from the same traditions (e.g. Mt. x. 26–33 = Lk. xii. 2–9; Mt. xi. 2–27 = Lk. vii. 18–28; xvi. 16; vii. 31–35; x. 13–15, 21–22; Lk. vi. 20–23, 27–49 = Mt. v. 3, 4, 6, 11, 12, 44, 39–42; vii. 12;

v. 46–47, 45, 48; vii. 1–2; xv. 14; x. 24–25; vii. 3–5; xii. 33–35; vii. 21, 24–27). Such passages can be explained only by assuming that Matthew and Luke used a second source besides Mk. This has not come down to us, but it can—in part at least—be reconstructed. As for the most part (though not exclusively) it contained spoken material it has generally been called the 'sayings source' or 'logia source' and referred to by abbreviation as Q (German *Quelle*). To what extent it was set down in writing, and whether Matthew and Luke had it in the same form, are still matters of argument.

A number of doublets in Mt. and Lk. make it clear that Mk. also, although he may not have known Q itself, was at least familiar with traditions which later found their way into Q (for example, Mt. xvi. 24 f. and Lk. ix. 23 f. are derived from Mk. viii. 34 f., but Mt. x. 38 f. and Lk. xiv. 27; xvii. 33 from Q). This brings before us for the first time the fact that even Mk. was not written spontaneously but employed source materials, but this is of no significance as far as the Two-Sources theory is concerned (see, however, section 11).

We cannot determine with any certainty the origin of the so-called special material (abbreviated as 'S'), that is, the traditions that are found either only in Mt. or only in Lk., particularly in the case of spoken material—for as Q has not come down to us we cannot say whether Matthew or Luke used their version of Q in its entirety or only in selection. As it seems, however, that Q contained no narrative material (one exception probably is Mt. viii. 5–13 = Lk. vii. 1–10), it is possible that the narrative parts at least of the special material in Mt. and Lk. come from other sources or from oral tradition, but could also in some cases have been compiled by the evangelists themselves (e.g. Mt. 1; ii; xiv. 28–31; xxvii. 19, 24 f.; xxviii. 16–20; Lk. i, ii; iii. 23–38; v. 1–11; vii. 11–17; xvii. 11–19, xix. 1–10; xxiv. 13–53).

The Two-Sources theory gives rise therefore to the following pattern:

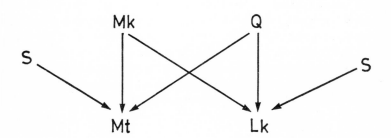

The question whether Matthew was familiar with Lk. or Luke with Mt. can be definitely answered in the negative.

This Two-Sources theory has been so widely accepted by scholars that one feels inclined to abandon the term 'theory' (in the sense of 'hypothesis'). We can in fact regard it as an assured finding—but we must bear in mind that there are inevitable uncertainties as far as the extent and form of Q and the special material are concerned. But this should not lead us into attempting to bring further sources to light. This attempt has sometimes been made,[10] but has not produced any convincing results.

The Two-Sources theory helps to explain both what the Synoptic Gospels have in common and also where they differ—but only as regards the literary relationships of the books to one another. But as the evangelists, even when they used models, did not copy them word for word, to demonstrate these literary relationships is really only a first step towards further findings.

(3) *The Significance of the Two-Sources Theory for the Exegesis of the Synoptic Gospels.* We shall consider later the question of the historicity of what is recorded in the Gospels (section 11), but we can already say that it is very unlikely that Matthew and Luke at least were direct witnesses of the life of Jesus, particularly in view of their dependence on literary models (on Lk. i. 1–4, see section 14, 2).

We need also to remember that for Matthew and Luke Mk. was in no sense 'canonical'. In fact they treated their model very 'critically' and took considerable liberties in altering the text (the same is probably true of their treatment of Q, although here we cannot trace the alterations so easily, as Q first has to be reconstructed). However, as this independent treatment of their sources by Matthew and Luke is not merely arbitrary, but is obviously connected with the standpoint they adopt, the Two-Sources theory has an important bearing upon exegesis in that the special features of these two writers are seen precisely where they vary from their models. This means that Mt. and Lk. have always to be expounded in the light of Mk. (and of Q) for it is these texts that form the background for the later documents.

When we realize this we see the danger of reversing the relationship. If we make a purely Synoptic comparison and place the parallel texts alongside each other we can easily overlook the fact that they represent not only something that can be compared side by side, but also a tem-

---

[10] E. Hirsch, *Frühgeschichte des Evangeliums, I: Das Werden des Markusevangeliums* (2 ed., 1951); *II: Die Vorlagen des Lukas und das Sondergut des Matthäus* (1941).

poral sequence. It is therefore a mistake to draw upon the later variations for the exegesis of Mk. and to produce in this way a harmonized text. The alterations in Mt. and Lk. have at best an indirect significance for the exegesis of Mk., for they can show under certain circumstances which of the statements in Mk. the later writers feel they no longer can or wish to make. Indirectly, therefore, the alterations do throw some light on Mark's statements, but we have to proceed with great caution in this respect, for the temporal sequence has always to be borne in mind.

If we do this, however, the use of the Two-Sources theory is of prime importance for the exegesis of Mt. and Lk. It is all the clearer the more we keep in view the contribution of the two Synoptic writers (cf. the appendix following section 14).

BIBLIOGRAPHY

G. Bornkamm, *Jesus von Nazareth* (4–5 ed., 1960), Appendix 1. (E.T. *Jesus of Nazareth*, Hodder; Harper, 1960).

G. Bornkamm, 'Evangelien, formgeschichtlich' and 'Evangelien, synoptische', *RGG*, II, cols. 749 ff.; 753 ff.

P. Wernle, *Die synoptische Frage* (1899).

F. W. Beare, *The Earliest Records of Jesus* (1962).

W. R. Farmer, *The Synoptic Problem: a Critical Analysis* (1964).

W. L. Knox, *The Sources of the Synoptic Gospels*, 2 vols. (1953–7).

J. H. Ropes, *The Synoptic Gospels* (2 ed., 1960).

B. H. Streeter, *The Four Gospels* (1924). (Cf. O. E. Evans, 'Synoptic Criticism since Streeter', *ET* 72 (1960–61), pp. 295 ff.).

See further: D. Guthrie, 'Some Recent Books on the Gospels', *VE* 4 (1965).

11. THE SYNOPTIC TRADITION

The study of the Synoptic Gospels, which reached a landmark around the turn of the century with the emergence of the Two-Sources theory, had always been carried out with the aim of trying to get as close as possible to the Jesus of history. When Mk. was now shown to be the oldest Gospel it was believed that this goal had been almost attained and that this book gave by and large an account of the course of Jesus's life.

Doubts, however, were soon raised. To which literary category should Mk. be assigned? It is neither a historical record nor a biography: on the one hand the linking of the various events into a narrative sequence is far too disjointed, and on the other hand everything that one would expect in a biography in the traditional sense is lacking—a description of Jesus' appearance, his character, his development from childhood onwards, etc. Therefore Mk. could not be interpreted either as a historical record, or as a biography. One could more readily interpret Lk. in this way, but this would mean that historical interest in the strict sense of the word developed relatively late. What can we say of Mk. in this respect?

Wrede[11] showed that Mk. by no means produced a historical record, but that he himself stood within the theology of the Church and was influenced by this theology in the account he wrote insofar as he expressed a particular theological conception in his work. Wellhausen,[12] however, pointed out that the sequences of tradition and the individual traditions brought together as a result of an editorial process in Mk. (and in the other Gospels) represented various stages. This gave rise to a new task, that of giving more attention to the separate units. But was it possible simply to isolate this element in the Gospels, particularly in Mk.?

The final proof of the justification of such an undertaking was provided by K. L. Schmidt.[13] He examined the 'framework of the story of Jesus' and showed that in Mk. there is a discrepancy between the framework and the statements made within the separate sections of narrative when they are considered from the historical standpoint. The references both to

[11] W. Wrede, *Das Messiasgeheimnis in den Evangelien. Zugleich ein Beitrag zum Verständnis des Markusevangeliums* (1901, 2 ed., 1913, reprinted 1962). (E.T. in preparation, James Clark).

[12] J. Wellhausen, *Einleitung in die drei ersten Evangelien* (1905).

[13] K. L. Schmidt, *Der Rahmen der Geschichte Jesu. Literarkritische Untersuchungen zur ältesten Jesusüberlieferung* (1919).

geography and chronology are not really consistent, and therefore the conclusion was inevitably drawn that the framework is secondary, and is the work of the evangelist. This made it clear that it might perhaps after all be possible to give an account of separate events in the life of Jesus, but not their historical sequence. To write a 'life of Jesus' proved in the end to be impossible, for the available material simply did not permit it.

The recognition of this fact is of the greatest importance for exegesis. It is not permissible when expounding a particular pericope to consider what happened before and what is to happen later and then to explain— perhaps from the psychological angle—why Jesus or those around him behaved in the way they did. The sequence is not a historical one, and the most we can do is to ask whether the evangelist is seeking to express some particular message through the sequence as he depicts it.

This evident lack of interest in the story of Jesus' life on the part of the Christian community in its early days seemed very strange. What kind of interest was there? This question could only be answered by a careful examination of the smaller units of tradition, which is what the so-called Form Criticism undertook. Before we consider this particular approach we will give a brief survey of the separate units—and try to arrange them.

(1) *Forms and Types.* The extensive and sharply differentiated material can be divided very roughly into narrative and sayings material.

(a) The miracle stories make up a large part of the narrative material, but we cannot speak of them as a uniform type. Alongside the nature miracles (e.g. the Stilling of the Storm, Mk. iv. 35–41 and the Walking on the Sea, Mk. vi. 45–52), the miracles of Feeding (Mk. vi. 34–44; viii. 1–9) and Peter's Draught of Fishes (Lk. v. 1–11) there is a great number of different kinds of healing miracles. The account is often very general and does not aim to relate what happened in the greatest possible detail, but aims rather to underline the miracle as such and so glorify the figure of Jesus. This comes out, for example, in the fact that the account of the miracles is given in a form for which both Jewish and Hellenistic parallels can be adduced, but most of all in the fact that it uses a general pattern. In the exposition the duration and seriousness of the illness is described and earlier fruitless attempts at healing are mentioned, etc. (Mk. v. 25 f.; ix. 18–22; Lk. xiii. 11). When the sufferer meets the miracle-worker the healing is described, in the course of which occasionally (although only seldom in the Gospels) the detailed manipulations or mysterious words are mentioned (Mk. vii. 33 f.; viii. 23). This is followed by the demonstration of the miracle that has been performed (paralytics carry their beds, Mk. ii. 11 f., those raised from the dead are given food, Mk. v. 43). Finally the 'refrain' refers to the astonishment of the crowd, sometimes linked with a word of praise (Mk. i. 27; ii. 12; Lk. xiii. 17).

If the purpose of these miracle-stories is to make clear—generally indirectly—who Jesus is, then the same purpose is achieved—but more directly—in another group of stories in which the person of Jesus is at the centre: the Baptism, the Temptation, Peter's Confession and the Transfiguration. According to their style these stories are legends (but this term is not meant to express any historical evaluation). In some of the other legends the connection with the person of Jesus is only indirect (e.g. Peter's Denial). The various Easter stories (with the Empty Tomb and the detailed accounts of the appearances) belong to this category, as well as the account of the so-called 'Institution' of the Lord's Supper.

(b) An intermediate stage between narrative material and sayings material is formed by the large number of shorter stories which contain a saying by Jesus in the framework of a brief scene. In some cases the saying interprets the scene, in others the scene illustrates the saying ('ideal scenes'). Among examples are the eating with publicans (Mk. ii. 15–17), the question of fasting (Mk. ii. 18–22), the blessing of the children (Mk. x. 13–16) and the story of the Tribute Money (Mk. xii. 13–17). The form here is often that of the dialogue or disputation, for which there are many parallels in Rabbinic literature.

It is characteristic of these stories that one can often trace in them the growth of tradition. There is evidence of secondary literary amplification (for example, Mk. ii. 23–26, 28; in view of the typically Marcan linking formula 'and he said unto them' v. 27 was probably inserted by the evangelist—i.e. at the last stage); in several instances we can actually follow the growth of these stories by the introduction of new motifs (for example, Mk. ix. 36 f. speaks only of the receiving of a child, but Mt. x. 40–42 of the receiving of disciples; cf. Mk. x. 13 f., 16 and v. 15. The pericope Mk. ii. 18–22 presumably referred originally in vv. 18–19a only to John's disciples, but later the Pharisees were introduced as opponents; vv. 21–22 give an interpretation of the reasons for rejecting fasting, whereas vv. 19b–20 envisage the resumption of fasting under certain conditions).

In this process which we can trace by literary analysis there is often evidence of a Christological interest. The attitude of the Church as it hands on the tradition becomes clear, for in the additions to the early tradition of Jesus the post-Easter faith in the exalted Lord expresses itself. What we find therefore are testimonies of faith, not historical reports.

(c) A large part of the sayings material is taken up by the parables. Here again we cannot speak of a uniform type, but have to draw distinctions. However, a number of mixed forms make it difficult to differentiate very sharply. The metaphor is the simplest form, in which one concept stands for another and the image and the object are identical (king=God; father=God; wedding feast=feast of consummation).

In the simile and the parable proper we have to consider the *tertium comparationis*, because in these cases the image stands alongside the object. In the simile the *tertium comparationis* is generally stated (Mt. x. 16), and in the metaphor (which we can call a rudimentary form of the parable) it is clear enough not to need to be mentioned (Mt. vii. 6).

The parables themselves present greater problems. What often happens is that an event from daily life is used as a parallel to something else, and the important thing is to find where the comparison applies at one particular point (Lk. xv. 1–10: joy at finding again—joy in heaven; Lk. xvi. 1–8: resolute action in view of a new situation that takes one by surprise). However, we have to resist the temptation to 'interpret' all the elements in the comparison and all the various ideas or people that are represented. This has often happened in the history of the interpretation of the parables, but since Jülicher's work[14] on the parables much more caution has been shown in this respect.

Sometimes the *tertium comparationis* is linked with a conclusion *a minori ad maius* (Mt. vii. 9–11; Lk. xi. 5–8). In the so-called parables of the Kingdom of Heaven the introductory phrase has often given rise to misunderstanding. It looks as though the comparison refers to the first word mentioned in the parable (merchant, hidden treasure, etc.), but in fact it refers to the whole action. The best translation therefore would be: 'The kingdom of heaven is as follows . . . (Mk. iv. 26, 30; Mt. xiii. 24, 31, 33, 44, 45, 47). In a number of parables we cannot say for certain what the *tertium comparationis* is, as the image could be applied to several possible points of comparison. As far as exegesis is concerned we could only be certain if we knew the situation—or could reconstruct it—in which the parable was originally spoken (cf. the reference to the circle of hearers in Lk. xviii. 9).

Parables seek to state an argument and thereby to convince their hearers directly. Allegory, on the other hand, seeks to encourage the hearer to ponder and reflect. It combines elements of the metaphor and the parable. There are no pure allegories in the Synoptic tradition, but there are some secondary interpretations of parables which show that at a

[14] A. Jülicher, *Die Gleichnisreden Jesu* (I, 1886, 2 ed., 1899; II, 1899, 2 ed., 1910).

later stage parables were understood as allegories and that these parables were to some extent allegorized (Mk. iv. 13–20; Mt. xiii. 36–43).

Finally we should note the exemplary stories (Lk. x. 30–37; xvi. 19–31), where the aim is to set out in the form of a paradigm right (N.B. Lk. x. 37) or wrong behaviour.

There are many parallels to the parables in the world contemporary with the New Testament, particularly in Judaism. There is, however, a characteristic difference: whereas in Judaism the parable almost always serves to expound the Law, the New Testament parables are not based on any given text, but are direct announcements. And although we cannot be absolutely certain in every case, for the most part we can trace the parables back to Jesus himself.

Here again we can follow the process of tradition. The parables were repeated not simply in order to preserve Jesus' message in as true a form as possible, but because they were used—at a later period—for the purpose of further preaching the Gospel. So, for example, an attempt was made to draw paranetic material from them (the 'exposition' in Lk. xvi. 9–13 completely misses the original meaning of Lk. xvi. 1–8); alternatively, secret theological relationships and implications were read into them (cf. the allegorizing in Mk. iv. 13–20 and Mt. xiii. 36–43). The parables which originally served the purpose of living proclamation have now become 'texts', from which one tries to deduce as much as possible to apply to the present. It was only on this assumption that the view could emerge that the parables were to be taken as 'dark sayings' of Jesus (cf. Mk. iv. 10–12, 33–34).

The remaining sayings material, which in general is much briefer, is very varied both in form and content, and it is very difficult to divide it into categories. We can mention some of the groups. In the prophetic-apocalyptic sayings, very often with borrowings from traditional concepts and material, the irruption of the reign of God is announced, and this can take the form of the beatitude (Mt. v. 3–12; xiii. 33–37) or the woe (Lk. vi. 24–26). It is important to be ready (Mk. xiii. 33–37) and to repent (Mk. i. 15), for the future judgement is coming now (Lk. ix. 26; Mk. viii. 38).

In the so-called 'Christ-sayings' the meaning of the hour is expressed in 'personal' terms. They include the group of 'I am come' sayings (Mk. ii. 17; Lk. vii. 49), and also the Son of Man sayings, which speak of the present and active Son of Man (Mk. ii. 10; ii. 28; x. 45; Mt. viii. 20; xi. 19; xii. 32) and of the suffering, dying and rising Son of Man (Mk. viii. 31; ix. 9, 12, 31; x. 33, 45). Most of these sayings, compared with

those of the group mentioned previously, have to be considered as
secondary, for what was expressed there in the fulfilment of Jesus'
ministry is now made the subject of reflection: from what Jesus does the
deduction is drawn as to who he is.

A similar development as in the 'Christ-sayings' can be seen when we
compare the sayings about the Law with the regulations for the Church.
Something similar took place in the Jewish tradition, but whereas there
the attempt was made to deduce ethical instructions from an exposition
of the Law, which often led to casuistry, and the Law became a means in
men's hands which they could use and so the direct relationship with
God was lost, here on the contrary the sayings about the Law, by attacking either the exposition (Mk. vii. 13) or the Law itself (Mk. x. 5–9),
confront men directly with the will of God—in contrast to any 'security'
through the Law. On the other hand, the Church itself later tries to draw
rules for its conduct from earlier traditions (cf. Mk. ix. 49 with Lk. xvii.
1 f., 3 f. and Mt. xviii. 6 f. and 15–17).

In the whole breadth of the various Synoptic materials that have come
down to us we can trace a history of tradition through which the materials
passed before they took form in the Gospels. In this process the different
types of material underwent considerable variations. The types went
through a process of development and in the course of this process new
types sometimes arose. Thus there is a correlation between the types and
the process of development, and it is this that Form Criticism attempts
to analyse in detail. It is to this that we shall now turn our attention.

(2) *Form Criticism.* The great liberty with which variations were introduced, which we have already noted in tracing the development of the
separate units of tradition, and also the adoption of traditional patterns
in the accounts (e.g. of the healing miracles) as well as the absence of
everything required for a biography (sequence of events, development,
Jesus' appearance, etc.)—all these show that the community that transmitted the traditions was obviously not interested in an historical record.
Its interest must have lain elsewhere. The survey of the material that we
have already made has shown from time to time what this interest
was.

We have to start from the fact that the tradition about Jesus, before it
was set down in writing, went through a process of oral transmission the
details of which can no longer be reconstructed. We need to remember,
however, that the transition from oral to written tradition was to a
certain extent fluid, so that the stage at which the material became

relatively fixed in oral tradition was almost simultaneous with the stage at which the tradition was also.fixed in writing.

It is important to note that this fixation did not take shape in a great variety of patterns corresponding to the variety of the actual events, but in quite definite and often similar forms. When, therefore, in certain forms the narrative is very brief but in others detailed and exceptionally vivid, we cannot conclude that in the one case very little happened, but in the other case much more. The particular form is linked with the intention underlying the telling of the story.

In passing we can make the general observation that any particular event—for example—a road accident, is described very differently in a letter to a friend from one of the people involved from what it is in an official police report, and differently again in an entry in a diary. In other words, it is the purpose for which the account is given that determines the form. On the other hand, if we have the different documents in front of us, even without knowing the background we can deduce the purpose from the form. As far as the historical question of what actually happened is concerned, however, it follows that the purpose for which the account was set down in some way always obstructs any direct access to the event. We can learn only as much of the event as is revealed by the form which the particular purpose determines.

If we find the same forms in the Synoptic material we can conclude with reasonable certainty that the same purpose lies behind them, that they have the same 'setting in life'. If, on the other hand, we can recognize one or more 'settings' then we have at least a provisional picture of the needs of the community that gave form to the traditions; and from there we can explain other forms as well. We need to look carefully at this particular approach, and the two works of fundamental importance are those of Dibelius[15] and Bultmann;[16] the difference is that Bultmann adopts the analytical, and Dibelius the constructive method.

We will consider now a few examples of Form Criticism. The accounts of the so-called Institution of the Lord's Supper, which differ considerably in the Synoptic Gospels, were at one time independent traditions (as is shown on the one hand by a literary examination of the framework, and on the other by 1 Cor. xi. 23–25). In the Synoptics they are set in the context of Jesus' Last Supper, but it is noticeable that the course of the

[15] M. Dibelius, *Die Formgeschichte des Evangeliums* (1919; 2 ed. 1933, reissued 1959). (E.T. *From Tradition to Gospel* (from 2 ed., 1933), Nicholson & Watson; Scribner, 1935).
[16] R. Bultmann, *Die Geschichte der synoptischen Tradition* (1921; 2 ed., 1930, reprinted with supplement, 1957). (E.T. *The History of the Synoptic Tradition*, Blackwell; Harper & Row, 1963).

meal (the details, the atmosphere, etc.) is not described; all that is mentioned is what was significant for the Church's celebration of the Lord's Supper. What we have, therefore, are not 'accounts' of Jesus' Last Supper, but 'liturgies', which show considerable differences from one another and show that the Supper was celebrated differently in the various churches and with a very varied interpretation. The setting in life of these particular traditions therefore is the cultus.

The position is quite different when we turn to the controversies. We can probably assume that in argument with his opponents Jesus used the traditional form of the disputation (Mk. ii. 23–26; xi. 27–33). On the other hand, however, older traditions are sometimes turned into a disputation (Mk. ii. 1–5a, 11–12 is expanded by the addition of vv. 5b–10, and so made into a disputation); on the other hand events which could have been elaborated into short stories and at the same time given a christological or soteriological significance have been set down as controversies between the disciples and the Pharisees (Mk. ii. 15–17), from which we can conclude that there were clashes between the early Church and its Jewish environment (of which we have evidence apart from these indications brought to light by Form Criticism). The setting in life of these controversies is therefore the apologia.

In the previous section we noted that the Church attempts with the aid of the traditions that have come down to it to order and regulate its own life. The setting in life in this case is that of Church organization. In this way we can bring to light a number of different settings in life, and Form Criticism can to some extent provide us with a clear insight into the life of the early Church. This is what is meant when it is said that Form Criticism has a 'sociological' bearing. For anyone who is interested in the historical aspect and is exclusively or primarily interested in finding out 'what really happened' this is to a certain extent disappointing. If the study of the Synoptics was undertaken primarily with the aim of getting as close as possible to the historical Jesus, we have to admit that it is not Jesus it has got close to, but the early Church.

There are two points, however, that we must bear in mind here. First we must see that we cannot simply ignore the methodical insights of Form Criticism (i.e. the reservation as regards the—supposedly direct—historical records concerning Jesus). We must never forget that the facts about Jesus have come down to us through the early Church. What the early Church is interested in—as the material clearly shows—is not in giving an account of who Jesus *was*, but who he *is* (Bornkamm); in other words, the early Church did not allow the life of Jesus to become a thing of the past, for it knew that its whole life was constantly determined by those events. This dependence finds expression in the form of the account. In other words, the story of Jesus' life is presented to us not as a historical record, but as 'kerygma'.

But this still does not tell us anything about the historicity of the story we read in the 'kerygma'. To pose the alternative: 'kerygmatic or historical' is the wrong approach, for it does not follow that what is set out in the form of kerygma is necessarily unhistorical. Therefore in spite of the insights that Form Criticism has provided, it is still possible to ask the question as to what the historical facts were, although of course it is much more difficult to arrive at any assured results than if we were dealing with material that is concerned simply with the past as such.

(3) *Early Compilations.* The process by which the Synoptic Gospels arose was not that Mark drew from the abundance of various material at his disposal and so compiled his Gospel and that Matthew and Luke then expanded Mk. with further units of material. What happened was that a process of compilation began even earlier, which—in part, at least—we can still trace. We can distinguish three stages in the gathering of material, which do not simply follow one another but are to some extent simultaneous and also at times overlap.

(a) The simplest type of compilation is when the same forms are assembled, as for example in the parable source which can still be traced as the background to Mk. iv (Mk. iv 2–9, 10, 13–20, 26–29, 30–32). The greatest part of the logia source (Q) probably belongs to this category, in so far as it was concerned with the collection of spoken material. This source cannot be reconstructed in its full extent, but some of its characteristic features can still be traced and can be linked as follows. The account of the 'teaching of Jesus', which is loosely put together, occupies most space (examples: The Lord's Prayer: Mt. vi. 9–15; Lk. xi. 2–4; the discourse on anxiety: Mt. vi. 25–33; Lk. xii. 22–31; teaching about prayer: (Mt. vii. 7–11; Lk. xi. 9–13; the would-be disciples: Mt. viii. 19–22; Lk. ix. 57–60; the commandment to confess one's faith: Mt. x. 26–33; Lk. xii. 2–9; woes: Mt. xi. 20–23; Lk. x. 13–15; rejoicing: Mt. xi. 25–27; Lk. x. 21–22; rejection of demand for a sign: Mt. xii. 39–42; Lk. xi. 29–32; the master of the house who keeps watch: Mt. xxiv. 43–44; Lk. xii. 39–40; the faithful and unfaithful servants: Mt. xxiv. 45–51; Lk. xii. 42–46, etc. Cf. also the Sermon on the Plain in Lk. vi. 20–49, which we find again in the Sermon on the Mount in Mt. v–vii and the mission address in Lk. x. 1–16, which is also found—somewhat expanded

—in Mt. x. In addition, Q also contained material concerning John the Baptist (the preaching of repentance: Mt. iii. 7–10; Lk. iii. 7–9; John's question: Mt. xi. 2–6; Lk. vii. 18–23; Jesus' words about John: Mt. xi. 7–19; Lk. vii. 24–35), traditions about the Christ (story of the Temptations: Mt. iv. 1–11; Lk. iv. 1–13), and a miracle story (Mt. viii. 5–13; Lk. vii. 1–10). It is surprising that there is no trace of any story of the Passion and that the Passion kerygma is not found in the separate traditions. It is the collection of Jesus' teaching that is most important in Q.

The editorial work on this simple form of collected material is restricted essentially to mere tradition, and this avoids any 'distortion' of the tradition. Yet we can see at least the onset of a problem that we shall meet later in the shape of the problem of the Canon. Such compilations were no doubt made for the purpose of proclamation and the instruction of the Church, but this same purpose was also served by the earlier separate units of tradition. But whereas we could see in that case that the Church in its proclamation possessed complete freedom to make variations, and preaching was therefore a living activity, as the result of collecting the material it now becomes fixed in a pattern that preaching took at one particular time. It was in *this* form that it was also used later: in other words, one now uses for the purpose of preaching a pattern of the kerygma which was originally addressed to a past situation. The question that arises is whether this older type of preaching will be effective at a later period.

As at first no great periods of time were involved, the problem was not a very serious one. It did exist, however, and there is evidence of it in the fact that what was originally living preaching became a 'text', which—in order to be of use for further preaching—needed to be expounded. We have already noted examples of such 'expositions': cf. Mk. iv. 2–9 and 13–20; Lk. xvi. 1–8 and 9 and 10–13; also when Mark expands his parable source, such exposition is being made. This means that it is no longer the life of Jesus proclaimed in the kerygma that determines the present existence of the Church, but the text 'kerygmatized' by means of exposition, the text which was once kerygma itself, but can no longer be heard directly as such. Here we can see in essence the problem of the Canon, insofar as the basis for later proclamation is no longer the event of Jesus itself, but a certain stage in the history of the proclamation of this event.

At the time, of course, this was not seen, nor were its implications considered, but for the very reason that the problem that now presented itself was not seen there was a danger—to use dogmatic terms—of a

K

'shift' of revelation: from history to the texts. The attempt was later made, with the aid of the doctrine of inspiration, to bridge this hiatus that had arisen. We cannot go into these problems here, but we have at least indicated where they arose.

(b) The second intermediate stage in the compilation of tradition is similar to the first, but it reveals one new element. This can be seen in the controversies source which Mark used and which can still be traced with a fair degree of certainty behind Mk. ii. I–iii. 6. At first sight it seems as though it were simply a matter of bringing together similar forms by a simple process of addition, but it is evident that the order of the passages is not altogether accidental, for particularly at the end (iii. 6) we can see that it works up to a climax as the opponents of Jesus— after the many clashes that have been related—plan to do away with him. It is clear therefore that the order of events plays a part here: in other words, there is evidence here of the beginning of a process of 'historicizing'.

The separate traditions were originally complete entities in themselves, and each of these entities expressed 'the whole Jesus'. If we add sayings material together it does not make much difference to it, but if we put together just two sections of narrative we create straight away a sequence of events and also the impression of a lapse of time. And when we consider this sequence we get a feeling of distance insofar as that which is narrated is itself distinct in time and what we have is the account of a sequence of past events. 'Historicizing' therefore simply cannot be avoided. This was not the intention either in the controversies source or in Q, where alongside the redaction which added the sayings material loosely together and arranged it thematically we also find a few narrative passages. The controversies source probably came into being in the 40's of the first century and was meant to help the Church in the confrontation with its opponents, whilst Q (which probably came into being not much later) was intended to serve directly the work of preaching and of instructing the Church. To this extent these compilations also serve a thoroughly kerygmatic purpose. But as the separate units of tradition by their very nature are resistant to any kind of joining together, when the process of compilation took place what was unavoidable had to be accepted.

The problem that faced the compilers now becomes plain: how can they retain the kerygmatic character of the material and at the same time avoid losing the kerygma to the past? We shall see that this was much simpler at the beginning—up to and including Mk.—than later, for the ever-increasing distance from the events of Jesus' life was then—together with the growth of the tradition into a 'text'—a strong factor favouring a 'historicizing' view.

(c) The third intermediate stage is again like the second, but its outcome is quite different. We can see it in the Passion story, where we have the earliest example of a continuous account, which, however, was not conceived straightaway in the form in which we now find it in Mk., but underwent several secondary expansions.

We can be quite sure that in many places historical recollection has been preserved in the Passion story. It is significant, however, that it still does not represent an originally continuous narrative thread, but is built up from separate traditions which again clearly show that they depict what happened in the form of the kerygma. In other words, we are once again faced with testimonies of faith.

We have to take care to distinguish here two theological themes which are often confused: the redemptive significance of the *Cross* and Jesus' *way* to the Cross. In the pre-Pauline and Pauline preaching the Cross of Jesus is often proclaimed as a saving event by being interpreted with the aid of Jewish ideas of atoning sacrifice and substitutionary sacrifice. The characteristic phrases are those linked with $\upsilon\pi\epsilon\rho$ or $\pi\epsilon\rho\iota$ (e.g. 1 Cor. xv. 3; 1 Thess. v. 10; Gal. iii. 13; 2 Cor. v. 14 f., etc.). Such statements, however, are not found in the Synoptic tradition (except Mk. x. 45; xiv. 24), nor in the Passion story. It could be questioned whether in certain passages this theological view is meant to be *illustrated* by the fact that the suffering Jesus is represented in such a way that the reader is reminded of the Suffering Servant of God in Is. liii. In this case it would be possible to trace—indirectly at least—the theme of vicarious suffering.

The striking thing, however, is that even these allusions are very rare, although generally speaking the Old Testament is widely used. It is not actually quoted, but the destiny of Jesus, the way he took, is described in such a way that the narrator (or narrators) repeatedly employs the language of the Old Testament and relates the path that Jesus took in phrases drawn from the Old Testament or at least affirms in general terms the Scriptural character of the way he takes (cf., e.g., Mk. xiv. 18 and Ps. xli. 10; Mk. xiv. 61; xv. 5 and Is. liii. 7; Mk. xv. 23 and Ps. lxix. 22; Mk. xv. 24 and Ps. xxii. 19; Mk. xv. 34 and Ps. xxii. 2). We cannot interpret these Old Testament passages as prophecies and Jesus' destiny as the fulfilment of them. The pattern of prophecy and fulfilment is not found until we come to Matthew and Luke. The point of using Old Testament language is rather to show that the way of Jesus' suffering—

from the human standpoint so puzzling—is the way of God (as is expressly declared later in the announcements of the Passion, which are later from the literary point of view—Mk. viii. 31; ix. 31; x. 33 f.).

Once we recognize this it becomes clear that the Passion story does not really aim to depict a path of suffering followed—after Easter—by glory, but it shows this path of humility paradoxically as the path of God and therefore also as the path of glory. Along this path the majesty of Jesus also comes to expression, not least by the emphasis upon his Messianic status (Mk. xiv. 61 f.).

We certainly therefore cannot read the Passion story as though it were a general illustration of the idea of atoning sacrifice and of vicarious sacrifice. It does not aim to describe the Cross, but Jesus—in spite of his death on the Cross. And when the Son of Man is mentioned in his acceptance of suffering, this is not meant to refer to his lowliness—as has often been thought—but is also to be taken as a title of majesty.

This is of course an interpretation made in the light of faith, which the Church could make only after Easter. It was Easter that reassured the Church that the apparently so meaningless death of the one whose majesty the disciples had experienced during his lifetime did not in any way detract from his majesty. We can therefore sum up the Passion story paradoxically as follows: the Risen Lord (the glorified One, the Son of Man, the Son of God) goes to his Cross. This makes it quite clear that the story is not meant to be read as the account of an historical sequence of events.

As, however, the bringing together of the separate traditions inevitably did create a sequence, there was a very real possibility at this point of the introduction of the historical element into the story of Jesus. If the death of Jesus is depicted as a path towards a goal then it must be possible to extend this path backwards—and this gives rise to 'passion narratives with extended introductions', as Kähler[17] describes the Gospels. We can really say this only of Mk., for Matthew and Luke had this Passion story 'with introduction' before them, and—as we shall see later—they interpreted it in a very different way.

In certain of the compilations therefore—particularly of narrative material—we can see a preliminary stage to the continuous account in Mk., but it is the Passion story that represents the really decisive stage. The question now is whether Mark, in extending the kerygma—that is,

[17] M. Kähler, *Der sogenannte historische Jesus und der geschichtliche, biblische Christus* (2 ed., 1896), p. 80; (reprinted 1956), p. 60. (E.T. *The So-called Historical Jesus and the Historic Biblical Christ*, Fortress Press, 1964, p. 80 n. 11).

the Passion story—backwards, can maintain its kerygmatic character, or whether he too will succumb to 'historicizing'.

BIBLIOGRAPHY

R. Bultmann, *Die Erforschung der synoptischen Evangelien* (4 ed., 1961). (E.T. in *Form Criticism: a New Method of New Testament Research*, Willett, Clark, 1934, Harper Torchbooks, 1962).

R. Bultmann, *Die Geschichte der synoptischen Tradition* (5 ed., 1961). (E.T. *The History of the Synoptic Tradition*, Blackwell; Harper, 1963, n.e. in prep.).

M. Dibelius, *Die Formgeschichte des Evangeliums* (4 ed., 1961). (E.T. *From Tradition to Gospel* (from 2 ed., 1933), Nicholson & Watson; Schribner, 1935).

E. Gräßer, *Das Problem der Parusieverzögerung in den synoptischen Evangelien und in der Apostelgeschichte* (1957).

K. L. Schmidt, *Der Rahmen der Geschichte Jesu* (1919).

On the logia source:

A. von Harnack, *Sprüche und Reden Jesu* (1907). (E.T. *The Sayings of Jesus*, 1908).

H. E. Tödt, *Der Menschensohn in der synoptischen Überlieferung* (1959), pp. 212 ff. (E.T. *The Son of Man in the Synoptic Tradition* (from 2 ed., 1963), SCM; Westminster, 1965, pp. 232).

B. Gerhardsson, 'Memory and Manuscript', *ASNU* 22 (1961), pp. 253 ff.

R. H. Lightfoot, *History and Interpretation in the Gospels* (1935).

E. B. Redlich, *Form Criticism* (1939).

H. Riesenfeld, *The Gospel Tradition and its Beginnings* (1957).

V. Taylor, *The Formation of the Gospel Tradition* (1933).

12. THE GOSPEL OF MARK

(1) *Contents and Structure.* The Passion story which Mark had before him, and which he himself expanded, may have begun originally at xiv. 1. It was compiled by means of joining together what were originally independent traditions, working backwards from the Cross. The 'history' that arose in this way depicted Jesus' path to the Cross, starting from xiv (cf. section 11, 3c).

We see these same conflicting trends in Mk. also in the fact that elements of tradition are included—and Mark is the first to do this—which speaks of the ministry of Jesus but have no connection direct or indirect with the Cross and with Jerusalem. In this way the rest of Jesus' public ministry is included, placed before the Passion story, and then before that are put traditions about John the Baptist, and the Baptism and Temptation of Jesus. There are therefore—though only roughly divided from one another—the three complexes: the 'introductory story' (i. 1–13), the ministry of Jesus up to his sojourn in Jerusalem (i. 14–x. 52) and the events in and around Jerusalem (xi. 1–xvi. 8).

Even though a sequence of events was created in this way, it is still clear that the account grew 'retrospectively': although the place references in xi. 1, x. 32 and x. 1 which point on towards the end in Jerusalem could be interpreted as the result of a conception of history that keeps its eyes fixed on the end (yet the method of redaction as we see it elsewhere would not support this view, so that it might be more accurate to see in it simply the evidence of a purely external linking of material), this is simply impossible as far as the announcements of the Passion in x. 33 f., ix. 31 and viii. 31 are concerned. They are rather concise summaries of the—familiar—Passion story, used in their particular context to introduce lessons about the path of suffering the disciples must follow.

There are therefore two trends interwoven in this Gospel: the one which can be traced backwards from the Passion story and is an expansion of the *kerygma*, and the other which is a *history* that can be traced forwards from John the Baptist. In these two trends moving in opposite directions we have the real problem of Mk. If we follow the sequence of the account, we get the impression of a report of the course of certain events; but if we consider the growth of the tradition retrospectively we see that what Mark aimed at was an expansion of the *kerygma*. Both aspects imply, however, that Mark wished to tell a story—but in the form of preaching. It is precisely this that is the characteristic of the type of literature created by Mark, the 'Gospel', although we must note straightaway that we cannot call the writings of Matthew and Luke 'Gospels' in this sense (cf. sections 13 and 14).

In view of this special way of linking the whole together that the evangelist used any further division of the work apart from the complexes mentioned earlier is hardly possible, nor indeed was it envisaged. Mark employs a variety of traditions or 'forms'. He relates the *deeds* of Jesus (healings: i. 23 ff., 40 ff.; ii. 1 ff.; iii. 1 ff., etc.; a raising from the dead: v. 22 ff.; stilling of the storm: iv. 35 ff.; walking on the sea: vi. 45 ff.; feedings: vi. 34 ff.; viii. 1 ff.). Jesus' *message* on the other hand is much less prominent. It is to be found—mostly very briefly—in a great variety of traditions. Mark himself has edited two 'discourses' (iv. 1–34; xiii). Here the material is arranged thematically, as it is occasionally elsewhere (e.g. controversies, ii. 1–iii. 6; miracles, iv. 35–v. 43; discourses and controversies in Jerusalem, xi. 27–xii. 37). It is possible that Mark found a considerable amount of this material already assembled in this way (cf. section 11, 3a, b).

All these separate traditions and compilations that Mark adopted were themselves meant to serve the purpose of proclamation. This meant, however, that they did not lend themselves to being used for an account of events in sequence which must lead almost inevitably to a 'historicizing' of the kerygmatic tradition—and it was precisely this kind of secondary 'historicizing' that Mark emphatically opposed. It is important to see how he did this.

As far as the purely formal aspect is concerned, Mark linked the material by a process of editing. He did not simply add the separate traditions to one another—this would have been to indulge in 'historicizing'—but the editorial work is always made to serve the purpose of an interpretation of the traditional material which will maintain its kerygmatic character. This interpretation, however, results in a definite conception which is determined by the point in history at which Mark stands. This is something similar to what we saw when considering Form Criticism (cf. section 11, 2). The various forms are determined by their 'setting in life', and from them in turn we can draw conclusions as regards this 'setting'. The editorial work of Mark, as of the other Synoptics, is similarly determined by a particular 'setting in life' (that of the editor), and so here again by studying the editorial work we can draw conclusions regarding its 'setting in life'.

(2) *The Editorial Process in Mark's Gospel.* Wrede's great distinction was that he was the first to point out that in composing his Gospel Mark was guided by a particular theological conception, which is expressed in the theme of the so-called 'Messianic secret'.[18] Mark sets out this theme by means of three closely linked 'stylistic devices'. In various forms Jesus gives commands to keep silent: the devils are forbidden to make known his Messianic nature (i. 34; iii. 12); the disciples are given similar instructions (viii. 30; ix. 9); and those who have been healed are forbidden to speak of the miracle that has been worked on them (i. 44; v. 43; vii. 36; cf. also viii. 26). Another device is the frequent emphasis on the disciples' lack of understanding, according to which we are led to believe that even those closest to Jesus were witnesses of his Messianic work and teaching yet did not understand (iv. 40 f.; vi. 52; viii. 16 ff.; ix. 10, 32). Finally, the so-called parable theory (iv. 10–12) has to be included, which appears to suggest that Jesus intentionally delivered his parables as dark sayings and explained them only to a very limited circle (iv. 33 f.).

All attempts to explain these three factors historically in the light of Jesus' life have failed on account of their inherent improbability. The commands to silence on the occasion of the healing of the sick simply could not be observed, and indeed in most cases we are told straightaway that the command was broken. The disciples' lack of understanding is also difficult to understand as a historical fact, particularly as according to the parable theory it is precisely the disciples—and only they—to whom Jesus explains everything. Almost certainly we can say in every case as far as the parable theory and the command to silence are concerned, and in most cases as far as the disciples' lack of understanding is concerned, that we have the results of an editorial process. From the literary standpoint, in other words, these elements have to be put to the account of the evangelist. This raises the question as to what he is seeking to say by this means.

Wrede's view was that this 'theory of the evangelist' was connected with the fact that Mark had before him various traditions which depicted Jesus as Messiah, but knew at the same time that Jesus' Messianic status was not seen until after Easter, not during his earthly life. He suggested that Mark tried to overcome this contradiction between the Messianic

[18] *Op. cit.*

stamp of the traditional material and the realization that the life of Jesus was not expressed in Messianic terms by means of this theory and by describing the life of Jesus in such a way as to imply that Jesus deliberately kept his Messianic status secret.

But can we accept this as a solution? Is it conceivable that anyone in the Christian Church, at the time when Mark wrote his Gospel and almost the whole of the tradition proclaimed Jesus as Messiah, would have been interested in cherishing the remembrance of a 'non-Messianic' life of Jesus (in so far as we can speak of such in any historical sense)? For whom would a compromise of this kind have been intended? Wrede is correct in his view that the theme of the Messianic secret corresponds with Mark's own viewpoint, but the more likely explanation is the exact reverse of his: that it was not the historical remembrance that troubled the evangelist, but the kerygmatic character of the various traditions.

By means of this theme of the Messianic secret Mark seeks to remove the difficulty that arises immediately one places alongside each other the kerygmatic units that have been handed down separately and so inevitably sets them out as a historical sequence. This would produce a history of Jesus which gave an account of a permanent, historically verifiable manifestation of his Messianic nature, but this is not what the evangelist wants. His work would then no longer have been a *kerygma*, but the account of a quite open and manifest revelation. In order that his work as a whole should remain what the separate traditions already were (i.e. *kerygma*) Mark makes use of his theory. In this way he prevents his work from becoming a historically verifiable sequence of epiphanies; instead we have secret epiphanies which now become manifest as they are proclaimed. Dibelius therefore described Mk. very aptly as the book of secret epiphanies. The fact that Mark himself is engaged in post-Easter proclamation in no way takes away from these epiphanies their secret character (N.B. ix. 9).

Earlier (section 11, 3c) we summed up the message of the (pre-Marcan) Passion story in the paradoxical phrase: the Risen Lord—the Son of God—goes to the Cross. We can now say the same about Mk. as a whole: through the proclamation which realizes his presence the Risen Lord is made manifest in the stories from his earthly life. As the whole Gospel of Mark has this same purpose as the pre-Marcan Passion story we can say of its contents as a whole—and not only of the edited material—that it is a Passion story with a full introduction.

This is further underlined by the meaning that the concept *evangelion* has in Mk., which we can consider as the main concept in the work. We need to note first of all that in every case the word *evangelion* can be traced back to Mark's editing (i. 1, 14 f.; viii. 35; x. 29; xiii. 10; xiv. 9). Matthew uses this concept only in passages where he is dependent on Mk., but Luke avoids using it. We do not find it in Q, although Q and Lk. do use the verb εὐαγγελίζεσθαι, which however has a different origin and a different meaning. The conclusion to be drawn is that the Synoptic tradition is not familiar with the concept of *evangelion*, and that it was only introduced by Mark. Previous to Mark we find the idea only in Paul's writings. It is derived from the milieu of Hellenistic Christianity and means the 'proclamation of a message of salvation', in which salvation is not only proclaimed but also offered. Paul often uses the idea in this sense almost as a formula standing for the salvation that is available in Christ and offered to the hearer as it is proclaimed. We find the same use of the term in Mk. In viii. 35 he expands the earlier saying 'Whosoever shall lose his life for my sake shall save it' by adding the idea of the *evangelion*; the 'and' that he inserts is Marcan exegesis, and the concept *evangelion* is an interpretation of 'for my sake' (as in x. 29 also). What Mark is saying is that what one does for the sake of the Gospel one does for Jesus' sake. In other words, Jesus is the content of the Gospel; Jesus is present in the Gospel; the Gospel 're-presents' him.

By his use of the concept *evangelion* in i. 1 Mark defines the character of his whole work. We can say that the Gospel that Mark writes is an illustrative commentary on the concept of *evangelion* as it is used—for the most part without explanation—by Paul. This makes it clear how Mark means the traditions that he includes in his work to be understood: they are not meant simply to preserve the memory of Jesus' ministry, but are intended to be an address, a proclamation that 're-presents' Jesus. In other words, in writing his Gospel Mark created a literary type that is unique. Before Mark it did not exist, and after Mark we do not find it again until we come to the Gospel of John, although very differently expressed—and this is the last example of it. The writings of Matthew and Luke are not 'Gospels' in this sense.

For an understanding of the editorial work of the earliest evangelist the concept of Galilee is also important, although scholars are not yet agreed as to the significance of this point. We must first note once again that (with the exception of vi. 21) all the references to Galilee are redactional (i. 9, 14, 28, 39; iii. 7; vii. 31; ix. 30; xiv. 28; xvi. 7). The traditions prior to Mark do of course refer to places that belong to Galilee, but they do not expressly say so and Mark is the first to make it clear. We can hardly assume that this is merely a matter of geographical elucidation on the part of the evangelist; the editing is too deliberate for this. Jesus' ministry begins in Galilee (i. 9, 14); the report of him went out into all the region of Galilee (i. 28); then we are told that Jesus ministered throughout Galilee (i. 39). In other words, Mark emphasizes that Galilee was the area of Jesus' activity. Is the evangelist merely depending on reminiscences, which are quite possibly historically correct? This seems unlikely, because in other passages the references to Galilee are obviously intentional. In Mk. xiv. 28 and xvi. 7 we read that the Risen Lord will go before his disciples—to Galilee. This raises the question whether Mark in his Gospel might be summoning the Christian churches to an assembly of some kind in Galilee, particularly in view of the fact that in iii. 7 ff. he makes out of a tradition which simply speaks of a withdrawal by Jesus (N.B. iii. 6) a great gathering by the lake—in Galilee! This seems all the more probable, as the order of events in the account cannot really lead us to consider the journey mentioned in xiv. 28 and xvi. 7 as being still awaited, whereas the gathering mentioned in iii. 7 ff. on the contrary is an event in the past story of Jesus. To do this would be to overlook the special characteristic of Mark's message as well as the fact that in the gathering mentioned in iii. 7 ff. the people come from the very places where there were in all probability Christian churches in Mark's time. We can therefore go so far as to say that the idea of Galilee is one of the links that Mark uses to prevent the various pericopes falling apart into a sequence that is simply provided by the account itself.

We can say therefore that the varied material that the evangelist assembles is held together by four links: by the way the Passion story is bound to the whole by means of the announcements of the Passion, by the theme of the Messianic secret, by the description of the work as *evangelion*, and by the geographical orientation towards Galilee. Before we can go into these questions any more fully we must consider the special problem of the ending of Mk.

(3) *The Ending of Mark's Gospel.* The manuscripts offer three different texts. They are all in agreement as far as xvi. 8; some break off at this point, a small group add a short postscript, and a larger group gives a further twelve verses after xvi. 8. Scholars are agreed that both the shorter and the longer ending are secondary additions which seek to bring Mk. into line with traditions from other Gospels.

Whereas on the one hand therefore the textual critics are unanimous that we can consider the text as original only as far as xvi. 8, on the other hand the question is often raised whether this is really the original ending of the work as intended by Mark. For one thing, there is a discrepancy between the two last verses which is not resolved: the angel's command to the women to tell the disciples of the Resurrection (v. 7) is followed in v. 8 by the statement that they kept silent, in other words, that they did not carry out the angel's command. At the same time there are no accounts of appearances of the Risen Lord such as we find in all the other Gospels. Mark must have known and used such Resurrection stories; the absence of them here is particularly surprising, as v. 7 seems to be preparing the way for them.

There are certainly real difficulties here, but it is very questionable whether we can remove them by suggesting that the ending has been lost. Bultmann,[19] for example, suggests that the original ending was removed for the reason that it contained statements that were not in keeping with a later standpoint, but this is not a convincing argument. It not only postulates an ending of which we really know nothing, but goes so far in defining the contents of this ending as to explain why this ending is now lost to us. It seems a somewhat improbable hypothesis.

It is of course possible that the ending was damaged; but at the same time it is surprising that both Matthew and Luke use Mk. only as far as xvi. 8—and presumably were familiar with it only up to this point. If the search for a lost ending arises solely from the fact that an ending at xvi. 8 creates exegetical difficulties, the cautious exegete will seek the deficiency in his own interpretation rather than in the corruption of the text; in other words, he will allow for the possibility that Mark really did intend to conclude his Gospel at xvi. 8. This is what we have to try to explain.

Ignoring xvi. 7 for the moment, the question that arises is whether it is in fact certain that the Gospel included accounts of appearances of the Risen Lord. There are two things we need to keep separate here: the evangelist's knowledge of the fact of 'Easter', which forms the basis of the standpoint from which the work is written—and giving expression to this knowledge by means of accounts of appearances. The latter, however, is by no means the only way of giving expression to the fact of Easter.

We can refer to Q in this connection, for here there is no mention of the Cross, and no explicit proclamation of Easter either. Easter here is only implicit—in the fact of the continuing preaching of the preaching of Jesus. The same was very probably true of the pre-Marcan Passion story, for this would hardly contain xvi. 1–8 (xv. 4b is not in keeping with the women's thoughts in xvi. 3 nor with their intention of embalming the

[19] *Op. cit.*, p. 309, n. 1 (E.T. p. 285, n. 2).

body—xvi. 1). It made a proclamation of Easter precisely by the way in which it described the path of the Son of God to the Cross.

The same is true of Mark's viewpoint: Easter is implicit in his whole message. If, therefore, the story of the Empty Tomb does not go any further than to refer indirectly to the Resurrection in the angel's command (v. 6), we cannot really speak of a 'lack' of accounts of Jesus' appearances. For one thing, this would be to make the ending of the other Gospels the norm for Mk., which would rob Mk. of its autonomy. We also need to remember that from the point of view of the history of tradition the appearance accounts that we have were developed from the ὤφθη ('he appeared') of 1 Cor. xv. 5, by way of illustration of this appearing of the Risen Lord. We cannot by any means say with certainty that this had already taken place by Mark's time, especially when we remember how little material Mt. offers that is different from Lk. In view of the material employed by Mark it seems more probable that even in his time at least the beginnings of the later appearance accounts were in existence. The question would still remain, however, as to whether Mark was familiar with such traditions, and the really decisive factor is that Mark—even if he did know them—could not include an account of an appearance. He proclaims the Risen Lord by means of stories from the earthly life of Jesus, and these would lose their character of direct proclamation if he gave an account of an event that was possible only after these had taken place. In spite of the redactional treatment pointing in the other direction, all the other stories would inevitably slip into a past distinct from the time of the Risen Lord after Easter. Mark would then have told a story—but all his editorial treatment of the material aimed precisely at avoiding this would not make sense at all.

Even though we have no adequate reason for surmising that there was a continuation after xvi. 8, the discrepancy between xvi. 7 and 8 is still a problem. From the point of view of literary criticism we have to conclude that v. 7 was inserted into this context as a result of the evangelist's editorial work. There are several reasons for doing this. Not only can the verse be taken out without disturbing the context, but there is also a close parallel to it in xiv. 28. It can certainly be taken to be redactional, as in both cases there is the reference to Galilee.

We must, however, follow the method of expounding the evangelist's editorial work in the light of his own standpoint, in other words in the light of the 'setting in life' of his work. The evangelist's aim is obviously to point his readers to Galilee (cf. iii. 7 ff.)—and to draw their attention to a 'vision' there. However, this can hardly refer to an appearance by the

Risen Lord. If Mark was acquainted with the traditions of the appearances of the Risen Lord, or even only with a rudimentary form of them, he would also have known that such appearances came to an end at a relatively early stage. In this case he cannot—as we have assumed—have wanted to draw his readers' attention at a much later period to this 'seeing' in Galilee. Therefore his references in xvi. 7 and xiv. 28 are to be taken as referring to an event that is in the future not only as far as the earthly Jesus is concerned but also Mark himself (especially as these statements are made by the Risen Lord himself). As our examination so far has provided many indications of the fact that Mark's aim was not to tell a story from the past, but to proclaim the Risen Lord, and also as an ending containing accounts of appearances is purely hypothetical it would be a mistake to corroborate the hypothesis of the lost ending on the basis of the obviously editorial verses xvi. 7 and xiv. 28, especially in view of the fact that such an ending would be contrary to the editor's intention. It is possible that Mark's references are meant to point to the *parousia* which he evidently expects will take place in Galilee and—as we can gather from various statements—in the near future.

The Gospel can therefore be described as standing between Easter and the *parousia*. The *evangelion* represents the life of Jesus from his first appearance in public up to the Cross as a proclamation; since Easter it has been possible to proclaim this event in Messianic terms (ix. 9). It is Easter that determines the account of the past as a secret epiphany—and in the same way the proclamation itself becomes a secret epiphany—and this is continued right up to the *parousia*. Ch. xiii shows that Mark does in fact go as far as the *parousia*, in the very passage in which Mark deals with this theme in the framework of his composition: in the last redactional section of any length immediately before the Passion story which was part of tradition.

(4) *Authorship, Time and Place of Composition.* The work was handed down anonymously, and it is ecclesiastical tradition that names Mark as the author. The earliest evidence for this is found in the so-called Papias fragment (Bishop Papias of Hierapolis about the middle of the second century, quoted by Eusebius, *H.E.*III 39, 15). According to this fragment, Mark was the companion and interpreter (presumably: translator) of Peter, whom he accompanied on his missionary journeys. Mark is said to have written down Peter's teachings from memory after his death, and to have made an effort to do this carefully, but without giving a correct (=historical) sequence of events.

This statement is historically worthless. The separate pericopes of the Gospel cannot possibly represent the preaching of Peter, for the findings of Form Criticism (the various forms with their different settings in life) simply preclude this. What seems most probable is that Papias is expressing the trend typical of his period—that of defending oneself against Gnosticism by appealing to the authority of a great apostle. When we have made allowance for this particular purpose behind Papias' statement, perhaps there is still something of value left. It appears that even before the time of Papias Mark was considered to be the author (otherwise Papias would presumably have suggested Peter himself as the author). The anonymous work was therefore probably attributed to Mark previously. We can assume that by Mark, the author of this work, was meant the man who was from time to time Paul's companion (Acts xii. 25; xiii. 5, 13; xv. 39; Phm. 24; 2 Tim. iv. 11; Col. iv. 10)—but this assumption does not really help us very much, for whatever name we assume to be that of the author does not really make the work any more or any less than it is in its anonymous form.

Rome is often suggested as the place of composition (Eusebius, *H.E.*II, 15), but this may possibly be a deduction drawn from 1 Pet. v. 13 (where 'Peter' sends greetings from Mark from 'Babylon'=Rome). But as the work is not connected with Peter, to locate it in 'Rome' is pure supposition, which cannot really claim support from the occasional Latinisms we find in the Gospel (xii. 14, 42, etc.). These are not derived from Mark, but from the tradition he took over—and indeed are found frequently elsewhere in the New Testament.[20] It is much more reasonable to assume that the author is writing in or near Galilee, as otherwise it is difficult to explain the great emphasis on this region—for would one write a 'Galilean Gospel' without having any connection with this area?

We can suggest a date for the composition with a greater degree of certainty. xiii. 5 ff. taken together with xiii. 14 points by means of 'signs' that are thought of as taking place in the present (wars, rumours of wars, etc.) to the period of the Jewish War (A.D. 66–70) before the destruction of Jerusalem (A.D. 70). Accordingly, the Gospel was probably written between A.D. 67 and 69.

(5) *Summary.* If it is true that the early Church did not seek to say by means of the Synoptic material who Jesus was, but who he is (Bornkamm) we can say that the same is true of Mark's intention. By his time of course this could no longer be done from the literary point of view in the same

---

[20] Cf. Blaß-Debrunner, sect. 5.

way as in the early Synoptic tradition. Between Mark and the early Synoptic tradition the texts have begun to be fixed and certain compilations have come into existence. At least implicitly this gives rise to an awareness of an interval in time. As a result of giving an account in sequence, which is inevitable when the material is linked, the past also appears as a succession of events. The result of this interval—and of this succession—is that the *kerygma* as it was expressed in the earlier units of tradition, which was meant to be a direct proclamation, succumbs to a process of 'historicizing'. Salvation comes to be presented as something belonging to the past.

The author of Mk. tries to withstand this process by his editorial work. His aim is to preserve the character of the work as proclamation—it is meant to remain *kerygma*. He achieves this aim by a very skilful linking of the varied material, so that the Gospel is not a series of sermons but *one* sermon, which in view of the evangelist's intention we should not divide again into sections. If we wish to expound particular sections nowadays we have in effect to ignore Mark's editorial alterations—which means that we are not really expounding pericopes from the work as a whole, but forms from the Synoptic tradition. (Cf. the appendix following section 14.)

The main message of Mk. can therefore be summarized briefly as follows: the evangelist proclaims the One who once appeared as the One who is to come, and who—in secret epiphany—is present now as the proclamation is made.

BIBLIOGRAPHY

E. Klostermann, *Das Markus-Evangelium* (Lietzmann, 4 ed., 1950).

E. Lohmeyer, *Das Evangelium des Markus* (Meyer, 15 ed., 1959).

J. Schniewind, *Das Evangelium nach Markus* (NTD, vol. 1, 9 ed., 1960).

H. Conzelmann, 'Geschichte und Eschaton nach Mk 13', *ZNW* (1959), pp. 210 ff.

W. Marxsen, *Der Evangelist Markus*, Studien zur Redaktionsgeschichte des Evangeliums (2 ed., 1959).

J. M. Robinson, *The Problem of History in Mark* (SCM; Allenson, 1957),

W. Wrede, *Das Messiasgeheimnis in den Evangelien* (1901, 2 ed. 1913. reprinted 1962). (E.T. in preparation, James Clark).

Commentaries: C. E. B. Cranfield, CGTC (1959); S. E. Johnson, Black (1960); D. E. Nineham, Pelican (1963); V. Taylor (2 ed., 1966).

S. G. F. Brandon, 'The Date of the Markan Gospel', *NTS* 7 (1960–1), pp. 126 ff.

P. Carrington, *The Primitive Christian Calendar* (1952).
A. M. Farrer, *A Study in St. Mark* (1951).
H. A. Guy, *The Origin of the Gospel of Mark* (1954).
R. H. Lightfoot, *The Gospel Message of St. Mark* (1950).
D. E. Nineham, 'The Order of Events in St. Mark's Gospel—an Examination of Dr. Dodd's Hypothesis' in *Studies in the Gospels, Essays in Memory of R. H. Lightfoot* (1955), pp. 223 ff.
P. Parker, *The Gospel before Mark* (1953).

L

13. THE GOSPEL OF MATTHEW

(1) *Contents and Structure.* The author of Mt. used as his sources Mk., Q and a source of special material, and as a result his work is considerably more extensive than Mark's. The author's aim, however, is by no means merely to extend the material, for he makes distinctive alterations to the traditional material, which reveal a deliberate editorial activity based on a definite theological standpoint.

(a) Mk's framework is extended backwards and forwards. Matthew places before the complex of stories about John the Baptist a prelude to the story of Jesus containing a genealogy (beginning with Abraham and leading up to Joseph: i. 2–17), a birth story (in which Joseph's fatherhood is expressly disputed: i. 18–25), the stories of the Wise Men from the East (ii. 1–12), the Flight to Egypt (ii. 13–15), the Massacre of the Innocents (ii. 16–18) and the return to Nazareth (ii. 19–23). From ch. iii onwards Matthew follows in essence the outline of Mk., apart from a few instances where the order and grouping are changed. The conclusion to the work —after the altered and expanded account of the Empty Tomb—is formed by the section about the appearance of the Risen Lord on the mountain in Galilee with the proclamation of his authority and the missionary command (xxviii. 16–20).

Even this outline is enough to show a certain 'historicizing' tendency, for Matthew sets his 'history' of Jesus in a vast context stretching from Abraham to the beginning of the Christian mission. That there are large gaps between the birth and public appearance of Jesus simply arises from the fact that the author had no material at his disposal, for at first the early Church was not interested in the biography of Jesus.

(b) Within the framework we can trace a grouping of the material according to theme. We can see this on the one hand in the bringing together of miracle stories (viii–ix) which were scattered in Mk., and on the other hand in the formation of larger complexes of sayings: the Sermon on the Mount (v–vii), the Mission Charge (x), the discourse in parables (xiii), the Church's discipline (xviii), teaching against the Pharisees and about the *parousia* and the Last Judgement (xxiii–xxv). That we have in these instances a deliberate composition of units of teaching can be seen from the stereotype phrases at the end of each section: 'And it came to pass, when Jesus ended these words . . .' (vii. 28; xi. 1; xiii. 53; xix. 1; xxvi. 1).

(c) Among further special features we can mention the frequent use of the Scriptural proof in the form peculiar to Matthew of the 'formula quotation' (i. 22 f.; ii. 5 f., 15, 17 f., 23; iii. 3; iv. 14 ff., viii. 17, xii. 17 ff.; xiii. 35; xxi. 4 f.; xxvi. 56; xxvii. 9 f.) and also the alteration of miracle stories which often has the effect—in some cases purely external—of abbreviation and greater austerity (cf., e.g., viii. 28–34 and Mk. v. 1–17; ix. 18–26 and Mk. v. 21–43).

These various editorial alterations of the traditional material lead us on to ask the question as to what the viewpoint was which was the driving force behind the alterations.

(2) *The Editorial Process in Matthew's Gospel.* When Matthew uses the Old Testament—particularly in the 'formula quotations'—for the purpose of Scriptural proof, he is going beyond the use of the Old Testament in earlier tradition, which is not yet familiar with the pattern of prophecy and fulfilment but uses the language of the Old Testament in order to express the eschatological character of what is happening (cf. section 11, 3c), and therefore makes it directly serve the purpose of proclamation. When it is turned into a Scriptural proof, this directness is lost, and its place is taken by argument, by means of which the demand is made intelligible. We can see here therefore a certain rational trend.

It does not follow, however, that Matthew has a stock of Old Testament prophecies for the fulfilment of which he seeks in the life of Jesus. His procedure is rather the reverse: starting from the fragments of tradition before him he looks for an appropriate passage in the Old Testament (i.e. 'formula quotation') which he quotes to make good the claim that the life of Jesus is a fulfilment. The trend of the argument therefore is in the reverse direction: from the Old Testament as the entity possessing a certain status to the life of Jesus as the entity to which a certain status is being attributed.

The Old Testament passages employed, however, are by no means always those which were originally meant to be prophecies. Matthew is not concerned with what meaning these passages had in their original context (cf. ii. 15); for the most part he is satisfied with a mere echo of the original, but sometimes we cannot even be sure which Old Testament passage he has in mind (ii. 23). In other words, the evangelist uses the Old Testament quite 'unhistorically', but in this respect he is merely adopting an 'exegetical' method common in his time. It is also significant that Matthew is not content to quote the Old Testament in connection with the fragment of tradition as it has come down, but he brings the quotation from the Old Testament to bear upon the fragment of tradition itself, which is sometimes altered in the light of the Old Testament (cf. Mk. i. 14 f. and Mt. iv. 15 f. and also Mt. iv. 12 f.; Mk. xi. 2 and Mt. xxi. 5 and also Mt. xxi. 2). This makes Matthew's 'historicizing' of the tradition very plain: what originally served the purpose of direct proclamation is now considered from the standpoint of what actually happened. What happened must correspond with 'prophecy', as otherwise the proof from Scripture would not be convincing. If it does not correspond with the prophecy found in the Old Testament, Matthew alters the 'event'.

We can see from this that Matthew interprets Mk. differently from the way in which Mark himself understood his work—i.e., no longer as *kerygma* but as a record. Matthew does not of course engage in 'historical research'; his 'historicizing' is guided by the dogmatic viewpoint that Jesus was the Messiah proclaimed in the Old Testament. As this has been confirmed to Matthew's mind and he is seeking to set out the evidence for what is to him an article of faith—and so bring others to the same understanding—he considers he is quite justified in correcting 'history'.

The same can be said as regards the arrangement of the material. Matthew took xi. 2–6 from Q. The original purpose of the passage was to express the fact that the ministry of Jesus was eschatological. This was done by an implicit use of the Old Testament: Jesus' deeds are set out in Old Testament terms (xi. 5), but no direct evidence is adduced (for all miracles as such can have various meanings). What we have here is rather an implicit evidence, which by no means dispenses with the question of faith (xi. 6). In other words, the whole section is *kerygma*. Matthew, however, uses this section along the lines of his Scriptural proof. We can see this from the way he arranges his material. The cycle of miracles (viii–ix) in which there is at least one example of all the mighty deeds mentioned in xi. 5, and also the Mission Charge in ch. x. (cf. xi. 5: the poor have good tidings preached to them) show that what was expected in the Old Testament in the last days has taken place through Jesus. His deeds, which correspond with the Old Testament expectations, prove Jesus to be the Messiah.

It is clear that the miracle stories have now been given an entirely different function from the one they had originally. It is not their kerygmatic character that is important for Matthew, but the fact that they actually happened. This means that he is in a position to make radical abbreviations, as a result of which the kerygmatic element is often lost. In ix. 18, for example, the ruler's daughter is stated to be 'even now dead', whereas in Mk. v. 21–43, by means of a circumstantial and detailed narrative as well as by the insertion of the pericope concerning the Woman with the Issue of Blood the tension is maintained as to whether Jesus will arrive in time.

After all these observations concerning Matthew's 'historicizing' the question naturally arises whether we can call Mt. a 'Gospel' in the same sense as Mk., or whether we should not call it a *Vita Jesu*. However, we have to note that Matthew does not only engage in 'historicizing', as we can see when we consider the cycles of discourses and also his recasting of the narrative material. Matthew does of course take over older traditions in his cycles, but he puts them together in such a way—or brings out their meaning in such a way—that they become proclamations addressed to his own time. In other words, he who proved himself to be Messiah by his former deeds now speaks to the Church.

A typical example is v. 17, which is an obviously polemical saying against what Matthew considers to be an undesirable liberty taken with the Law. It is obvious that there was a problem here for Jewish Christianity: it is necessary to resist the reproach that the Law has been abrogated in the Christian Church, but at the same time it is important to bring out the difference between the Church and Judaism. But according to Matthew the reproach to be levelled against the Jews is not that of the 'righteousness of works': the scribes and Pharisees are not wrong in defending the Law (N.B. xxiii. 3), but in not fulfilling it (ch. xxiii). Therefore the righteousness of Christians must exceed that of the scribes and Pharisees (v. 20). According to Matthew, therefore, the Law is binding. The antitheses in the Sermon on the Mount (v. 21 ff., 27 ff., 31 f., 33 ff., 38 ff., 43 ff.) are not to be interpreted as an abrogation of the Law but as a radical statement of it. In other words, when Jesus says that he came not to destroy the Law or the prophets, but to fulfil (v. 17), this does not mean that he himself in his own life carried out all the precepts of the Law (vicariously for all Christians). Here 'fulfil' means to bring out the full meaning. It is this Law—its full meaning brought out, and thereby 'radicalized'—that Christians have to observe (v. 18). The Law comes to its climax in the commandment to love (v. 43 ff.), which Matthew underlines with a number of editorial comments (vii. 12; ix. 13; xxii. 7; xxii. 40; xxiii. 23).

In other words, the indicative which makes it possible to perform the imperative is to be found in Jesus, not because Jesus br ought the new aeon, but because by re-interpreting the Law he taught such behaviour (v. 17 ff.; xxiii. 23), argued about it with his opponents (xxiii) and commanded such behaviour (xxviii. 20). According to Matthew, therefore, the Sermon on the Mount gives instructions for right conduct; it is a Law and—like the Mosaic Law—is delivered on a mountain (v. 1; cf. also the typological parallel between Moses and Jesus in ch. ii especially: persecution by a king opposed to the will of God, massacre of children, Egypt; cf. ii. 20 and Exod. iv. 19, etc.).

The other cycles of discourses can be described similarly. They contain proclamations such as were made in the time of Matthew, but they are presented to us as 'discourses of Jesus'. Matthew's special purpose now becomes clear: by a process of 'historicizing' he vindicates Jesus' claim to be Messiah and therefore as the one who is entitled to give instructions and proclaim his teachings. This vindication is made quite plain: Jesus fulfilled Old Testament prophecies. The towns that have seen his mighty deeds should therefore have listened to him—and repented (xi. 20). At the same time, however, Matthew formulates the contents of Jesus' teaching in such a way that the disciples he addresses appear as representatives of the later Church of Matthew's time, to which the teaching is made to apply directly.

The same can be said of the narrative passages. Matthew turns miracle stories as they have come down to him into illustrative didactic stories, with the result that from the conduct and faith of the original disciples we are shown by way of example what is required of the later Church in conduct and faith. We can see this, for example, in the theme of 'little faith' which Matthew introduces into passages where his source speaks of unbelief or hardness of heart (cf. viii. 26 and Mk. iv. 40; xvi. 8 and Mk. viii. 17). Matthew is not concerned with the question of becoming a Christian (unbelief—belief) but with the building up of the Christian life (belief—little belief). We must of course bear in mind that this 'ecclesiastical adaptation' of the traditional material cannot always be clearly seen in each alteration that is made, but rather emerges as a general impression from the tendency that finds expression in all the alterations.

Matthew's literary technique brings to light the ecclesiastical aspect of the work (cf. xvi. 18; xviii. 17). The significant thing, however, is that—in contrast to earlier tradition—the idea of the 'presence of salvation' is relegated to the background by the strong emphasis upon the provisional character of the Church. The Church is never identified with the Kingdom that is to come, and it is in keeping with this that the cycles of discourses always conclude with an eschatological outlook (vii. 21 ff.;

x. 40 ff.; xiii. 49 f.; xviii. 35; xxv. 1 ff.). The End will bring judgement—upon the Church too—according to one's deeds and separate those who are chosen from those who are called (xvi. 27; xix. 30; xx. 16; xxi. 43).

Mt. therefore proves to be a carefully planned work in which the traditions that are used have been thoroughly recast in the light of one main standpoint. We can in fact no longer describe it as a 'Gospel'. We never find the concept *evangelion* in Mt. used absolutely—in contrast to Mk.—but always with modifications: 'the gospel of the kingdom', iv. 23; ix. 35; 'this gospel', xxvi. 13; 'this gospel of the kingdom', xxiv. 14. The context suggests that Matthew thinks of the preaching of Jesus, particularly the cycles of discourses, as gospels. Jesus delivers them, but himself no longer forms the content of them.

On the other hand, we cannot really describe the work as a *Vita Jesu* either. Matthew himself calls it βίβλος γενέσεως Ἰησοῦ Χριστοῦ (i. 1). It is unlikely that this phrase in the sense of 'the book of the beginning (or origin) of Jesus Christ' merely refers to the genealogy (including the birth story). It is rather an echo of Old Testament phrases (cf. esp. Gen. xxvii. 2). The meaning therefore is: the book of the history of Jesus Christ, but not history just in the sense of reported information about the past, but as something having a bearing upon the present. By means of this phrase therefore the work is presented almost as 'Holy Scripture'—by analogy with the Old Testament—to which one can appeal and from which one can take one's bearings if one wishes to observe or teach others to observe what Jesus commanded (xxviii. 20).

This gives us an indication of the Christology of Mt. Jesus is the Teacher of the Church; he is this because he is the Messiah, the King of Israel, who has proved himself to be such by the fulfilment of Old Testament prophecies. He does not only teach, of course, but himself walks in the way he teaches, in humility and lowliness (xi. 29; xxi. 1 ff.), and so himself fulfils all righteousness (iii. 15). His path leads him in the first place only to Israel (xv. 24; cf. x. 5), but the extension of the sphere is soon hinted at (viii. 11; xxi. 43), although we do not find it clearly set out until xxviii. 16 ff. At his future *parousia*—which is no longer thought of as imminent—he will sit in judgement (chs. xxiv f.).

The special feature of this Christology is that it no longer serves the purpose of proclamation directly, but only indirectly. Its interest is no longer primarily soteriological, for it serves in the first place to vindicate the One who makes the proclamation. In Mt., therefore, the preacher and the message are to some extent separated. The message itself is not really eschatological: it is eschatological because it is the message of the

Messiah. This standpoint is certainly connected with the fact that the interval since the time of Jesus has grown longer. One can no longer merely say who Jesus is—for the benefit of the present—one must now also say who he was. It is true that this is not said just as a matter of past history but as part of a 'historicizing' process, the purpose of which is to preserve the continuity of the past with the present. In other words, 'Jesus' delivered the discourses which are to be made in the present—and in speaking them to the disciples he has spoken them to the Church.

The viewpoint which Matthew presents is therefore quite different from the earlier outlines. By making a direct comparison between the two we can point to particular differences, e.g. in the attitude to the Law, and certain one-sided distortions, e.g. in Christology, but such a 'verdict' would fail to appreciate the extraordinary achievement of the author. By means of his literary endeavours and his interpretation of tradition he succeeds in raising questions and problems facing his contemporaries and in providing the answer to them in a consistent theological framework. To pass a theological or dogmatic judgement on this framework is not the task of exegesis.

(3) *Authorship, Time and Place of Composition.* The work has come down anonymously, but according to ancient Church tradition the author was Matthew, one of the twelve disciples. The Papias fragment mentioned in section 12, 4 includes besides the remarks concerning Mk. the statement that Matthew collected the logia in the Hebrew language and that everyone interpreted them as well as he could (Eusebius, *H.E.*III 39, 16). Even if we do not try to make too much of the term 'logia' and assume that this is a statement about the Gospel, it can hardly be correct, for the author of Mt. not only wrote the work in Greek (it is out of the question to consider it as a translation from Hebrew or Aramaic), but also used sources written in Greek (Mk., Q). We can therefore understand Papias' statement only against the background of a period in which efforts were being made to find guarantees for the Church's tradition.

The author in fact remains completely unknown to us. The fact that in ix. 9 the name of the tax-collector who is called to be a disciple is given as Matthew and not Levi as in Mk. ii. 14 is not a veiled indication of the author but is connected with the fact that there is no Levi in the list of disciples in x. 2 ff. It has recently been suggested that the work is not that of a single author but of a 'school' (K. Stendahl), but it is impossible to produce any detailed evidence for this. It is conceivable—perhaps even probable—that Mt's. viewpoint was the common property of a kind of Christian scribal school (cf. xiii. 52), in which for example his special method of Scriptural proof was practised and his view of the Law was developed. It is difficult to imagine, however, that the work was written only for this group. It is aimed rather at the Church, and it is most probable that the redaction was made by an individual, someone we can no longer trace. He was certainly not an eye-witness of the life of Jesus, because if he were his dependence on the sources would be incomprehensible. In that case he could not have made any use of his experience as an eye-witness.

Mt. looks back to the destruction of Jerusalem (xxii. 7), and some time has probably elapsed since the composition of Mk. Mt. therefore could have been written in the 80's of the first century. As the place of origin the only possibility is a Jewish Christian area, and we have probably to consider somewhere in Syria. It is conceivable that it originated in Pella in the region to the east of the Jordan where the Jewish Christian community in Jerusalem found a new meeting place after the flight from the city shortly before its destruction in A.D. 70, but this is no more than a possibility.

BIBLIOGRAPHY

E. Klostermann, *Das Matthäus-Evangelium* (Lietzmann, 2 ed., 1927).

E. Lohmeyer, *Das Evangelium des Matthäus* (Meyer, Sonderband, 2 ed., 1958).

G. Bornkamm, 'Matthäus als Interpret der Herrenworte', *ThLZ* (1954), pp. 241 ff.

G. Bornkamm–G. Barth–H. J. Held, *Überlieferung und Auslegung im Matthäusevangelium* (2 ed., 1961). (E.T. *Tradition and Interpretation in Matthew*, SCM; Westminster, 1963).

R. Hummel, *Die Auseinandersetzung zwischen Kirche und Judentum im Matthäusevangelium* (1963).

K. Stendahl, *The School of St. Matthew and its Use of the Old Testament* (1954).

G. Strecker, *Der Weg der Gerechtigkeit*, Untersuchung zur Theologie des Matthaus (1962).

W. Trilling, *Das wahre Israel*, Studien zur Theologie des Matthäusevangeliums (1959).

Commentaries: W. C. Allen, ICC (3 ed., 1912); A. H. McNeile (1915); F. V. Filson, Black (1960).

B. W. Bacon, *Studies in Matthew* (1930).

B. C. Butler, *The Originality of St. Matthew* (1930).

G. D. Kilpatrick, *The Origins of the Gospel according to St. Matthew* (2 ed., 1950).

K. Stendahl, 'The School of St. Matthew', *ASNU* 20 (1954).

14. THE GOSPEL OF LUKE

(1) *Contents and Structure.* The author of Lk. used as his source Mk., Q and considerable special material. Again, however, his aim—like that of the author of Mt.—was not simply to increase the amount of material, but he deliberately altered and edited the traditions that were handed down so that once again we have to consider the problem of the editorial process in the work.

As his basic material Luke adopts the Marcan outline, especially that of chs. i–xiii, and this can still be traced in Lk. iii–xxi. Luke prefaces this with an introductory section (i–ii) which had previously been compiled from various traditions. In the Passion story (xxii–xxiii) Luke shows great independence in altering his source and decisively shifting the emphasis. In the final ch. xxiv he makes use of much special material. This use of a considerable amount of special material is typical of Lk. There is, for example, the so-called small interpolation (vi. 20–viii. 3) and the so-called 'journey report' (great interpolation: ix. 51–xviii. 14). A typical feature of the special material in Lk. is the theme we meet quite frequently of the saving love of Jesus for sinners, the poor and the despised.

These materials, however, which are very varied in origin, are not simply added one to the other in Lk. We find in this work a much more thorough shaping of the whole into a unity than we find in any of the other Synoptic Gospels—or than we have yet been able to trace. The structure therefore stands out very clearly. After the preface (i. 1–4), the introductory account (i. 5–ii. 52) and the preparation for Jesus' ministry (iii. 1–iv. 13) there come three great sections: A—Jesus' ministry in Galilee (iv. 14–ix. 50); B—Jesus' journey to Jerusalem (ix. 51–xix. 28); C—Jesus in Jerusalem (xix. 29–xxiii. 49). The concluding section contains an account of the Burial and accounts connected with Easter and the Ascension (xxiii. 50–xxiv. 53).

(2) *The Editorial Process in Luke's Gospel.* In trying to discover Luke's own viewpoint we need to bear in mind that he adds a continuation to his 'Gospel' in the Acts of the Apostles (Acts i. 1 ff.). This fact is of great importance, and has a bearing upon the exegesis of the first part of the two-volume work. We can see this when we consider that by contrast

with Luke the standpoint of both Mark and Matthew make any kind of continuation unthinkable. Of course Matthew (and—with certain reservations—also Mark) could have written a Church history; however, this would not have been a continuation of their original works, but a history of the continuing influence of these works, which is something quite different. By writing Acts Luke makes it plain that his 'Gospel' is meant to be understood as part of a historical account. The story of Jesus is now told as something belonging to the past, and for the first time the historical sequence is stressed. Luke himself draws attention to this fact when he sets out his intentions: he states in his introduction (i. 1–4) that, after many others have attempted to draw up a narrative (διήγησις) of the events that have been 'fulfilled', he himself is now going to undertake the work in order that Theophilus (presumably a wealthy patron, to whom the work is dedicated, but not to be thought of as the only intended reader) might be convinced of the reliability of the things that he had been told. As Luke is using a traditional formula here, we should not press the details of his statement too far. Luke certainly did not have before him 'many' works similar to his own, but only the sources we have already mentioned, but his aim is clear: he wants to do 'better' than his predecessors (his work therefore is not meant to stand alongside, but in place of the others!) and as a criterion of what he can do 'better' he mentions historical reliability.

We need to take care in evaluating these personal statements. Luke's assertion by itself does not mean that we have in Lk. historically more reliable information; it merely tells us something of his intentions. Luke was not like the modern secular historian, and therefore we should not think of him as such, nor should we tacitly assume that his writings were the outcome of modern methods. The question we have to consider is whether, and how, Luke could achieve the aim he set himself. The sources at his disposal were in no sense historical sources, but proclamations; nor did the outline adopted from Mk. provide a faithful historical sequence of events. According to our standard of measurement, therefore, Luke simply could not achieve what he wanted, as his sources did not provide what he required.

When we bear this in mind it is clear, however, that Luke reads his sources from the standpoint of the aim he himself is pursuing. His aim is to write past history, and to do this as accurately as possible, and he reads his sources—although with a critical eye—as historical records. If Luke wishes to be a 'historian' he can only achieve this by writing history, and he therefore sets out the units of proclamation as a succession of past events, but at the same time he characterizes the story by describing the events as 'fulfilments', and as fulfilments of a Divine plan of salvation which has unfolded itself in a sequence of history. Luke sets the story in the context of secular history (ii. 1 ff.; iii. 1 ff.), but he does not allow it to merge into it. As a 'historian' he is always the believer, and his account of history is always determined by his 'belief'.

This helps us to understand his division of history into three epochs: the period of Israel (the Law and the prophets), the period of Jesus as the 'centre of time' (Conzelmann) and the period of the Church. Luke marks the divisions very clearly. The first epoch reaches up to and including John the Baptist. This is explicitly stated in xvi. 16, but it can also be deduced from the way Luke arranges his material, for the arrest of John (iii. 19 f.) is put before the Baptism of Jesus (iii. 21 f.). We can see from this instance how the traditional material goes against Luke's conception, but at the same time how Luke's belief—that John is really only a forerunner—determines his 'historical' arrangement. Finally we can see the effect of Luke's 'de-eschatologizing' of John in the fact that he omits the Elijah passage in his source (Mk. ix. 11). The 'early history' of Jesus is also included in this first epoch.

The 'centre of time' begins at iv. 14. Its characteristic is that it is a period 'free from Satan'. After the Temptation the devil leaves Jesus ἄχρι καιροῦ (iv. 13), and from then on there are no more temptations (cf. x. 18). The *kairos* of Satan does not begin again until xxii. 3, when he enters into Judas during the farewell discourses before the Last Supper. This brings to an end the 'centre of time' (N.B. the Cross is not included in this period).

The third epoch, the period of the Church, begins at Pentecost (Acts ii. 1 ff.; cf. Lk. xxiv. 49), and therefore does not follow directly upon the second epoch. The significance of this interval—which Luke does not trouble to fit into the overall pattern—will be considered later.

We can see what is special in Luke's viewpoint most clearly when we compare it with Paul's, and also with Matthew's. Mark declares by means of stories from the past the immediate significance of the exalted Lord for the present, Matthew writes as a historian, as his Old Testament quotations in particular show, but makes the past appear relevant for the present both directly by showing its character as 'fulfilment' and also indirectly by virtue of the fact that it provides an example. For Luke, however, the period of Jesus really belongs to the past, and is sharply distinguished from the period of the Church. The eschatological element present in the proclamatory character of the pre-Lucan tradition is eliminated. Luke's 'historicizing' is therefore at the same time a process of 'de-eschatologizing'. This raises the question as to what meaning the past has for the present in which Luke lives. Some indication of this is given in the description of the 'centre of time' as a period 'free from Satan'.

In the period of the Church Satan is once again active, but it is expected that in the Last Days he will finally be destroyed. Luke looks forward to this time, and this is the substance of his hope, a hope which springs from the fact that Satan has already been deprived of power once before. The period of Jesus is therefore an eschatological period in so far as it already contained what is to come later. As a foretaste of the future in the centre of time this provides the basis for the expectation of the final fulfilment. It is therefore characteristic that the eschatological element in the period of Jesus is represented as having taken place in the past, but it does not take the form of direct address. By turning to the past viewed in this light one can experience the 'certainty' of that which one has been taught (i. 4), and can become sure of one's belief, because here one can learn what is to be expected of the future fulfilment.

The future itself, however, is postponed, and the expectation of an imminent *parousia* is abandoned (cf. the complete alteration of Mk. i. 14 f. in Lk. iv. 14 ff., and the warning about those who claim that the time is at hand which Luke inserts in xxi. 8 into his source Mk. xiii. 6, and also the indication that wars and tumults do not mean that the End is 'immediate'—see Lk. xxi. 9 in comparison with Mk. xiii. 7). By projecting into the distant future the *parousia* which was previously thought of as imminent, although he still speaks of it in apocalyptic images (cf. xvii. 22–37; xxi. 28), he gains time for the period of the Church.

In this way, however, Luke solves only one problem which the delay of the *parousia* had posed inescapably, and in considering the questions raised by his procedure we must not overlook this fact. Luke of course cannot describe the present in which he lives as the Last Days in the way in which Paul did (2 Cor. vi. 2) and as Mark did by means of the standpoint he adopted. The truth is that the Last Days were once there (in the ministry of Jesus)—and they will come again (at the later *parousia*). Luke therefore can no longer describe the change from the old age to the new as having taken place in the past, as Paul did, for the past merely provides the basis for the hope of a future transition. This is the goal of redemptive history, which unfolds according to the Divine plan and is 'fulfilled' from stage to stage (cf. i. 1; iv. 21—the 'today' is the past 'today', but not that which is eschatologically present; ix. 51; xxiv. 25 ff.; Acts ii. 1).

The 'centre of time' is *one* section, but a particularly significant section, of this redemptive history, and is itself sub-divided into three. It begins with the assembling of the witnesses in Galilee (iv. 14 ff.—the significance of this is shown particularly by Acts i. 21 f.), then gives an account of the path Jesus takes towards his Passion, by means of the journey theme (ix. 51–xix. 28) and concludes with the Passion story (xix. 29–xxiii. 49), in the midst of which—not after—the 'centre of time' comes to an end (N.B. xxii. 3). The Cross, therefore, does not belong to the 'centre of time', nor does the Last Supper. Even during the discourses during the Supper there is a glance back to the period of salvation, now in the past (xxii. 35) and forwards to the period of affliction that is to come (xxii. 32, 36), which has to run its course according to God's plan (xxii. 37; cf. xxiv. 26 f.; 44 ff.).

The alterations which Luke makes in the Passion story clearly show how he understands it—as a legal murder by the Jews, but not as the ground of salvation. A false accusation is laid before Pilate (xxiii. 3— without parallel in Mk.), but it is not discussed at all (xxiii. 3—here Luke follows tradition; and again the difference between tradition and Luke's conception becomes clear). The governor finds no fault in Jesus and tries to have him set free (xxiii. 4, 13–16—again without parallel in Mk.). It is only under pressure from the crowd that Pilate hands Jesus over to 'the will of the people' (xxiii. 25: contrast Mk. xv. 15). It is therefore the Jewish High Priests and rulers who brought about the death of Jesus (N.B. xxiv. 20). The guilt of the governor—and therefore of the Romans —is reduced as far as tradition will allow.

It would be a serious mistake if we were to interpret Luke's alterations in the Passion story as evidence of anti-Semitism. His aim is rather to come to terms with the *Imperium Romanum*, but this would be impossible if all the emphasis were laid on the guilt of the Romans. Correspondingly all the persecutions in Acts, even those which were instigated by the authorities, are described as being stirred up by Jews. The aim Luke pursues, therefore, is not that of vilifying the Jews but of exonerating the Romans, and it is this that gives rise to the emphasis on the guilt of the Jews. In the period of the Church, according to Luke, the only choice open to the Jews is that of becoming Christians or of remaining Jews. The 'problem' of Israel and the Church does not exist as far as he is concerned, for redemptive history finds its continuation after the 'centre of time' no longer in the Jewish sphere, but in the sphere of the Church.

Although the Cross is depicted as a legal murder by the Jews, it still takes place according to the Divine plan, and the purpose of it is to glorify Christ (xxiv. 26). Here again Luke the historian splits the Easter message which was originally complex: the Cross is followed by the Resurrection, a time limit is set to the appearances of the Risen Lord which are concluded by the Ascension, and this in turn is followed by Pentecost. The meaning of these events between the second and third epoch is that they make possible the Church to which Luke belongs. In the 'centre of time' Jesus is the only bearer of the Spirit (cf. the alteration of Mk. i. 12 in Lk. iv. 1; also Lk. iv. 14), but after the Ascension the Spirit comes to the Church at Pentecost. In other words, it is the Spirit who provides the continuity between the period of Jesus and the period of the Church.

There are also other themes which express this continuity. In Lk., for example, the course to be taken by the missionary preaching is set out in advance (Lk. x. 1 ff.). It is important to note the geographical references. The early part of Jesus' ministry is in Galilee (iv. 14 ff.). In ix. 51 the journey to Jerusalem begins, but it does not take Jesus to Samaria; the rejection comes in ix. 53, after which Jesus never again goes to Samaria.

According to Luke's geographical conceptions Judaea (alongside the Mediterranean) and Galilee (to the East) are directly adjacent (cf. Lk. iv. 38 ff., then iv. 44 and immediately afterwards v. 1). Samaria is envisaged as being to the North of both these regions; according to ix. 52 Jesus attempts to go to Samaria, but is rejected in ix. 53 and according to xvii. 11 is still on the way to Jerusalem between Samaria and Galilee. Luke restricts Jesus' ministry to Galilee and Judaea, and omits any activity outside Palestine (cf. Mk. viii. 27 and Lk. ix. 18). In the one instance that is an exception, the healing of the demoniac, the proximity to Galilee is emphasized (viii. 26); this is followed by a further rejection (viii. 37).

All these geographical references are a foreshadowing of the Church's mission. According to Acts it extends to Samaria and lands beyond Palestine, but not to Galilee. The result of this viewpoint can be seen in the skilful alteration of Mk. xvi. 7 in Lk. xxiv. 6: the reference to Galilee is turned into a reminiscence of something said in Galilee. Here again we can see the deliberate transformation of the whole conception. Luke has often been reproached with 'de-eschatologizing' the 'Gospel'. The fact is that he did not write a 'Gospel'—he avoids the concept—but something more akin to a 'Life of Jesus'.

He presents the period of salvation as belonging to the past, but we shall not understand Luke's approach correctly if we assume from this that he is interested in the past as such. The question that concerns him is how the Church of his time, which no longer expects an imminent *parousia* and realizes that the period of Jesus belongs to the distant past, can remain in continuity with this past. Therefore if we are to pass judgement on Luke's procedure we should not start by asking: what has Luke made out of his models? (nor what has Luke made of the Pauline theology?—he certainly did not adopt it) but we must start by considering his 'setting in life', for it is this that determines the way he uses and alters tradition. And at a time when a non-historical Gnosticism was abandoning the connection of the Christian message with history, the viewpoint on which Luke's work is based represents a protest against this trend. At the same time we must emphasize that Luke offered this solution to the problems of his time precisely for his time, and not for the whole of subsequent Church history. It would be a completely unhistorical approach to Lk. if we were to judge the author's achievement by the extent to which it is applicable to the dogmatic problems of today.

(3) *Authorship, Time and Place of Composition.* Once again we have to begin by noting that the work is anonymous. There is no Papias fragment about Luke. The earliest reference is found in Irenaeus, who states that Luke, the companion of Paul, set down in a book the gospel proclaimed by Paul (*Adv.Haer.*III, i. 1, in Eusebius, *H.E.,V* 8, 3). The statement in the Muratorion Canon is similar. Here Luke is explicitly described as a doctor (cf. Phm. 24, Col. iv. 14; 2 Tim. iv. 11). We have already seen that Paul can in no way be considered as the guarantor for this work, and we therefore have to make the same reservations about these statements as in the case of Mk. and Mt. We shall have to consider the question again when dealing with Acts (cf. section 15, 4).

As the author is writing for Greek readers, we can perhaps best say where he probably did not write—in Palestine or Syria. The time of writing was probably in the third Christian generation, round about the year A.D. 90.

BIBLIOGRAPHY

E. Klostermann, *Das Lukasevangelium* (Lietzmann, 2 ed., 1929).

K. H. Rengstorf, *Das Evangelium nach Lukas* (NTD, vol. 3, 9 ed., 1962).

H. Conzelmann, *Die Mitte der Zeit*, Studien zur Theologie des Lukas (4 ed., 1962). (E.T. *The Theology of Saint Luke* (from 2 ed., 1957), Faber; Harper, 1960).

E. Lohse, 'Lukas als Theologe der Heilsgeschichte', *EvTh* (1954), pp. 256 ff.

M

Commentaries: J. M. Creed (1930); A. R. C. Leaney, Black (2 ed., 1966);
W. Manson, Moffatt (1930); A. Plummer, ICC (5 ed., 1922).

C. K. Barrett, *Luke the Historian in Recent Study* (1961).

H. J. Cadbury, *The Making of Luke–Acts* (1927).

V. Taylor, *Behind the Third Gospel* (1926) and 'The Proto-Luke Hypothesis', *ET* 67 (1955–6), pp. 12 ff.

APPENDIX: THE EXEGESIS OF THE SYNOPTIC GOSPELS

The examination we have made in sections 10–14 has shown that the Synoptic material passed through a long process of proclamation. At the beginning separate units of tradition were formed, and then they were expanded and modified. Early compilations came into being, and then Mk., which itself in turn became a model for Mt. and Lk. Both the formation of the separate units of tradition and also the further developments, the compilations and finally the continuous linking of material in the 'Gospels' served the purpose of proclamation in the particular period in which they arose. The variations spring from the differences in the historically conditioned situations.

We have direct literary evidence of only the last stages in this development, in which the Church's message was embodied in three 'literary types': the Gospel, the book ('Holy Scripture') and historical writing from the standpoint of faith (*Vita Jesu*). From this point of view it seems questionable whether we can speak of 'the Synoptics'. It is true that—as far as the contents are concerned—we find to a large extent the same material in the three works, but it is presented in very different forms or literary types. If we wish to bring out the message the authors sought to convey in their works we need to bear this in mind. The Synoptic aspect is of only indirect assistance in the work of exegesis. It only helps us to determine the alterations made by Matthew and Luke in individual passages, alterations which they make in their model Mk. and also in Q, but this leads us into a vicious circle, as the original text of Q can only be deduced by reconstructing it from Mt. and Lk. It is only by taking account of the alterations in *all* the passages that we can gain a complete picture of the authors' message, and this complete picture must in turn be kept in mind if we are to form a correct judgement as to the significance of the individual alterations.

Once we have understood this, it becomes obvious where the real difficulty lies in Synoptic exegesis—in the relationship of detailed exegesis to general exegesis. The one is not possible without the other, but the material before us—which is very obviously made up of what were originally separate sections—leads us to give preference to detailed exegesis, and to give more attention to it. This is also encouraged by the fact that exegesis is generally pursued in order to arrive at a 'Christian message', e.g. in preaching, Bible study and private Bible reading, and therefore tends to select particular pericopae and concentrate on isolated sections. It is precisely here that the problem arises.

As Mark almost always links together the separate units of tradition by very simple literary means and without any great alteration of the material, these editorial processes can be easily traced. The same is often true in Mt. and Lk. in the case of the special material, and often also of Q, where there is only a loose linking. We can therefore arrive relatively simply at the traditional material in the form in which it existed before it was incorporated into the Gospels. But as they really were separate units in their original form, we can still approach them from the point of view of exegesis as separate sections. (Examples: Mk. ix. 2–8; x. 13–14, 16; xvi. 1–6, 8; Mt. xi. 2–6; xiii. 44–46; xiii. 47–50; xviii. 23–34; Lk. iii. 10–14; vii. 11–17; vii. 18b–20, 22–23.)

If we can trace in these separate sections subsequent alterations or expansions which took place before they were incorporated into the Gospels we can make a second exegesis in which the message of the first exegesis is modified. (Examples: Mk. ii. 2–5a, 11–12 and Mk. ii. 2–12; Mk. iv. 3–8 and Mk. iv. 3–10, 13–20; Mk. x. 13–14, 16 and Mk. x. 13–16, etc.) In general, therefore, we can say that in so far as we can reconstruct the history of Synoptic traditional material as proclamation before it was taken up into the Gospels, we can make an exegesis of each stage in its development, but always in its separate units.

Exegesis becomes more difficult, however, when dealing with a pericope which in the form in which we find it never existed as a separate section, but was taken out of a larger unit. We have to bear in mind the fact that none of the evangelists offers us merely a collection of separate sections strung together, but a complete work which, if we take into account the author's own viewpoint underlying the work, cannot be subsequently split up again. If we overlook this fact, the danger is that we may conclude from our knowledge that the material used in these works was once separate units of proclamation that we can treat it as separate units in its new context and extract it. The attempt is then made by exegesis to draw out the message of such pericopae, without realizing that we have before us only the broken fragments of what should be treated as a whole.

The problem presents itself differently in the various instances, but we can distinguish two main types. In the first type the *scopus* lies outside the pericope. This applies, for example, to the miracle stories in Mt. viii–ix (altered by Matthew), which are used as 'Scriptural proof', as becomes clear in Mt. xi. 2 ff. The section Mt. viii. 1–xi. 6 is a unity to the extent that the *scopus* of each miracle story, in the form in which they are presented by Matthew, is not only the same, but can only be formulated in connection with Mt. xi. 5. If, for example, we wish to make an exegesis of Mt. ix. 18–26, we can only do this either by tracing Matthew's alterations backwards—which means in effect making an exegesis of Mk. v. 21–43—or by going far beyond this pericope itself. As an isolated pericope Mt. ix. 18–26 simply cannot be expounded. The same is true of practically all the sections in Mt. where the evangelist altered his course.

We find the same situation in Lk. In this case we can take as an example the Passion story (cf. section 14, 2). The traditions Luke used once had their *scopus* in themselves, as separate pericopae, but pericopae such as Lk. xxiii. 1–5 or xxiii. 13–25 never stood on their own, and they can be expounded only in the context of the whole. As it is Luke's aim, however, after the 'centre of time' has come to an end, to continue the account of redemptive history up to the outpouring of the Spirit, the *scopus* of the Lucan Passion story lies strictly speaking in Acts ii. 1 ff. It cannot therefore be expounded in isolated sections.

Nor can it really be preached. The primary reason for this lies not so much in Luke's theological conception of the Cross of Jesus—although of course systematic considerations do play a part here; it is to be found rather in the fact that the pericopae (in isolation—and then in their Lucan significance) are not capable of exegesis. If we do not bear this in mind, we can very easily introduce ideas from Mk. or the pre-Marcan Passion story, or even from the still earlier separate traditions. If we wish to make an exegesis of them, then we must turn to the texts in which they are found.

In other cases the *scopus* does not lie outside the pericope, but in it—but only partly so. Mk. ix. 2–9 is a good example of this: up to v. 8 we have the Marcan model, but in v. 9 we find the command to keep silent, which is part of Mark's conception of the Messianic secret. This itself can only be expounded if we consider the whole complex, which is scattered throughout the whole Gospel. As far as exegesis is concerned, therefore, the alternatives are either to restrict it to vv. 2–8, and so as a result to bring out the pre-Marcan message or to include Mark's message (vv. 2–9) in which case we have to take into account the whole complex of the Messianic secret.

We find a similar situation when we turn to the Matthean miracle stories, which not only serve the purpose of Scriptural proof, but have also been turned into illustrative stories for the later Church. The disciples have become representatives of the Church (cf. section 13, 3). If we expound a miracle story from chs. viii–ix, for example, on the one hand the *scopus* lies outside the story in xi. 5 (see above), but there is a different editorial emphasis in part at least in the story itself. It is true that this emphasis is not fully expressed in any single miracle story, and it is often only hinted at; we get a full impression of it only when we examine the editorial work of the evangelist in all the stories. In order to discover the *scopus* expressed by this particular emphasis we need to refer to the whole complex of these typical alterations in so far as they have a bearing on the individual story. As pericopae—first in isolation, and then in the interpretation Matthew gives them—they can only rarely be expounded.

The same, finally, applies to Lk. If, for example, iv. 16–21 refers to the fulfilment of Scripture that was then taking place, then what we have is a partial statement of Luke's conception of the course of Divine history within secular history. Exegesis has to bear this in mind, and therefore can expound this pericope only in the context of the whole work, otherwise it would be in danger of interpreting the 'today' in the sense of 2 Cor. vi. 2.

To sum up our findings, we can say as a general rule that exegesis can only succeed when it is made in the framework of the particular context of proclamation. This may be the pre-literary one, if we can succeed in reconstructing the earlier independent units, but if we turn to the passages in the form in which we find them in the New Testament, then in each case it is the complete work that forms the context of proclamation. To break up the complete works into small sections—which is usually done in an attempt to fix them into some general scheme—means destroying this unity, which is all the more serious the more the editors altered the traditional material in the process of composition. This applies much more to Mt. and Lk. than to Mk., and so it is in the former two Gospels that the customary practice of dividing into pericopae has a serious effect, because although it does not completely prevent real exegesis (as the cautious procedure outlined above is still possible) it does make it considerably more difficult. Systematic Theology, and Homiletics in particular, has to draw its own conclusions from these facts.

15. THE ACTS OF THE APOSTLES

(1) *Contents and Structure.* According to the title, which was not given to it by the author ('Acts of the Apostles', in most manuscripts 'Acts of the Holy Apostles', later often abbreviated to 'Acts', Acta) the aim of the work appears to be to give an account of the deeds of these men, in particular Peter and Paul. The title, however, is not in keeping with the author's intention. His aim is not to describe the activity of men; the real agent is the Lord, now exalted, or—to be more exact—it is the Spirit, who works in the Church through men (i. 8; ii. 33; iv. 8; vi. 3; xiii. 2, etc.). This is enough to show that Acts is a continuation of Lk. (cf. also Acts i. 1). As Jesus was previously the only bearer of the Spirit, the Spirit can now be called the Spirit of Jesus (xvi. 7), or reference is made to the effect of the name of Jesus (iii. 16; iv. 12, 30, etc.).

The framework is clearly set out in i. 8: the disciples are to be witnesses of Jesus in Jerusalem, in the whole of Judaea and Samaria and to the ends of the earth. The road leads from Jerusalem to Rome, where Paul preaches the kingdom of God and 'the things concerning the Lord Jesus Christ' without hindrance (xxviii. 31).

Within this framework there is a twofold division. The first section, in which Peter is the main figure, covers chs. i–xii. After the Ascension, the replacement of Judas (i), Pentecost and the beginnings of the Church (ii), the account of its spread and its life in Jerusalem (iii–v), we hear of the first persecution of a part of the Church, the martyrdom of Stephen (vi–viii. 3), and the start of the Gentile mission in Samaria and Syria (viii–xii, including in ch. ix the conversion of Paul). The second section contains first the story of Paul's missionary activities, and it is he who now takes over the main rôle (First Journey: xiii. 1–xiv. 28; Apostolic Council: xv. 1–35; Second Journey: xv. 36–xviii. 22; Third Journey: xviii. 23–xxi. 14); this is followed by the story of his imprisonment (Jerusalem: xxi. 15–xxiii. 22; Caesarea: xxiii. 23–xxvi. 32; journey to Rome: xxvii. 1–xxviii. 15; stay in Rome: xxviii. 6–31). In spite of all opposition the 'word of God' increased (vi. 7; xii. 24; xix. 20) and finally reached the capital of the Empire.

(2) *Sources.* It seems quite clear that Luke used sources, as he did in the first part of his work. Scholars have tried for a long time to discover what

these sources were by literary critical methods, but without arriving at any unanimous findings. This possibly arises from the fact that Luke thoroughly alters and recasts his sources—to a far greater extent than in his Gospel—and then joins them together. A clear-cut separation of the sources is therefore for the most part simply impossible.

A somewhat more promising approach is offered by the so-called 'We-passages', where the narrative suddenly falls into the first person plural (xi. 28—but only in the Western text, xvi. 10–17; xx. 5–15; xxi. 1–18; xxvii. 1–xxviii. 16). With the exception of xi. 28, these are all accounts of Paul's journeys, and it would be natural to assume that we have here the notes of an eye-witness which the author has inserted into his work. To assume this, however, presents certain difficulties. As Luke himself was certainly not an eye-witness of the events (see section 3 below), but these 'We-passages' clearly reveal evidence of being modified by him, the question is why—in spite of other modifications—he left the 'We' references. If we assume that he did it for the sake of the liveliness of the account, the converse of this question arises, namely, whether Luke did not perhaps create this 'We' precisely for this reason, particularly as this would be in keeping with his general method of description. In this case we could not assume with too much certainty the existence of a 'We' source.

The same applies to the assumption that the author had at his disposal an itinerary of Paul's journeys for chs. xiii–xxi, containing brief notes about places he stayed at, his hosts, etc.[21] Here again we cannot make any separation of sources with any degree of certainty. In other words, we can define the extent of the sources only in very general terms. The author had at his disposal separate stories in which Peter and Paul played the main parts, also lists of names (i. 13; vi. 5; xiii. 1) and perhaps a few other detailed references. We have to try and determine the extent and limits of these sources in each case. However, they are now firmly embedded in the carefully thought-out and meticulously planned work of the editor.

(3) *'Setting in Life' and Standpoint of Acts.* If we compare the picture of Paul given in Acts with the impression we gain from the genuine Pauline letters, there are considerable differences which call for explanation. That the apostle was a great worker of miracles, and that this activity

---

[21] M. Dibelius, *Aufsätze zur Apostelgeschichte*, edited by H. Greeven (1951), p. 64. (E.T. *Studies in the Acts of the Apostles*, SCM; Scribner, 1956, p. 69). See also E. Haenchen, 'Das "Wir" in der Apostelgeschichte und das Itinerar', *ZThK* (1961), pp. 29 ff.

was used directly in the service of his missionary work (xiii. 6–12; xiv. 8–10; xix. 12; xx. 7–12, etc.) exactly fits the picture of Peter that Acts gives, but not that of the historical Paul. That the latter was an outstanding speaker (cf. xiii. 16 ff.; xxi. 40 and xxii. 1 ff.; xxiii. 1 ff., etc.) is expressly contradicted by his own statements (cf. 2 Cor. x. 10; xi. 6). It is also very surprising that for the sake of the Jews Paul should have circumcised Timothy (xvi. 3—contrast Gal. ii. 3 f.), similarly that he should have taken a Jewish vow (xviii. 18; xxi. 24–26). Again, without hesitation Acts makes Paul—as a Christian and in his defence—appeal with pride to his Pharisaic past (xxvi. 5; contrast Phil. iii. 7 f.). It is true that there are still traces in Acts of the realization that Paul was 'against the law' (xxi. 21, 28), but we are not told why he was. Strangely, this is not the reason for the Jewish accusation against him either, but his preaching of the resurrection of the dead (xxiii. 6). This, however, even wins him the sympathy of the Pharisaic scribes, so that of the contrast between Paul and the Jews all that remains is a contrast between Paul and the Sadducees (xxiii. 8 f.). It is expressly emphasized that Paul's preaching is no different from Jewish preaching—when properly understood (xxvi. 27 f.). No account seems to be taken of Paul's passionate struggle against the righteousness that is of the law.

It is also puzzling to see how the apostle's position as regards the Twelve is described. In contrast to Gal. i. f., Paul has already been to Jerusalem once before the Apostolic Council, where Barnabas has to present him as a Christian and he is then recognized as such (ix. 27 f.). Peter is acknowledged as the first missionary to the Gentiles (xv. 7), and after the Apostolic Council Paul takes the so-called apostolic decree to Antioch, in which he himself is described as the apostles' emissary, and thus dependent upon them (xv. 25; contrast Gal. i. 1, etc.). But it seems impossible that Paul should even have associated himself with the contents of such a decree. It is true that the Gentiles are set free from observing the whole law, but not from the regulations which according to the law had to be observed by Gentiles (xv. 20 f., 23–29; xxi. 25). It is in keeping with the impression given here of Paul's dependence upon the apostles (who are always the Twelve) that Paul himself—with the exception of xiv. 14 and, indirectly, xiv. 4—is never called an apostle.

From all these facts—and they could easily be multiplied—it is quite clear that the author of Acts could not possibly have been a companion of Paul, and also that he has no clear idea of the apostle's aims. From this it follows that it is impossible to use Acts directly as a historical source, but this of course does not mean that it does not often contain information that is historically correct, but each instance has to be critically examined.

As the author of Acts seeks to give an account of the beginnings of the Church, and does it from the standpoint of a later age, the question arises as to what his aim was in the work. In the first place and in general terms we can say that his aim is to write an edifying work for Christians, which will at the same time present the case for Christianity to Gentiles. This comes to light in many different ways. The author is a very skilful narrator, and possesses a great gift for dramatic presentation. We can see this not only in the composition of the narrative passages, but also in the speeches particularly, those which comprise about a third of the whole work. What we have here of course are not shorthand reports of speeches actually delivered, but something entirely composed by the author. For example, Peter's speeches (i. 16–22; ii. 14–36, 38–39; iii. 12–26; iv. 8–12; v. 29–32; x. 34–43; xi. 4–17; xv. 7–11) are to a large extent built on a very similar pattern to Paul's (xiii. 16–41; xiv. 15–17; xvii. 22–31; xx. 18–35; xxii. 1–21; xxiv. 10–21; xxvi. 1–23; xxvii. 21–26; xxviii. 17–20), but there is a distinction between speeches made to Jews and those made to Gentiles. It is possible that Luke is following a set type of preaching, which actually did not exist in the time of Peter and Paul, but only developed in the course of time. More important to notice, however, is the fact that the speeches do not take into consideration the situation of the audiences addressed in Acts. As far as content is concerned they are closely linked with the narrative framework. The hearers in fact are the readers of Acts, and the purpose of the speeches is to bring the past to life. In other words, the ultimate aim behind Luke's account of history is not so much to present the past but rather to speak to the present. The author achieves this by turning 'history' into 'stories'.[22] It is in this way that the Church is 'edified', for it learns how the Word of God has triumphed over all opposition and can therefore be confident that it will continue to triumph. We can see here the missionary aim coming to the fore.

It is noticeable that the aim here is to show that Christianity is not something 'done in a corner' (xxvi. 26). Its success is carefully brought out by references to the numbers of converts (ii. 41; iv. 4; vi. 7; cf. xi. 21; xviii. 10; xxi. 20). It is also emphasized that influential people have either become Christians themselves or have entered into serious conversation with the missionaries (x. 1 ff.; xiii. 7; xviii. 12 ff.; xxii. 25 ff.; xxiv. 1 ff.; xxv. 1 ff., 13 ff.; xxviii. 7 ff.). This is of course meant to make the Christian faith more attractive, but there is obviously a further special

[22] E. Haenchen, 'Apostelgeschichte' in *RGG*, I, col. 502.

intention here. The author does not seem to be thinking any longer in terms of a sweeping success in the mission to Jews (xxviii. 28), but he emphasizes the fact that the Christian message is not opposed to the Jewish (xxiii. 6 ff.; xxvi. 5 f.). There is no real reason ultimately for Christian–Jewish tensions, for they spring from envy at the success of the Christians (xiii. 45; xvii. 5); therefore it is always the Jews who instigate persecutions. It is they who bear the guilt for the disturbances. If the account is read from the Roman standpoint, it follows that Christians can expect the same tolerance from the State as the Jewish religion enjoys. Thus the account of the past becomes in many respects something addressed to the present.

At the same time, however, we are given some idea of the Church at the time of Luke, in so far as it is reflected in the account in Acts. For example, the Church has presbyters (xi. 30), and in missionary churches Paul and Barnabas have to appoint presbyters (xiv. 23). Offices are conveyed by the laying on of hands (vi. 6). In view of these statements, which, compared with Paul, certainly reveal a considerable advance towards the institutionalizing of the Church and its offices, Luke's standpoint has sometimes been described as 'early Catholic', but this is not really correct. We should only speak of early Catholicism where such institutionalizing is systematically represented as an arrangement valid for the future. It is true that Luke envisaged a fairly long period of time for the continuance of the Church; however, he does not project the line of succession into the future, but merely points out the evidence for it in the past. A typical example of this can be seen in Paul's farewell address to the elders at Miletus (xx. 17 ff.), which is expressed in the traditional terminology of the attack upon heretics. The grievous wolves referred to here, the men who arise within the Church teaching perverse things and summoning to apostasy, indicate difficulties which arose in the time of Luke. It is the task of the officials to protect the Church from such errors, and they can trace their office back to the beginning. In consequence of this line of succession which runs back to the beginning Paul becomes a representative of the 'apostles' (xv. 25), but only one who was an eye-witness can actually be an apostle (i. 21 f.). The concept of succession in Luke therefore does not serve to lay down a pattern for the future, but to provide a basis for the 'certainty' of doctrine in the present (cf. Lk. i. 1–4).

(4) *Authorship, Time and Place of Composition.* Here we need to bear in mind what was said in section 14, 3. As the author gives a picture of the early Church as it was around the end of the first century, Luke the companion

of Paul is out of the question. Even if we trace some of the sources back to him, as has sometimes been attempted, this does not really help us as we cannot in any case reconstruct them with sufficient certainty to be able to deduce from them Luke's message. We have therefore still to accept the anonymity of Acts. Nor have we any evidence for suggesting what was the place of composition either. The work was probably written in the last decade of the first century, certainly before the Pastorals (cf. section 18).

(5) *The Text of Acts.* Acts has come down to us in two forms, a shorter one and a longer one (the latter the so-called Western text). At one time it was sometimes assumed that the author brought out two editions of his work, but this assumption breaks down because of the fact that the variant readings sometimes contradict one another (xv. 20). As the amplifications in the longer text serve partly to illustrate (cf. xii. 10; xix. 28), to correct mistakes (cf. iii. 11—Solomon's porch lay outside the 'Beautiful Gate', which the longer text makes clear) and to insert liturgical phrases (vi. 8), generally speaking the shorter text is to be preferred.

BIBLIOGRAPHY

E. Haenchen, *Die Apostelgeschichte* (Meyer, 13 ed., 1961). (E.T. in prep., Blackwell).

M. Dibelius, *Aufsätze zur Apostelgeschichte*, edited by H. Greeven (4 ed., 1961). (E.T. *Studies in the Acts of the Apostles*, SCM; Scribner, 1956).

E. Gräßer, 'Die Apostelgeschichte in der Forschung der Gegenwart', *ThR*, NF (1960), pp. 93 ff.

E. Haenchen, 'Apostelgeschichte' in *RGG*, I, cols. 501 ff.

E. Haenchen, 'Das "Wir" in der Apostelgeschichte und das Itinerar', *ZThK* (1961), pp. 329 ff.

E. Lohse, 'Die Bedeutung des Pfingstberichtes im Rahmen des lukanischen Geschichtswerkes', *EvTh* (1953), pp. 422 ff.

Commentaries: F. F. Bruce (2 ed., 1952); F. G. Foakes-Jackson, Moffatt (1932); C. S. C. Williams, Black (2 ed., 1964).

H. J. Cadbury, *The Book of Acts in History* (1955).

B. S. Easton, *The Purpose of Acts* (1936).

F. G. Foakes-Jackson and K. Lake (Eds.), *The Beginnings of Christianity*, 5 vols. (1922–33).

W. L. Knox, *The Acts of the Apostles* (1948).

See further: D. Guthrie, 'Recent Literature on the Acts of the Apostles', *VE* 2 (1963).

On the textual problem: A. C. Clark, *The Acts of the Apostles* (1933); E. J. Epp, *The Theological Tendency of Codex Bezae Cantabrigiensis in Acts* (1966).

III. The Pseudo-Pauline Epistles

We describe as 'pseudo-Pauline' those letters which claim to have been written by Paul—or, in the case of Heb., where Church tradition accepted Paul as the author—but where there is such doubt as regards this claim or accepted tradition that we have to call it in question. We have already considered 2 Thess. in section 3 on account of its connection with 1 Thess., but it really belongs to this category. By including six other letters here we are of course making an historical judgement upon them in advance that has still to be established. It is more important of course to understand each letter as a theological statement in its own particular situation than to pass a historically negative judgement upon it—and this in fact is the real theological problem of New Testament Introduction. We have already seen in connection with 2 Thess. that any doubt as to its Pauline authorship did not lead to the 'loss' of the letter, but on the contrary led to a real understanding of it.

16. THE EPISTLE TO THE COLOSSIANS

The letter falls into four sections. In the first place (i. 1–ii. 5) what we might call a 'position' is set out (the idea will be explained in the course of the account); ii. 6–23 deals with a particular heresy; iii. 1–iv. 6 contains various exhortations. The conclusion (iv. 7–18) contains a surprisingly long list of greetings. In considering the most important problems of Introduction we shall follow these divisions.

(1) *Contents.* The 'position' can be further divided into four sections.

(a) It begins with Preface, Thanksgiving and Intercession (i. 1–11). The Preface (i. 1–2) is brief, and names Paul as the sender, in association with 'Timothy our brother'. The recipients are the 'saints and faithful brethren in Christ which are at Colossae'. In other words, there is no explicit reference to an ἐκκλησία (church). There is a certain parallel to this in Phil. i. 1 and Rom. i. 6. The greeting is briefer than we usually find in Paul. Colossae is a town in the south-west of Phrygia, in the valley of the upper Lycus, on the great trade route from Ephesus to Cilicia and Syria. The nearest towns to the west were Laodicea, the more important town, which overshadowed Colossae economically, and Hierapolis.

The Thanksgiving (i. 3–8) provides us with a few interesting facts. Paul has heard (N.B.) of the faith of the brethren and of the love they have to all the saints (v. 4). This gives the impression of a harmonious community, but this does not of course exclude the fact that there were problems within it or around it which will be dealt with later. v. 7, where Epaphras is mentioned for the first time, poses a problem for textual criticism: 'Even as ye learned of Epaphras our beloved fellow-servant, who is a faithful minister of Christ ὑπέρ ἡμῶν' (on our behalf); in other words, Epaphras is Paul's representative in the church. Or according to other readings, ὑπέρ ὑμῶν (for your sake), meaning that Epaphras has proved to be a faithful servant of the Church. To come to a decision on this textual question is not altogether straightforward, but it is important for determining the position Epaphras held in the church.

We need to ask therefore what we can learn either directly or indirectly about Epaphras. We might begin by assuming that he founded the church, for vv. 5 f. speak of the beginnings and v. 7 follows on with καθώς ('even as'), but we cannot be certain of this. We learn from ii. 1 that before the writing of this letter Paul had not visited either Colossae or

N

Laodicea. As Epaphras is mentioned in iv. 12 as one of those who send greetings, at the time of writing he is obviously not in Colossae, and yet he is specifically mentioned as a member of the church there. The question that arises is why he is not associated with the sending of the letter, as this would have seemed the natural thing. Perhaps he is the deliverer of the letter, or at least thought of as such. We shall see that as the letter is partly concerned with him there were good reasons why he could not be referred to as the joint sender. As the letter goes on another question arises. In ii. 8 ff. an attack is made upon errors that are threatening the church. Epaphras evidently stands on the side of orthodoxy. Is it the aim of this letter to give Paul's support to Epaphras' 'doctrine'? In that case this document would be in effect an apostolic authorization of Epaphras, and it would also give meaning to the ὑπὲρ ἡμῶν (on our behalf) in v. 7. The doctrine of Epaphras corresponds to the doctrine that was taught in Colossae at the founding of the church. This makes ὑπὲρ ἡμῶν seem the more probable reading in v. 7. Epaphras is recognized by Paul as a fellow-servant who works in the church 'in the place of' the apostle. As this was not understood at a later period, copyists substituted ὑμῶν for ἡμῶν, making Epaphras the representative of the church.

It is surprising that Paul, although he neither founded the church nor ever visited it, indirectly claims the right to direct it, or at least feels responsible for it. There are no parallels to this anywhere else in Paul's writings. We cannot draw a comparison in this respect with Rom., for Paul does not intervene so directly there. But this is certainly not sufficient evidence for us to decide whether the letter is genuine or not. What we have to consider is the meaning of what is said about Epaphras, if Paul is not the author. In this case it could be that an attempt is being made to defend Pauline Christianity against error, or to attack this error by appealing to what Paul said about Epaphras. It is hard to say which of these two possibilities is the correct one, but in fact they both amount to the same thing: that the Pauline type of teaching is set out in opposition to an error.

Right at the beginning of the letter therefore there is evidence of a problem which the church has to face, but we cannot be altogether certain of the historical background of it. All we can be sure of is that Epaphras' position in the church has to be supported. This is done in an exceptionally emphatic way, for Paul never showed such esteem for a fellow-worker as he does here for Epaphras.[1] All this is interwoven

[1] Cf. E. Lohmeyer, *Die Briefe an die Philipper, an die Kolosser und an Philemon* in Meyer (11 ed., 1956) on Col. i. 7.

CONTENTS

with the Thanksgiving, to which is then added (vv. 9–11) an Intercession.

(β) The second sub-section contains the hymn-like outline of a Christology (i. 12–20). The transition is not abrupt, but the syntax of the section is not always clear. Christ is described as the 'Son of (God's) Love' (v. 13), who brings redemption and forgiveness. He is the image (εἰκών) of the invisible God, the firstborn of creation, for 'in him' all things were created in heaven and earth, things visible and invisible, thrones, dominions, principalities and powers; all things were created through him and for his sake (v. 16). The whole creation consists in him (v. 17). He is the head of the body, the ἐκκλησία (church), the firstborn from the dead (v. 18). In him dwells the fulness of God (v. 19).

It is not easy to find a parallel to such ideas anywhere else in Paul. There are certain resemblances here and there, but taken as a whole this passage is unique. What is the origin of these ideas? i. 15–20 could possibly be a Christian adaptation of a pre-Christian hymn, deriving from the realm of cosmic mythology. Whether it was first linked with vv. 12–14 by the author of Col.,[2] or whether he found the two sections already joined together[3] we cannot say for certain.

It is significant that whoever adapted the hymn did not deny the existence of the cosmic powers, but merely 'christianized' the concept. The whole structure of the cosmos is interpreted as σῶμα Χριστοῦ (body of Christ). It is to be noted however, that Christ is not described—as in the genuine Pauline letters—by the concept σῶμα (body), but as the 'head' of the body, and the body is made to refer to the Church (i. 18). The aim behind this whole conception, therefore, is not primarily to develop fresh speculative, cosmological statements about the Church; the reverse of this is the case, for the cosmological statements are presupposed, and the adaptation asserts that Christ is head even of this cosmic structure. In other words, the cosmological statements about the Church are set out not for their own sake, but are formulated only in order that the cosmic powers—the existence of which is assumed—can be brought under the Lordship of Christ. The examination of the editorial process therefore shows the significance of these statements and their

[2] M. Dibelius, *An die Kolosser, Epheser, an Philemon*, edited by H. Greeven in Lietzmann (3 ed., 1953) on Col. i. 14.
[3] E. Käsemann, 'Eine urchristliche Taufliturgie' in *Festschrift für Rudolf Bultmann* (1949), pp. 133 ff. Reprinted in *Exegetische Versuche und Besinnungen*, I, pp. 34 ff. (E.T. *Essays on New Testament Themes* (selections from *Exegetische Versuche und Besinnungen*), SCM; Allenson, 1964, pp. 149 ff.). R. Bultmann, *Theologie des Neuen Testamentes* (3 ed., 1958), p. 508. (E.T. *Theology of the New Testament*, SCM; Scribner, 1958, II, p. 150).

underlying purpose. Ideas are expressed here which derive from the heretical world of thought, but now they are transcended—from the literary standpoint by an editorial process, as far as content is concerned by being 'christianized'.

(γ) In the third sub-section this Christology is applied and the consequence drawn for the reader (i. 21–23). All this has taken place for the benefit of those who were once enemies and estranged (v. 21), but have now been reconciled 'in the body of his flesh through death', in order that they might be presented before him holy and spotless (v. 22), if (N.B.) they hold fast to the faith, 'grounded and steadfast, and not moved away from the hope of the gospel' that they have heard and of which Paul was made a minister (v. 23).

Here we see the link with the statements about Epaphras, for now Paul's position is emphasized. He is minister, and Epaphras his fellow-minister, and it could be said that here it is the office that comes to the fore. 'The Church is bound not only to its confession of faith, but at the same time to the apostolic office'.[4] The whole opening section of this letter shows therefore that it is a kind of pastoral letter, although its form is different from that of the three pastoral letters we shall be considering later (section 18). These are addressed to Timothy and Titus, but Col. is delivered by Epaphras himself—at least this is the impression we get—although here again the aim of the letter is to support his authority. The purpose is therefore the same in each case: the authority of Paul is claimed for the authorization of other men. Here we can see the germ of a problem that had to be dealt with quite early in the post-apostolic period: How can apostolic authority be preserved when the apostle is no longer living? Is it enough to appeal to the Gospel, or must the authority have a personal basis? Who is to enter upon the 'succession' of the apostles? The apostolic message? Or does it need for its support an authority the same as that of the apostles or similar to it, or at any rate an authority that is personal?

It is here that the most serious doubts as regards the Pauline authorship arise. It would be possible to try and explain how Paul could use a different terminology from that we are familiar with elsewhere in his letters, and we know from other examples that he does on occasion incorporate already formulated material in his letters. It cannot be disputed that there are in Col. echoes of Pauline ideas, but that Paul himself should have attacked heresy by this kind of emphasis upon the apostolate —tantamount in effect to the doctrine of 'apostolic succession'—is open

[4] E. Käsemann, 'Kolosserbrief' in *RGG*, III, cols. 1727.

to very serious doubts. Any reference to 'Paul' therefore in what follows has to be thought of as being in inverted commas.

(δ) In the last sub-section, following on from v. 23 we are given a discussion of the apostolic office (i. 24–ii. 5). Paul speaks of his sufferings, by which he makes up for what is lacking in the afflictions of Christ (v. 24). The apostle has been entrusted with stewardship in order to fulfil the word of God to the Colossians. The mystery that was kept secret for ages has now been revealed and delivered to him. This ministry means a struggle for Paul, which he continues to wage even when he is not seeing the churches. He states all this in order that no one should mislead the Church by deceptive speech. Although absent in the body, he is still present in the spirit and rejoices in the good order that prevails in the church.

We used the word 'position' in the heading of this first part of the letter. It is used in a two-fold sense, and first as it applies to the contents. A cosmological hymn is adopted, christianized (i. 15–20) and then applied to the immediate situation (i. 21–23). It is possible, in the light of i. 12–14, that it is connected with a baptismal hymn.[5] The other sense in which the word is used is a personal and institutional one. The church, which Paul neither founded nor has visited, is nevertheless under his responsibility. His conflict and suffering is—and was—conflict and suffering on its behalf. The authority which Paul is given is now handed on to his fellow-servant Epaphras, whose teaching is identical with the teaching that was laid down when the church came into being. The 'position' therefore is based on tradition, and is something that was given, is handed down and continues to be taught. Its guarantors are Paul and now Epaphras as well.

(b) The 'position' is important, as the second section (ii. 6–23) now shows, for the defence against heresy. vv. 6 f. are almost like a heading: 'As therefore ye received Christ Jesus the Lord, so walk in him . . . established in your faith, even as ye were taught.' The 'tradition' is 'received' (N.B. παραλαμβάνειν). The corresponding concept (παραδιδόναι=to pass on) is modified to 'walk' (περιπατεῖν). This is as it were the application of the position, first with regard to doctrine and then with regard to conduct (iii. 1 ff.). In this section Paul deals first with doctrine. The argument is set out in two stages: in ii. 8–15 Christ's superiority to the world elements (στοιχεῖα) is set out, and in ii. 16–23 the implications of this are drawn over against the errors.

(a) The first sub-section begins with a warning against being misled

[5] Cf. E. Käsemann, 'Eine urchristliche Taufliturgie', *loc. cit.* (E.T. *Essays on New Testament Themes*, *loc. cit.*).

by philosophy, which is described as the tradition of men. Then the στοιχεῖα τοῦ κόσμου ('world elements' thought of in a personal sense) are mentioned, which as personal forces can enslave men. Christ, in whom the fulness of the Godhead dwells bodily, is set over against them. He is the head of all principalities and powers, in him the Colossians are circumcised with a circumcision that is not external, in him they are buried in baptism and in him they are raised again. The ordinances (δόγματα) are torn up at the same time as the list of debts. The powers are deprived of their power, they are publicly exposed and are led along in a triumphal procession.

Again we must beware of reading these statements in too objective a sense. The terminology of the heretics is adopted, but their standpoint is not refuted, as it is, for example, in Gal., but merely christianized. The confrontation therefore is not critical—as in Paul—but more of a compromise. This means that basically there is not a complete rejection, but rather that the victory of Christ is extended through a wider sphere.

(β) The second stage of the argument (ii. 16–23) contains a kind of practical application. The fact that Christ is Lord has consequences for the Church. No one has the right to pass judgement on its members. Eating or drinking, feast days, new moons or sabbaths—all these are only 'a shadow of what is to come'. Here again we see the theme of transcendence, for the body, which is more than a shadow, is the body of Christ. Therefore the Christian can no longer subject himself to these powers either, and he may no longer serve them. Visions and the worshipping of angels are rejected, for he who has died in Christ to the elements does not burden himself with ordinances as though he was still living in the former age.

It is not easy to define the errors precisely, but we can recognize certain features of them. The observance of feast days, new moons and sabbaths (ii. 16) points to Gnostic Judaism, or Judaism with a Gnostic colouring. This is reminiscent of the opponents in Galatia, where we also met 'world elements' and circumcision, which although it is not attacked in Col., is given a Christian re-interpretation with reference to baptism. Again the question arises, whether Paul would have adopted this line of approach. We cannot point to Rom. ii. 28 f. in support, for there he argues on the basis of the practice of circumcision, and describes as the true Jew the one who is circumcized not externally, but in the heart. In Col., however, circumcision belongs to the heretical practices. We can see from Gal. how Paul argues in this case.

However we judge and arrange the details from the standpoint of the history of religion, in exegesis we have to beware once again of taking the concepts and ideas we find as expressing the actual attitude of the author. He does not really wish to indulge in speculation, for this would ultimately land him in syncretism, but wants to remain a Christian in the midst of and in spite of the cosmological mythologies. The fact that he does not really defeat the heresy, but only takes it over and christianizes it, shows the limits and the ultimate inadequacy of the confrontation.

(c) An admonitory section follows (iii. 1–iv. 6), containing first of all (iii. 1–17) a further practical application. As the readers have been raised with Christ, they should set their minds on the things that are above, in other words they should act as those who have been raised up, and lay aside malice, anger, slander, etc. Their behaviour must be determined by the resurrection that has taken place.

This idea of the resurrection as having already taken place again shows how close we are to Gnostic thought, which however is held in check from the Christian standpoint both by the ethical demand and also by the expectation of the visible appearing of Christ. Whilst Paul describes the not yet completed salvation of the Christian mainly in temporal categories, here the thought is in terms of spheres. The situation evidently is that the heretics claim to be risen but that they do not draw any ethical consequences from the fact. Their libertinism does not come out very clearly in this letter, but it seems reasonable to assume that this was their attitude because the ethical consequences are drawn from the assertion of these people that the resurrection has already taken place, and because the letter now goes on to exhortation, which is no doubt not merely a coincidence.

The catalogue of virtues is based on the reminder that the Colossians are called 'in one body'. This is followed by a list of duties of members of a household (iii. 18–iv. 1), in which exhortations are addressed to wives, husbands, children, fathers, servants and, almost as an afterthought in iv. 1, to masters. This list is 'surprisingly poor in original Christian material'[6] and contains a considerable amount of older material. What is specially important is the christianizing of the instructions (N.B. iii. 23 f.), but not the 'moral principles governing family life in popular Greek philosophy and Jewish Halacha' (Dibelius) which did in fact as a result of a legal interpretation of the rules become the normal Christian ethic. Exegesis has therefore to concern itself not with the edited material, but with the message this material is used to convey, in other words with the ethical 'appendix' (vv. 23 f.).

[6] Dibelius, *op. cit.* on Col. iv. 1.

(d) After some general exhortations concerning prayer and correct conduct (iv. 2–6) there follows in the fourth section (iv. 7–18) the conclusion of the letter with its long list of greetings. Among the people mentioned are the 'fellow-servant' Tychicus, whom Paul has sent to the church, Onesimus (cf. section 6), Aristarchus, who is described as a fellow-prisoner, Mark, the nephew of Barnabas (cf. section 12) and Luke, the beloved physician (cf. section 14). Epaphras is again praised at length. Greetings are sent to the brethren in Laodicea and also to a house church in Colossae. Somewhat unexpectedly, Archippus is exhorted to take care to fulfil his ministry properly. The final greeting is explicitly stated to have been set down in Paul's own hand.

(2) *The Situation of the Church and the Question of Authorship.* The situation in Colossae is clear to a certain extent. The church is threatened by a Jewish Gnostic heresy, but we cannot be sure how far this has penetrated or whether it has led to open conflict. But obviously help from outside is needed, and so Paul, who had not himself previously visited the church, takes steps to help. The manner in which this support is given in the battle against heresy is significant for the second generation. The position is expounded, explained in the light of tradition—the doctrine taught at the founding of the church—and supported by the strengthening of the authority of Epaphras, behind whom Paul stands. In other words, the authority of the apostle is in the end used in the service of the battle against heresy.

In view of the great number of indications that Paul was not the author of Col. we cannot assume that this was the kind of argument Paul used. The language itself is peculiar. Thirty-four words which occur only once elsewhere in the New Testament and twenty-five which occur only once elsewhere in Paul have been counted in this letter. Although one should be cautious in drawing conclusions from statistics of vocabulary, the abundance of peculiarities here is certainly striking. To suggest that these are due to the ageing apostle, to his long imprisonment and his declining power of expressing himself (Feine-Behm) seems rather odd. The author in fact shows himself to be a man who is not only familiar with the terminology of the heretics, but who also knows how to use it—in other words he possesses to a marked degree the power to express himself. But how did Paul come to know of the heresy at Colossae? From Epaphras? But would it then be likely that he would adopt not only the terminology but also the actual material of his adversaries and christianize it although he knew it only indirectly through Epaphras? The greatest difficulty for the acceptance of the Pauline authorship, however, is the interpretation of ministry within the Church linked with the idea of tradition. The long list of greetings is also strange, and only Rom. xvi. offers a parallel (cf. section 9, 4). There are certain similarities to the list of greetings in Phm. Epaphras is mentioned there also (Phm. 23) as a 'fellow-prisoner', whereas in Col. iv. 10 it is Aristarchus who is referred to as such. It is hard to imagine that, as Michaelis suggests, both men should have shared alternately Paul's imprisonment.

E. Schweizer[7] makes the interesting point that in all Paul's letters— even in Gal.—we often find the mode of address 'brethren', but that it is completely missing in Col., Eph. and in the Pastorals. Is this accidental? It is of course possible that a third person, writing a 'Pauline' letter could adopt the apostle's practice, e.g. in 2 Thess., where the address is used seven times, but it is strange that Paul should have abandoned his practice in these disputed letters.

The request that the letter should be exchanged with the Laodicean letter is rather surprising. It was the custom later to read the letters aloud during worship, but was this the practice as early as this? On the relationship with Eph., see section 17.

We are faced by so many reasonable doubts and uncertainties here that it is impossible to assume that Paul was the author. There is of course the possible solution offered by the so-called secretary hypothesis, which suggests that Paul, who is of course represented as a prisoner (iv. 10; cf. i. 24), left the writing of the letter to a secretary and himself only wrote the final greeting (iv. 18). But in this case we could not really call it a Pauline letter, for its very peculiarities would prove the writing to be marked out as the secretary's own work.

Although certain questions still remain open, we have managed to get a reasonably clear idea of the questions raised by New Testament Introduction. This is important from the point of view of exegesis, which seeks to bring out the meaning of the work by bringing to light the actual situation in which it arose.

BIBLIOGRAPHY

H. Conzelmann, *Der Kolosserbrief* (NTD, vol. 8, 9 ed., 1962).

M. Dibelius, *An die Kolosser, Epheser, an Philemon,* edited by H. Greeven (Lietzmann, 3 ed., 1958).

E. Lohmeyer, *Die Briefe an die Kolosser, an Philemon* (Meyer, 12 ed., 1961).

[7] *ZNW* (1956), p. 187.

G. Bornkamm, 'Die Häresie des Kolosserbriefes', *ThLZ* (1948), pp.11ff. Reprinted in *Das Ende des Gesetzes* (3 ed., 1961), pp. 139 ff.

E. Käsemann, 'Eine urchristliche Taufliteratur', *Festschrift für R. Bultmann* (1949), pp. 133 ff. Reprinted in *Exegetische Versuche und Besinnungen*, I (1960), pp. 34 ff. (E.T. *Essays on New Testament Themes*, selections from *Exegetische Versuche und Besinnungen*, SCM; Allenson, 1964, pp. 149 ff.).

E. Käsemann, 'Kolosserbrief' in *RGG*, III, cols. 1727 ff.

Commentaries: J. B. Lightfoot (with Philemon) (6 ed., 1882); C. F. D. Moule (with Philemon), CGTC (1957).

G. S. Duncan, *St. Paul's Ephesian Ministry* (1929).

E. R. Goodenough, 'Paul and Onesimus', *HTR* 22 (1929), pp. 181 ff.

J. Knox, 'Philemon and the Authenticity of Colossians', *JR* 18 (1938), pp. 144 ff.

17. THE EPISTLE TO THE EPHESIANS

(1) *Its Relation to the Epistle to the Colossians.* To go on to make a merely cursory reading of Eph. after reading Col. shows, in spite of a different train of thought and various differences of detail, an extensive relationship between the two, which is all the more striking as it is this very fact that distinguishes these two letters from the rest of the Pauline letters. There is a very close similarity where Tychichus is mentioned as the deliverer of the letter who is to tell the recipients how Paul is faring and comfort their hearts (vi. 21–22; cf. Col. iv. 7–8—but the long list of greetings in Col. is missing in Eph.). As there are twenty-nine words the same in the two passages whereas in other parallel passages the identity runs to only seven words, it seems reasonable to conclude either that the two letters were written directly after one another out of the same situation—although we cannot be sure of the order—or that the author of the one letter knew or made use of the other letter. In any case there is obviously a dependence of some kind. We cannot determine which of the two possibilities is correct here, for on closer inspection the problem reveals itself to be more complicated, as a comparison of the hymn-like material used in the two letters rather suggests that there is no direct dependence. The position seems to be that they both derive from the same traditions, which, however, are more faithfully reproduced in Eph. than in Col.[8] So the question arises as to whether the same author wrote both letters and merely gave a different form to the same material, or whether someone else modified the themes and ideas of Col. with which he was familiar in his own way and from a new standpoint.[9] In this case he would have had to be familiar both with Col. and also with the hymn-like material that was already available to the writer of this letter.

In spite of the considerable similarity of language, style and terminology, however, the theme of each of the two letters is different. In Col. the emphasis was on the polemic against heresies, but in Eph. there is only a faint suggestion of the problem of heresy. The readers are exhorted rather to attain to unity in the faith, to become a 'fullgrown' man, to attain the 'measure of the stature of the fulness of Christ', so that they should no longer be like children, 'tossed to and fro and carried about with every

---

[8] Cf. G. Schille, 'Der Autor des Epheserbriefes', *ThLZ* (1957), pp. 325 ff.; see also Schille's dissertation, *Liturgisches Gut im Epheserbrief* (1953).

[9] The view expressed by E. Käsemann, 'Epheserbrief' in *RGG*, II, cols. 517 ff.

wind of doctrine by the sleight of men' (iv. 13 f.). The theme of heresy, therefore, is not only not central, it is also treated in a different connection than in Col. Whereas Col. starts from the fact that the church stands—or stood—fast in the faith, but is now threatened by heresy, in Eph. the threat is really only a potential one, and is linked with the fact that the readers are not yet fully established in the faith, but are—according to the author's idea—people who are on the way from the immature to the 'fullgrown man'. It is true that they have 'faith in the Lord Jesus' and 'love toward all the saints' (i. 15), but this needs to be deepened. It is this deepening and strengthening that the writer is concerned about. The effect of such strengthening will be that heresies that may possibly arise later will be less dangerous to the readers. It is clear, therefore, that in contrast to the quite specific situation that is envisaged in Col., the approach in Eph. is much more general. What is set out here is really applicable to any of the young churches.

The opening Thanksgiving, in which normally there are definite references to the situation of the church, is set out in such general terms that it would fit any situation. Then we cannot help noticing that there is no evidence of personal affection between the writer and his readers. i. 15 might suggest, in spite of the similar phrase in Phm. 4 f., that the readers do not know the writer personally, but they have heard of the ministry of grace that has been granted to him (iii. 2). As Paul spent three years in Ephesus (section 1, 1) the readers must have known of this in any case.

With the exception of the preface, the prayer, the reference to Tychichus and the concluding blessing this document lacks all that we normally associate with a letter. We cannot but doubt whether it is really to be considered as a letter at all, and whether what we have is not rather 'a treatise with a uniform theme and a systematic construction merely clothed in the form of a letter'.[10] As far as the content is concerned we could call it a 'mystery address' or a 'wisdom address', as Schlier suggests,[11] although he still wishes to regard it as a letter.

But to whom would one send a 'wisdom address' or treatise of this kind? One thing is quite certain—this is not a letter sent by the apostle Paul to Ephesus. Such a letter could only have been written before his stay in Ephesus—this was pointed out by Theodore of Mopsuestia at the beginning of the fifth century—but to suggest it is such an early Pauline letter is ruled out by the contents. Nor can it have been sent to Ephesus

[10] E. Käsemann, op. cit., col. 517.
[11] Der Brief an die Epheser (1957), p. 21.

by the apostle after his stay there, in view of its impersonal character. The first question we have to consider therefore is that of the recipients of the letter.

(2) *The Address.* The Preface (i. 1 f.) has come down in two forms. The great majority of manuscripts read, apart from small changes of order or slight additions: Paul, an apostle of Jesus Christ, 'to the saints τοῖς οὖσιν ἐν 'Εφέσῳ καὶ πιστοῖς ἐν Χριστῷ 'Ιησοῦ (which are at Ephesus, and the faithful in Christ Jesus), grace to you. . . .' A smaller group of manuscripts —and also Marcion—gives the same preface, but without mentioning Ephesus. The reference to the recipients then reads: τοῖς ἁγίοις τοῖς οὖσιν καὶ πιστοῖς ἐν Χριστῷ 'Ιησοῦ (to the saints which are . . . and the faithful in Christ Jesus).

The various suggestions that have been made in an attempt to solve this problem cannot all be dealt with here. None has met with general acceptance. We shall simply set out here a few considerations which need to be borne in mind in seeking a solution and which are important for the exegesis of this letter. As it is far more conceivable that a missing place-name should be added later than that a definite place-name should be omitted without making any replacement, according to the rules of textual criticism the preface without the mention of Ephesus must be regarded as original. This does not of course by any means solve the problem, for the question that now arises is what the meaning of this apparently defective reference to the recipients τοῖς ἁγίοις τοῖς οὖσιν καὶ πιστοῖς (to the saints which are . . . and the faithful in Christ Jesus) can be.

We must first try to make sense of the text as it stands. This is what Origen attempted to do. He suggested that εἶναι (to be) was not an auxiliary verb but an independent verb, as for example in 1 Cor. i. 28: God chose the things that are despised and the things that 'are not' that he might bring to nought the things that 'are' (τὰ ὄντα). But this is a rather improbable explanation, because we would then have to translate: to the saints 'that exist'. What could this possibly mean? Another possibility that has been put forward is that the καί (and, also) should be treated as emphatic. This would mean that the letter is addressed to the saints who are *also* believers in Jesus Christ. In other words, the recipients are distinguished from the saints of the Old Testament. Neither of these solutions is really convincing.

The difficulty would be removed if we were to adopt the more frequently expressed suggestion that Eph. is an encyclical, and that each time it was read aloud the appropriate place-name was inserted, or, assuming it was a circular letter of which a number of copies were made, that the place-name was written into each copy. But is this probable? If this were an encyclical which Tychichus takes round with him, it would be more reasonable to expect that the address would have been formulated in more general terms. If, on the other hand, it is a circular letter of which copies were made, then we would have besides the Ephesus edition only the 'rough draft' or a 'copy for the records'. Neither suggestion seems very likely.

It is significant that these theories are mainly put forward by those who take Paul to be the author, but if Eph. is an encyclical or circular letter the Pauline authorship is excluded. The receiving churches are described in such a way as to suggest that the author is not familiar with them. Is it likely, however, that Paul would have sent this 'circular letter' only to the churches he had not visited, and that—apart from the model for all the others—the only copy that has come down to us is the one for the town in which we know that Paul spent three whole years? Apart from the doubts which the contents of the letter arouse, the Pauline authorship would be a possibility only if the letter were really intended for a church with which Paul was not familiar. In this case the absence of the place-name in the preface would be very strange.

We need to examine our conclusions in the light of textual criticism as to the originality of the shorter text more closely. This only applies of course to the manuscripts as we know them. It is true that the earliest stage we can reach is that in which the name Ephesus still does not appear, but it is conceivable that the original—and of course we do not possess the original of any of the New Testament writings—had a different text. The question, therefore, is on the one hand whether an original place-name has dropped out (that is, between the original and the earliest copies) and on the other hand how the name of Ephesus was introduced into the preface (that is, between the earliest copies and the later ones).

If we wish to consider whether there was a place-name in the original and do not wish to indulge in pointless guess-work, for in theory a great number of names could be suggested, there is only one possibility that is worth serious discussion—Laodicea. This name has to be considered, because Marcion calls Eph. the Laodicean letter. Further support for this—although only very indirect—is to be found in Col. iv. 16, according to which the Colossians are to receive a letter from Laodicea and are to send theirs to Laodicea. On account of the relationship between Col. and

Eph. it has been assumed that Col. iv. 16 refers to the letter to the Ephesians as we know it. This, however, is no more than a supposition, which perhaps Marcion himself realized, for it is noticeable that he does not give the place-name in the preface but only designates the letter as the letter to Laodicea in the *inscriptio* or the *titulus*, in other words in the title. Marcion is therefore familiar with the shorter text, and the most we can ask is whether in describing Eph. as the letter to the Laodiceans he was restoring something that was there originally—or was he also simply putting two and two together?

This question can only be answered—if at all—if we can explain why the original reference to Laodicea should later have been omitted. An attempt has been made to explain it by reference to Rev. iii. 14 ff., where Laodicea is described as a 'lukewarm' church.[12] The suggestion is that objection was taken to the fact that this of all churches should have received a letter from Paul, and that for this reason the name was omitted. In this case it would be an early example of *damnatio memoriae* together with *evasio nominis*. The theory has not found much acceptance, and it is unlikely. If Paul was the author, as Harnack and Roller assume, why did he write a letter to an unknown church without any evident reason, such as there was for the writing of Col.? Even if we interpret this letter as a 'wisdom address', as Schlier does, containing deeper perceptions than had yet been revealed to Paul (iii. 3 ff.), there is still no reason for writing of these things to a church with which he was not familiar. It would perhaps be conceivable if in this unknown church questions had arisen about Paul's preaching and that he had heard of these things and was now telling them of the further revelations that had come to him, but the letter itself provides no support for such an assumption. We must therefore conclude either that the letter was written by Paul—in which case it was not addressed to Laodicea, or that it was meant for that church—in which case it was not written by Paul. The theory really holds little interest for us, as this place-name does not signify anything at all, and could in fact be replaced by any other name. We have no further information about the church.

There are also internal difficulties to the theory. Col. iv. 16 presupposes the existence of a letter to Laodicea. If this refers to the Eph. we know, then we would have to assume that it is earlier than Col. There is no mention of an exchange of the two letters in Eph., nor are any greetings

[12] A. Harnack, 'Die Adresse des Epheserbriefes des Paulus', in *Sitzungsberichte der preußischen Akademie der Wissenschaften* (1910), pp. 669 ff. O. Roller, *Das Formular der paulinischen Briefe* (1933), pp. 199 ff., 520 ff.

sent to Colossae; there is only an allusion to a possible threat from heretics. According to the theory, the author must have heard of the appearance of the heretics in Colossae after writing 'Ephesians' (to Laodicea), must then have written Col., sent greetings to Laodicea (and Hierapolis) and suggested the exchange of letters. In this case both the letters, in view of the reference to Tychichus, must have been written close together. But as we have already seen that Paul cannot have written this letter to Laodicea, the reference to Tychichus must be an invention. Apart from this, there are a number of indications that Eph. was written later than Col.[13] This means that the author must have had Eph. in mind when he wrote Col.; otherwise he could not have asked to have it sent. But why is there no corresponding request in Eph., and why are no greetings expressed in Eph.? Many of these questions remain obscure. If there was an original address, it is now irretrievably lost—unless one day older manuscripts are found in the sands. Until that day we have to assume that the letter did not contain any specific statement as to who the recipients were.

What, then, can we say is the meaning of the two verses of the Preface? It would be strange if, after we have ascertained from the contents of the letter that it is not addressed to any specific situation, we should express our surprise at finding this view confirmed in the Preface. Presumably the author has no particular church in mind. He is meditating, and developing certain thoughts—and clothes them in the form of a letter. He wishes to be 'Pauline', as we shall see when we come to discuss the contents of the letter, and develops certain Pauline ideas (N.B. iii. 3 ff.), but by adopting the literary form of the letter he finds himself in difficulties as soon as he has to provide an address. He leaves this space 'blank', and so the Preface simply reflects the lack of particularity that we find in the letter as a whole.

What is the significance of this as far as exegesis is concerned? The Preface confirms the type of the document which we had already assumed from certain indications as regards the contents: that it is not really a letter, but a treatise or a 'wisdom address'. In this case we should abandon the attempt to interpret it as a letter. It is not a statement addressed to a particular situation, but an essay the character of which as a 'personal document' has to be remembered when making our exegesis. To pass a theological judgement on the statements contained in the treatise is therefore not the responsibility of the exegete, but of the historian of dogma and the systematic theologian.

---

[13] Cf. Dibelius, *op. cit.*, on Eph. iv. 16.

The other question which we mentioned earlier, how the name Ephesus found its way into the Preface, can be answered quite easily, for even in the manuscripts which have no reference to a place-name we find in the *inscriptio* at least: to the Ephesians. It was quite natural for scribes to copy the title in the Preface. How the *inscriptio* came into being we can only guess. Did it arise from the fact that people knew of Paul's long stay in Ephesus and were surprised that there was no letter addressed to the church there? Or is there a connection with the place where the Pauline letters were assembled? Or did the assertion that it was a letter to the Ephesians only arise out of the desire to engage in polemics against Marcion, who was propagating 'Laodiceans', i.e. a church which did not have a good name in the church as a whole (Rev. iii. 14 ff.)? In opposition to such trends one would want to appeal to a church that was in good standing, which Ephesus certainly was. These are all possible explanations, but we cannot be certain as to the answer.

In a series of Latin Biblical manuscripts and translations from Latin there is a 'letter to Laodicea', no doubt based on Col. iv. 16, which represents the work of a crude forger and is made up of a mosaic of Pauline quotations, from Phil. in particular. This 'letter' is quite without value.

(3) *Contents*. The aim of this treatise is to give instruction concerning the *Una Sancta*.[14] The Preface (i. 1–2) is followed by Thanksgiving (i. 3–14) and Intercession (i. 15–23). As far as form is concerned, therefore, the letter adopts the traditional pattern, but as far as the contents are concerned the sections differ from the corresponding ones in other letters in that they do not go into particular circumstances.

The theme of the Thanksgiving is praise for the grace whereby even Gentiles (cf. ii. 11) are included in the creation that has been eschatologically renewed. This Thanksgiving has been called 'the most monstrous conglomeration of sentences in the Greek language'.[15] The grammatical constructions are the most confused that we find anywhere. The theme of the Intercession is that Christians should more and more grasp with enlightened hearts the great hope that awaits them, as they now belong to the Kingdom of which Christ is the head. All powers are subject to him, as a result of his having been raised from the dead by God.

The first section of the treatise covers chs. ii–iii, where the 'notae ecclesiae' are set out.[16] ii. 1–10 follows directly on the preceding passage. Previously the readers were dead in their sins, they lived under the

---

[14] E. Käsemann, *op. cit.*, col. 517.   [15] *Ibid.*, col. 519.   [16] *Ibid.*, col. 517.

O

powers of this world and were by nature children of wrath, but now God has raised them up as well. This is solely a work of grace; it has not taken place on the basis of works, so that no one should glory. This idea is developed in ii. 11–22: all this applies particularly to the Gentile Christians (the readers are explicitly envisaged as such). Formerly they were strangers, but have been made 'nigh' through the blood of Christ, who has taken away the dividing wall (the law) so that now both Jews and Gentiles have access in Christ to the Father in one Spirit. In other words, the Gentiles have received citizenship, they are fellow-citizens and members of the same family with the saints, built on the foundation of the 'apostles and prophets'. Christ is the corner-stone of the Church, which is itself described in the image of a building.

In iii. 1–13 all that has been set out so far is described as a Pauline mystery and therefore is meant to be taken as a continuation of earlier revelation. 'If so be that ye have heard of the dispensation of that grace of God which was given me to you-ward (εἰς ὑμᾶς); how that by revelation was made known unto me the mystery, as I wrote afore in few words, whereby, when ye read (N.B.), ye can perceive my understanding in the mystery of Christ, which in other generations was not made known unto the sons of men, as it hath now been revealed unto his holy apostles and prophets in the Spirit' (iii. 2–5). Paul is the least of the saints, but to him was given the grace of preaching to the Gentiles. The Gentiles are therefore now fellow-heirs, they belong to the body and have a share in it. There follow (iii. 14–21) further petitions, concluding with a doxology. Paul prays that the members of the church may have understanding and be strengthened in the inner man, so that Christ may dwell in their hearts through faith.

Following the 'dogmatic exposition' the second section (iv. 1–vi. 20) consists of a series of exhortations systematically set out. iv. 1–24 could almost be described as 'ethical foundations'. These are based on ecclesiology, which in turn is based on Christology. The point of intersection is the idea of the σῶμα (body). Great emphasis is placed upon unity (one body, one Spirit, one hope, one Lord, one faith, one baptism, etc.—iv. 4–6), a unity which is given, but has constantly to be won again and preserved. The exalted Lord has bestowed gifts. First the basic functions in the Church are mentioned: apostles, prophets, evangelists, pastors, teachers. Their task is to equip the saints for service. But every Christian also receives a share in these gifts. The Christian therefore should no longer be like a child, exposed to the influence of every heresy, but should become a perfect man. In this way he will—and this is significant—grow again into the body, the head of which is Christ. In other words, the unity of the body is the starting-point and the goal of the whole movement—to which, however, Christians can only belong if they no longer behave like Gentiles. The old man must be put away (iv. 17 ff.). The exhortation that follows is built on this foundation that has now been laid down. In iv. 25–v. 2 the most elementary requirements of Christian brotherhood are mentioned (e.g. that one should not be angry, should no longer steal or indulge in evil speech), and are summed up in the words: 'Be ye therefore imitators of God, as beloved children; and walk in love, even as Christ also loved you' (v. 1, 2a). The idea is developed, first negatively (v. 3–7) in a catalogue of vices and then positively (v. 8–21) in a catalogue of virtues. The catalogue of vices is followed by the demand to keep oneself free from all such things, and in the catalogue of virtues the missionary note is sounded. A hymn-like conclusion follows. v. 22–vi. 9 contains a section on domestic morality in which the author discusses the mystery of marriage, which he compares with the relationship between Christ and the Church, and finally points out the duties of children and slaves. The second section closes (vi. 10–20) with the passage on 'spiritual armour', which again includes a summary and a strong admonition, with regard both to what is given and what is demanded ethically.

We have already referred to the conclusion of the letter, the reference to Tychichus (vi. 21 f.) and the two greetings of peace and grace. The outstanding feature of this letter is its extraordinary internal consistency.

(4) *The Question of Sources.* The author used an abundance of existing material, which he incorporated to such an extent that it cannot always be constructed with the certainty we would like. Behind i. 5–8, 9–12a there probably lies an original hymn with two verses.[17] There are obvious echoes of baptismal themes here, as also behind ii. 19–22 and v. 14, where a baptismal hymn has been conjectured. The exhortation is also made up to a considerable extent from traditional material, and the same is probably true of the section on domestic morality. Although compared with Col. the author may not have altered the hymn-like material of his sources as much, nevertheless taken as a whole the very independent treatment of it is a striking feature. The way it is fitted into the whole framework is for the most part very skilful, and in this respect the author has become to a remarkable extent the master of his material. As far as

---

[17] *Ibid.*, col. 519. For a different view, see E. Lohmeyer, *Die Briefe an die Kolosser und an Philemon, ad loc.*, who sees the whole section i. 3–14 as a hymn. See also the discussion in Dibelius, *op. cit.* on Eph. i. 3.

exegesis is concerned, this means therefore that the material has to be considered not so much as quotation but as the statement of the author. We can see therefore from the example of Eph.—and Col.—that there are various stages between quotation pure and simple and independent adaptation or fresh presentation. It is impossible to lay down any systematic rules; in each case one has to try and clarify the degree of independence for the purpose of exegesis.

(5) *The 'Setting in Life'.* The author writes as 'Paul' and thereby indicates that he wishes to stand in the Pauline tradition. This is in fact the case, for he does adopt Pauline ideas, for example the doctrine of justification (ii. 1 ff.), statements concerning charismatic gifts (iv. 7 ff.) and the repeated emphasis that the Church is made up of Jews and Gentiles. It is significant, however, that in spite of all the similarity, he goes beyond Paul. Using Gnostic terminology, he interprets the Church as a body, which is a Pauline idea, but he then adds the idea of the head—Christ is the head of the body. This is an idea that is not found in Paul.

The author is not only aware that he is developing certain ideas, but explicitly says so. 'Paul' has already written briefly before, and one can read what he wrote (iii. 3 f.). We can of course interpret this as referring to the first two chapters,[18] but this does not seem a natural interpretation. But even if this were the case, it would not alter the fact that earlier views are being developed and that this development is described as a mystery, which goes beyond the initial revelation. In any case, therefore, we find an 'advanced theological development', as even Schlier admits, although he still feels the Pauline authorship can be upheld. He writes 'Paul had gained understanding in the mystery of Christ' (iii. 4), which now comes to light in the mystery of the Church (iii. 9) as the 'eternal mystery of God's will' (i. 9), through the 'mystery of the gospel' (vi. 19). This understanding can be seen in his letter, as he himself states (iii. 4)'.[19] The author of this letter, in other words, is fully aware of what is new or more profound in the understanding the letter reveals. In other words, this means—to express it cautiously—that compared with the 'earlier Paul' a development has taken place. Is Paul himself the originator of it? The way in which the writer of this letter speaks of the apostle provides the answer to this question.

We have already seen in connection with Col. that the apostolic office is linked with the idea of tradition, and that we can therefore trace the first stage in the 'apostolic tradition'. The apostolic authority is 'dele-

[18] H. Schlier, *op. cit., ad loc.*   [19] *Ibid.*, p. 10.

gated' there. In Eph. the problem is rather different. The Church is built upon the foundation of the 'apostles and prophets' (ii. 20), and reference is made to the 'holy apostles and prophets' (iii. 5). We should not try to interpret the prophets mentioned here as Old Testament prophets, and indeed the sequence rules this out. The reference is to the Christian prophets, who followed the apostles. This is quite clear from the order: apostles—prophets—evangelists—pastors—teachers, who equip the saints for service (iv. 11). The Church therefore is already 'standing'. It is based upon apostles and prophets, to whom its members look back. The description 'the holy apostles' indicates that it is men belonging to the past who are envisaged. At the time of the author there are evidently no longer any apostles, or prophets. But as only apostles and prophets are the recipients of revelation (iii. 5) and the author is developing this revelation further, we can see why it is impossible for him to write under his own name. However, as he does not think of his account as a new revelation, but as an unfolding—of the earlier one made to Paul, he is acting entirely in good faith when he makes 'Paul' write this 'letter'. At that time this was by no means an unusual procedure, and we should therefore not judge it by our criteria.

It could be said that it is not the task of the apostle as the sole bearer of the revelation that is described in an un-Pauline fashion, but his status.[20] Yet even this statement has to be modified a little, for from the standpoint of a later age the description of the 'status' of the apostle does bring out the 'substance' of the apostolate. Revelation as a revelation in history is in fact tied to the apostolic testimony. The author gives expression to this fact when he speaks retrospectively of the 'holy apostles' as the sole bearers of revelation and thus adheres to the belief that the apostolic office cannot be transmitted. A personal succession is excluded here—in contrast to Col.—and also the idea of a continuing direct revelation in 'post-apostolic' times. Thus the author, as far as his own period is concerned, remains entirely within the framework of the genuinely Pauline conception. This description of status, attributed by a later writer to Paul, can be described as 'un-Pauline' only if one interprets it as meant to be an actual judgement upon the apostle. But this is not the intention of the author, who is merely appealing to the authority of the apostle for the justification of his own statements in the post-apostolic period. The problem which confronts not only the author of Eph., but also ourselves, is this: How can the Church remain an apostolic Church in a period when the apostles are no longer living? The author's way of

[20] E. Käsemann, *op. cit.*, col. 519.

solving it is by developing and interpreting Pauline ideas—in the form of a 'wisdom address'—and expounding them as such under the authority of the apostle. It is clear that this solution is possible only in the immediate post-apostolic period, in which the apostolic tradition is still 'fluid'. When after a considerable time it became a historically complete entity, this solution of the problem which the author adopted becomes no longer possible. This gives us the decisive factor for determining the 'setting in life' of this treatise—in the early post-apostolic period.

BIBLIOGRAPHY

H. Conzelmann, *Der Epheserbrief* (NTD, vol. 8, 9 ed., 1962).

M. Dibelius, *An die Kolosser, Epheser, an Philemon*, edited by H. Greeven (Lietzmann, 3 ed., 1958).

H. Schlier, *Der Brief an die Epheser* (2 ed., 1960).

H. Chadwick, 'Die Absicht des Epheserbriefes', *ZNW* (1960), pp. 145 ff.

E. Käsemann, 'Epheserbrief' in *RGG*, II, cols. 517 ff.

G. Schille, 'Der Autor des Epheserbriefes', *ThLZ* (1957), pp. 325 ff.

Commentaries: T. K. Abbott (with Colossians), ICC (1897); E. F. Scott (with Colossians and Philemon), Moffatt (1930).

R. Batey, 'The Destination of Ephesians', *JBL* 82 (1963), pp. 101 ff.

J. Coutts, 'The Relationship of Ephesians and Colossians', *NTS* 4 (1957-8), pp. 201 ff.

F. L. Cross (Ed.), *Studies in Ephesians* (1956).

E. J. Goodspeed, *The Meaning of Ephesians* (1933).

E. J. Goodspeed, *The Key to Ephesians* (1956).

P. N. Harrison, 'The Author of Ephesians', *Studia Evangelica* II, TU 87 (1964), pp. 595 ff.

C. L. Milton, *The Epistle to the Ephesians* (1951).

18. THE PASTORAL EPISTLES

1 and 2 Tim. and Tit. differ from the other New Testament letters which are written or claim to be written by Paul in that they are addressed to individuals. The same is true of Phm., but that is more of a private letter than one in which an 'apostolic' ruling is given about a 'private' concern of Philemon, whereas in these three letters the recipients are addressed as officials, as 'pastors'. For this reason they have been known since the eighteenth century as the 'Pastoral Epistles'. The name does not describe the letters completely, for they contain not only exhortations and advice for those who hold the pastoral office, but also what are in effect rulings concerning the organization of the Church. These matters, however, are always related to the pastors themselves, so that the concept of the 'Pastorals' seems justified, and in addition it brings out clearly what these three letters have in common. It seems logical therefore, to discuss them together, as the problems they raise overlap to a considerable extent.

(1) *The Recipients.* 1 and 2 Tim. are addressed to Timothy, who is called in 1 Tim. i. 2 γνήσιον τέκνον ἐν πίστει (true child in faith) and in 2 Tim. i. 2 ἀγαπητὸν τέκνον (dear child). The address to Titus corresponds to that to Timothy in 1 Tim. (Tit. i. 4: γνήσιον τέκνον κατὰ κοινὴν πίστιν—true child after a common faith). This purely formal similarity is in keeping with the considerable agreement in substance between 1 Tim. and Tit., in which however both differ from 2 Tim.

Timothy—according to Acts xvi. 1, the son of a Jewish Christian woman and Gentile father from Lystra—presumably became a Christian through the influence of Paul (1 Cor. iv. 17). In 1 Thess., Phil., 2 Cor. and Phm. (cf. also 2 Thess. and Col.) the apostle mentions him as the joint-sender of a letter. He was obviously a close colleague of Paul's, and was also used by him as a messenger. In this capacity he was sent to visit the churches at Thessalonica (1 Thess. iii. 1 ff.), Philippi (Phil. ii. 19 ff.) and Corinth (1 Cor. iv. 17; xvi. 10). On these occasions Paul tells the churches with pride of his loyalty and reliability. The picture that Acts gives of Timothy is in essential accordance with the one Paul gives (Acts xvii. 14 f.; xviii. 5; xix. 22; xx. 4), but there are considerable doubts about some of the details: for example, it is impossible that Paul should have circumcised him at Lystra (Acts xvi. 3; cf. 1 Cor. vii. 17–20; also Acts xv. 1–29). According to ecclesiastical tradition Timothy later became bishop of Ephesus. We shall consider this point, and the statements concerning him in the Pastorals, later.

Titus was a Gentile Christian. He went with Paul to the Apostolic Council at Jerusalem, where Paul won his point that Titus should not be circumcised (Gal. ii. 1, 3)". He was also used by Paul as a messenger, and visited the church at Corinth when it was in conflict with Paul (2 Cor. vii. 6, 13 f.; xii. 18). He no doubt had the gift of conducting negotiations skilfully, for he evidently succeeded in restoring the relationship between the church and the apostle. Paul later sent him there once again for the final preparations for the collection (2 Cor. viii. 17; cf. 2 Cor. viii. 6, 16, 23). Acts makes no mention of Titus. According to ecclesiastical tradition he later became bishop of Crete, where he is said to have died at Gortyna at the age of 94.

(2) *Contents.* (a) In 1 *Tim.* the preface (i. 1–2—see below) is followed (i. 3–20) by a 'pastoral section' in which Timothy is exhorted to keep watch over the preaching of the Gospel. 'I exhorted thee to tarry at Ephesus, when I was going into Macedonia, that thou mightest charge certain men not to teach a different doctrine' (i. 3). The meaning of τροσμεῖναι is disputed, but it is significant for the situation that is reflected —or at least is to be assumed—in 1 Tim. 'Every unbiased reader will translate τροσμεῖναι as "stay", not as "hold fast" ';[21] but this implies that Timothy stayed on in Ephesus when Paul left Ephesus for Macedonia. Michaelis,[22] on the other hand, suggests that this does not refer to Paul's departure from Ephesus, but from some other place, because it would be superfluous to repeat in writing a message that had been given by word of mouth. But this argument is not convincing, for in Tit. i. 5 a corresponding situation is to be found. When we also remember that the parallel between 1 Tim. and Tit. goes much further than this, in spite of certain variations in detail, we cannot but accept what appears to be the obvious meaning that Paul has departed from Ephesus, left Timothy behind and is now 'repeating' in writing the instructions already given by word of mouth.

There are evidently certain people in Ephesus who are proclaiming heretical doctrines (i. 3–7). The church, on the other hand, must hold fast to Paul's Gospel, which is very briefly set out (8–12), and then follows (13–17) by way of example a description of Paul's character,

---

[21] M. Dibelius, *Die Pastoralbriefe*, edited by H. Conzelmann in Lietzmann (3 ed., 1955), *ad loc.*

[22] *Einleitung in das Neue Testament* (3 ed., 1962), p. 260.

CONTENTS 201

which was formerly that of a persecutor, until he obtained mercy as he
was acting out of ignorance. Finally Timothy is exhorted (18–20) to
fight the good fight in faith with a good conscience. There are some who
have not done this. Hymenaeus and Alexander are mentioned, whom
Paul delivered to Satan, in order that they might learn by being chastised
not to blaspheme. Ch. i. therefore contains nothing that Timothy would
not already have known. Paul is merely confirming what he has said
before.

The pastoral section is followed by a section of instructions (ii. 2–iii. 13).
It deals first (ii. 1–15) with prayer, which Timothy is to offer (1–7) for
all men, and 'for kings and all that are in high place; that we may lead
a tranquil and quiet life in all godliness and gravity'. This is briefly
explained as being the will of God, who seeks to help all men and for this
reason has appointed Paul as herald and apostle. ii. 8 refers to the men's
prayers, and vv. 9–15 to the prayers offered by the women, who are not
to adorn themselves ostentatiously, but—as Eve was created after Adam
—should keep silent in church and not teach or interrupt the men. Women
should find their salvation through child-bearing.

Exhortations to the officials follow (iii. 1–7: the qualities of a bishop;
8–13: the qualities of a deacon), in which it is presupposed that these two
offices are institutions that have already been in existence for some
considerable time; however it is not so much the duties involved in the
offices that are described but rather the holders of the offices that receive
ethical exhortation—or, ethical requirements are laid down for those who
desire office.

There is a further pastoral message in iii. 14–16. Paul writes in the hope
of coming to see Timothy soon, but if he is delayed, then Timothy will at
least know how people ought to behave in the house of God. Again the
question arises—Would not Timothy have known all this already? After
all, he has already carried out a number of commissions on his own—
Thessalonica, Philippi, Corinth. The section closes with a hymn which
extols the mystery of εὐσέβεια (= the Christian religion).

There now follows a further section of regulations for the Church or
for the Christian life (iv. 1–5), the special feature of which is that it refers
to a future to which the 'Spirit' points. In later times some will fall away
from the faith, and the signs of this will be false preaching, the pro-
hibition of marriage and abstinence from certain foods.

When we consider that in vv. 3–5, 7 these 'future' heresies are refuted
and that strange doctrines—present ones—are mentioned as early as
i. 3 f., and finally that in i. 20 Paul has already delivered 'heretical

leaders' to Satan, it seems reasonable to ask whether the description of
the heresy as future is not merely a fiction, and whether it is in fact
already present and is now being attacked, then it will seem as if its
emergence in the last days has already been prophesied by Paul. This
would be strong evidence against the Pauline authorship.

This would also help us to understand the other puzzling element that
we have already noted, the fact that the recipient is told about things
with which he is already familiar, so that we can see it as a variation of
the method of attacking heretics in the sphere of doctrine and Church
order: in other words, present problems are dealt with by reference to
Paul. To adopt the form of Pauline letter is a way of using the apostolic
authority for decisions in the post-apostolic Church.

The theme is continued in iv. 6–10. Timothy is called to resist the
godless old wives' fables, and instead to teach the brethren and so be a
good minister of Christ. Here again we can see that the fiction of future
heresy is not maintained. This is underlined in a further pastoral section
(iv. 11–v. 2). Timothy is told how he should preach and teach (iv. 11).
No one is to despise his youth; he himself, however, should set an example
and take heed to himself and his teaching. Timothy is reminded that he
has received a charismatic gift through the laying on of hands (='ordination'), and he is instructed how to deal properly with older and
younger men and women.

This leads again into a section on the ordering of the Christian life
(v. 3–vi. 2), which deals first with widows (v. 3–16) and then with
presbyters (v. 21–25). A pastoral section is introduced (v. 21–25) which
contains a number of instructions which do not always seem to have much
connection with one another: Timothy is to act without prejudice and
not lay hands on anyone hastily, and should not drink only water but
also take a little wine for the sake of his stomach. Then (vi. 1–2) the
question of the ordering of the Christian life is touched upon again:
slaves should honour their masters, especially if they are Christians.

The final passage (vi. 3–21) contains a loosely connected series of
pastoral instructions and instructions on living the Christian life. After
some general warnings against heresy and greed for money (3–10) there
follows a renewed exhortation to avoid all such things and fight the good
fight of faith (11–16), a reminder to the rich that they should rely not on
their wealth but on God (17–19) and finally (20 f.) a call to Timothy
entreating him to guard that which has been committed to him and to
avoid false *gnosis*. The letter concludes with the benediction: 'Grace be
with you'.

In spite of its looseness of construction the letter as a whole has a real unity. The letter is not meant for one individual (N.B. plural in vi. 21b), although it is addressed to one person. It presupposes that there are heresies in the church and calls on the leader of the church to exercise his office correctly and on the other members—indirectly at least—to fulfil the duties of their calling.

If we imagine for a moment that what is written here to Timothy was written throughout in the third person (as it is in fact in part—cf. the qualities of the bishop and the deacon, etc.), we could describe the whole letter as a summary of regulations for the Church, or as the early form of a 'Church constitution'. From this angle we can describe the letter in the following terms: it is a collection of questions concerning Church organization which—together with occasional infrequent allusions to a heresy—are sent clothed in the form of a letter to the leader of the church. If Paul is suggested as the author of the letter, this is no doubt intended to give the regulations laid down the necessary apostolic authority. We will return later to some of the other questions that arise.

(b) In *Tit.* the preface (i. 1–4) is rather more detailed than in 1 Tim., but the similarity in the address (cf. 4a) is striking. The letter again consists of alternating pastoral sections and sections concerning the organization of the church.

The external occasion (i. 5 f.) is described in the same terms as in 1 Tim. Titus is to stay behind in Crete in order to put in order the things that Paul had not been able to deal with. In each town he is to appoint presbyters, of whom an orderly way of life is required. i. 7–9 sets out the qualities of the bishop, expressed here more briefly than in 1 Tim. Emphasis is placed, among other things, on the duty of preaching sound doctrine and the ability to convince opponents.

A pastoral section which follows (i. 10–16) takes up the theme of 'opponents'. There are on Crete many such disorderly people and conceited fanatics, who are more precisely defined as 'they of the circumcision'. They ruin whole families and teach for the sake of mean gain. A saying of Epimenides, who is described as one of their prophets, is quoted in support: 'Cretans are always liars, evil beasts, idle gluttons.' The heretics are then further described: they follow Jewish fables and commandments; their mind and conscience is defiled; they claim to know God, but deny him in their works; they are of no use for any good deeds. By contrast the exhortation addressed to Titus (ii. 1) reads: 'But speak thou the things which befit the sound doctrine', and this is followed by a passage resembling the list of duties for the members of a household.

This juxtaposition is significant for the line of argument, which is as follows. The heretics are depraved people; Titus must oppose them with pure doctrine which, however, is not expounded any further; instead there follows immediately the list of household responsibilities. In other words, the argument is based more on ethics than on doctrine.

In the list of household responsibilities (ii. 2–15) the following are addressed in turn: the older men (2), the older women (3) who should be 'priestly' in their attitude so that they can train the younger women properly (4 f.), then the younger men (6–8), to whom Titus is to set an example, and the slaves (9 f.) who are to be subject to their masters in every way. The theological foundation for this list of duties is finally set out (11–15) in the fact that the grace of God has been manifested for men's salvation and that it instructs all men to renounce ungodliness and lusts and lead an honourable, upright and devout life.

The final chapter (iii. 1–15) again contains a loose collection of pastoral sections and sections on the ordering of the church. The church is to be admonished to be subject to the authorities, to avoid conflicts, and be peaceable (1 f.), and this is then explained theologically (3–7). At one time even those who are now Christians lived in foolishness, disobedience and error, but then there appeared the 'kindness of God our Saviour, and his love toward man', which brought salvation—not by works, but by the washing of regeneration and by the Holy Ghost. The pastoral section (8–11) is an exhortation and warning about heresy. One should avoid unnecessary arguments and discussions, and Titus must repel any man who seeks to create factions, after giving him one or two warnings. Finally a few instructions are given (12–14): when Artemas or Tychichus arrives, sent by Paul, Titus is to come quickly to Nicopolis, where Paul has decided to spend the winter. Titus must see that Zenas and Apollos have all they need for their winter journey. After greetings from all those who are with Paul and to all 'them that love us in faith' the letter concludes (15) with the plural form of blessing ('Grace be with you all'), for which the preceding greetings provide more reason here than in 1 Tim.

There is a clear resemblance to 1 Tim. The situation—that of the 'bishop' who has been left behind—is the same, and also the mixture of pastoral sections and those dealing with the organization of the church. Therefore the question arises here again as to whether the letter form and the mention of Paul as the sender is meant merely to provide authorization for the organization of the church.

This of course raises the further question: why has this to be expressed by two letters? If these are not in fact Pauline letters—which we have only surmised so far—and we therefore cannot assume the actual situation in Ephesus and Crete, then one letter would have been sufficient to lay down the pattern of Church order on a foundation of apostolic authority. We shall have to consider this point later, but in the light of the contents of the two letters we can already make one suggestion: that 1 Tim. presupposes a relatively organized church, but Tit. one that still needs to be organized. The effect of this is a certain difference of tone. A clear picture is given of how a church should be organized: those already in existence should be guided by it (1 Tim.), and those still developing should be encouraged to grow in this direction (Tit.).

(c) *2 Tim.* The preface (i. 1 f.) is followed (3–14) by a grateful remembrance of the Christian tradition in which Paul and Timothy stand by descent. Timothy is reminded of the charismatic gift he received through the laying on of hands by Paul—although according to 1 Tim. iv. 14 Timothy was 'ordained' by the elders. In other words, Timothy stands within a tradition, in which one can understand and bear suffering, as Paul is now doing as a prisoner. For as an apostle one must suffer; but God has not given the spirit of fearfulness, but of power and love and discipline. This is followed by certain personal observations (15–18): all the Christians in Asia have turned away from the apostle, including Phygelus and Hermogenes; Onesiphorus, on the other hand, has often refreshed Paul and, when he came to Rome, sought out the apostle diligently until he found him. Timothy himself is well aware of all that he did at Ephesus. The reference to the fact that Paul is imprisoned in Rome—or is he looking back on the experience?—is important for dating the letter. In any case the letter must have been written late.

Timothy is now exhorted (ii. 1–13) to fight worthily, for the only one who receives the crown of victory is he who has fought faithfully. Such a conflict brings suffering, but suffering leads to salvation. This is underlined by the words of a hymn. This battle has to be fought well, especially with regard to the heretics (ii. 14–26). Timothy must avoid their godless ways of speech and repudiate foolish and ignorant arguments, for a servant of the Lord should not enter into disputes. Hymenaeus and Philetus are mentioned as heretics; their heresy consists in the assertion that the resurrection has already taken place. The instruction that Timothy should not allow himself to be involved in fruitless discussion throws a peculiar light on this 'battle against heresy'. Elsewhere Paul certainly does not ignore his enemies, but enters into argument with them.

In a section of 'prophecy' (iii. 1–5) the coming of difficult days in the last times is announced. The heretics are described by quoting a long list of vices, but once again the prophecy is not carried to its logical conclusion, for Timothy is called upon to avoid these people, although in the long run they cannot have any success (iii. 6–9).

This is followed by an urgent appeal to Timothy (iii. 10–iv. 8). In spite of all his trials he has adhered to the apostle's doctrine, conduct, aims, faith, patience, love, constancy, persecutions and sufferings, and he must now hold fast to what he has learned and remember from whom he has learned from his childhood onwards. Again we see the theme of tradition being employed, in order that one might endure in present trials or when endangered by heretics. Timothy must preach the Word, whether there is a demand for it or not. Again we find the element of 'prophecy' (iv. 3 f.): the time will come when men will seek teachers to their own liking. However, Timothy must endure suffering as Paul has done, who is already being offered as a sacrifice. The apostle has fought the good fight, finished the course, has kept faith; now there awaits him the crown of righteousness.

The conclusion of the letter (iv. 9–22) is couched in very personal terms. 9–12 describes the situation in which the apostle finds himself. Timothy must hasten to come to Paul. He is to bring Mark with him, for he can be valuable to Paul now that he is alone. Demas has left the apostle, out of love of the world, Crescens has gone to Galatia and Titus to Dalmatia, and Tychichus has been sent by Paul to Ephesus. Only Luke is with him at present. This account of the lonely apostle seems rather curious as it is in complete contradiction to v. 21, according to which Paul is by no means alone, but conveys greetings from Eubulus, Pudeus, Linus, Claudia and all (N.B.) the brethren. The intention in this passage, therefore, is to stress the apostolic loneliness—a situation of suffering—as taking the form of actual isolation.

Timothy is then given instructions (13) to bring from Troas the cloak and books, but particularly the parchments, which Paul left behind there. In vv. 14 f. he is given an explicit warning about Alexander the smith. In the news about Paul that follows (16–18) the theme of loneliness recurs. At his first defence no one supported him, but the Lord was by his side and saved him from the mouth of the lion. The Lord will do the same in the future and bring Paul to his heavenly Kingdom. (The meaning of ἀπολογία here is a matter of controversy.) Paul now conveys his greetings (19 f.), mentions that Erastus stayed in Corinth and that he had to leave Trophimus behind in Miletus ill. Linked with the greetings there is a renewed request to Timothy to come quickly (21) and then the final greeting: 'The Lord be with thy spirit. Grace be with you' (22).

This letter gives an entirely different impression from the other two. It would be possible to explain 1 Tim. and Tit. relatively easily as constructions, but it seems more difficult to do this with 2 Tim. on account of the abundance of personal references. However, these do not give rise to other questions, because of their inner inconsistency and discrepancy when compared with the details given in the other letters of Paul.

Can we find, nevertheless, in the light of the contents of the letters, a common key to the understanding of all three? One common factor is to be found in the attack upon heretics, but this does not really stand in the forefront of any of the letters. 1 Tim. and Tit. are concerned rather with codified 'rules' or 'rules' requiring to be codified, for the ministry among other things. 2 Tim. also deals with the ministry, not in the sense of laying down rules, but rather that Timothy in fulfilling his ministry should follow the example of Paul. In this respect—particularly as regards his suffering—Paul is the model for the 'bishop'. In the light of this we can understand the more marked personal character of 2 Tim.

The common factor, therefore, lies in the bearing of the three letters upon Paul. In 1 Tim. and Tit. a variety of previously existing material (for example, lists of household responsibilities and lists of duties) is employed and used as a basis for ordering the life of the church. By means of the letter form in which everything is clothed apostolic authority is claimed for this ordering. In 2 Tim. Paul himself and his suffering is taken as the basis for the fulfilment of the bishop's office—or, to sum the position up briefly: in 1 Tim. and Tit. 'Paul' expounds Church order, whereas in 2 Tim. he expounds 'himself'.

This does not really throw much light on the question of authorship, particularly as we find both elements in the Pauline letters. The apostle often adopts already existing material and reproduces it, interpreting it at the same time; and he also interprets his own apostolate (cf. 2 Cor.). Nevertheless we have already noted certain elements that make us doubt Paul's authorship, for the style of argument in the Pastorals is often essentially different from that with which we are familiar in the Pauline letters. This is a problem to which we shall have to return.

(3) *The Situation.* According to 1 Tim. Paul and Timothy have so far been working together in Ephesus (see 2a above). Paul then went to Macedonia, leaving Timothy behind in Ephesus, but plans to return there soon (iii. 14; iv. 13). However, this poses a psychological problem,

as it is difficult to understand why Paul should have written this letter. The apostle does not really convey anything that would not already have been known in Ephesus. There are already bishops and deacons there—is it likely that the need has only now arisen to lay down moral instructions for these officials? There is no indication that anything that has happened during Paul's absence has now made it necessary to refer to such matters. The guidance that is given is of permanent validity—but Paul could have waited until his return before giving it, even if it was unfamiliar. We cannot avoid, therefore, questioning these references to the situation. The difficulty disappears, however, as soon as we assume that a stylistic device is being employed here by means of which the laying down of Church order can be traced back to Paul.

We still need to consider, however, whether the situation that is indicated can be fitted into the events of Paul's life as far as we know them. Acts tells us that Paul went to Macedonia (xix. 21; xx. 1 f.) after a stay of three years in Ephesus (xix. 8, 10; xx. 31). At that time, however, Timothy did not stay behind in Ephesus, but Paul sent him on ahead to Macedonia (xix. 22). Paul intends then to go on to Corinth and later to Jerusalem, but does not go to Ephesus again, as is made plain in 1 Tim. This could of course be connected with a change of route for the journey after the writing of 1 Tim., but this raises a further difficulty: if Timothy accompanied Paul on the journey to Jerusalem (Acts xx. 4 ff.) he could not have stayed in Ephesus (1 Tim. i. 3). The letter therefore cannot be fitted into the situation as indicated. The question remains whether 1 Tim., even if it was not written by Paul, is nevertheless meant to presuppose the situation. The fact that a three-year stay in Ephesus by Paul could well be linked with the beginnings of organizing the church's life lends support to the idea. In this case the author must either not have known or have overlooked the tradition that Timothy was sent on in advance to Macedonia.

If we look for other possibilities whereby the situation revealed in 1 Tim. can be fitted into the events of Paul's life, there are no more known dates that can help us. One solution would be to assume the period after Paul's imprisonment in Rome. In this case the apostle, after being released, must have travelled to Spain and later to the East again. This solution is the one suggested by all those who accept 1 Tim. as Pauline. Whether it is a possible solution can only be considered in connection with the other Pastorals.

(b) According to Tit., Paul and Titus have been working together in Crete, and the apostle has left his companion behind in churches which are not yet fully organized (i. 5). Titus is to complete this work and apply himself in particular to the struggle against heresy (i. 10 ff.; iii. 9 ff.), but after the arrival of Tychichus or Artemas he is to leave the island and join Paul, who intends to go to Nicopolis in the winter (iii. 12). The mention of Nicopolis might be a useful pointer, but we cannot rely on it too much as there are several towns of the same name. We cannot therefore go beyond supposition. When, however, did Paul's stay in Crete take place? Certainly the statements in Acts xxvii are out of the question here, and there are other indications either in Acts or in the Pauline letters we possess.

If it is not a Pauline letter, we need to consider whether the author is thinking of the statements in Acts xx. 3, where there is a reference to a voyage by Paul to Syria. It is possible that the author of Tit. assumed that this journey would take him via Crete.[23] It is noticeable that as regards both 1 Tim. and Tit. it is possible to reconstruct situations with which we are familiar from Acts. However, this reconstruction cannot be maintained. The question still remains: Was the author of the Pastorals familiar with Acts? If, on the other hand, we still wish to assume that Paul was the author of Tit., here again the only solution is to suggest that Paul stayed in Crete after his imprisonment in Rome. This idea seems reasonable also on account of the connection as regards content between Tit. and 1 Tim. In any case the two letters cannot be fitted into the phase of Paul's life with which we are familiar.

(c) The situation reflected in 2 Tim. is even more complicated. We have to assume that Timothy is still in Ephesus (i. 18). The greetings addressed to Aquila and Priscilla (iv. 19), who according to Acts xviii. 18 f., 26 and 1 Cor. xvi. 19 live in Ephesus, are a further indication of this. It is more difficult to determine the place, actual or assumed, where Paul is staying. i. 16 f., which refers to Onesiphorus' visiting Paul in Rome, seems to provide us with one pointer at least. The letter can have been written only after Paul had been in Rome, on at least one occasion. In any case, therefore, it is later than Rom. But according to 2 Tim. Paul was in prison at the time (i. 8; ii. 9), and therefore the question that arises is whether we have to think here of this 'first' imprisonment in Rome.

This assumption, however, raises considerable difficulties. It would mean that the stay in Troas, where Paul left behind his cloak, books and parchments (iv. 13) and also the stay in Miletus, where he left Trophymus behind ill (iv. 20) took place three years previously. Is it likely that Paul

[23] Cf. Dibelius, *op. cit.* on Tit. iii. 14.

P

would only now ask for the things, particularly as he feels his end is approaching (iv. 6 ff., 18)? An even greater difficulty is posed by the question whether it would seem necessary to send Timothy news from Rome of the illness of his fellow-worker, when he was in Ephesus and not far from Miletus. This seems very improbable. We can conclude that it is out of the question to think of the letter having been written during Paul's imprisonment on his first visit to Rome.

Is there any evidence that Paul is in fact writing from Rome? i. 17 does not necessarily imply this. There are various references to be noted: according to iv. 13 Paul has been in Troas, and according to iv. 20 in Corinth and Miletus. According to Acts xx. ff. he covered the same route Corinth—Troas—Miletus when he went to Jerusalem for the collection. Here he was brought before the Sanhedrin, but escaped any direct injury (Acts xxiii. 1–11). Could iv. 16 f. be a reference to this? (Cf. especially Acts xxiii. 11 and 2 Tim. iv. 17). It seems reasonable in fact to assume that Caesarea was Paul's place of imprisonment at the time. In this case the earlier companions would have gone from here to Thessalonica, Galatia, Dalmatia (iv. 10) and Ephesus (iv. 12). We can see therefore a remarkable agreement between the events and centres of activity described in Acts with those that are presupposed in 2 Tim.

In this case the letter cannot be Pauline, for at the time of his imprisonment in Caesarea Paul had not yet been to Rome, which is presupposed in i. 17. The author—as we have already noted in connection with 1 Tim. and Tit.—had a fairly close acquaintance with Acts or with the traditions used there. He made this his starting-point, but did not maintain the fiction—perhaps could not maintain it, as certain material (though not all the material) was at his disposal. One difficulty, for example, is that Paul should tell Timothy, who is at present in Ephesus, that he has sent Tychichus 'to Ephesus' instead of 'to you' (iv. 12).

The question of the situation in which the Pastorals were written presents us, therefore, with a peculiar set of circumstances. Because of the connections with Acts they seem to point to a period before Paul's imprisonment in Rome, but they cannot be assigned to such an early date either because discrepancies make it impossible or—in the case of 2 Tim. —because there is an explicit reference to a visit to Rome by Paul.

(4) *The Imprisonment in Rome.* If in the light of the observations we have made so far one still does not wish to accept the pseudonymity of the Pastorals, the only solution that remains is the hypothesis of a second

imprisonment of Paul in Rome. If this could be proved it would certainly dispose of many of the difficulties, for there is no comparative material available for this period, and therefore there is no question of contradicting other traditions. We would have to assume that after Paul had been released from Rome he completed a further extensive programme of journeys. Are there any indications that he did this?

We must consider first the evidence of the Pastorals themselves, and 2 Tim. in particular, for there would surely be some indication here. 2 Tim. iv. 16 ff. refers to Paul's first 'defence' when he had no one to support him but was saved from the mouth of the lion by the help of the Lord. 'The Lord will deliver me (sc. "in the future") from every evil work, and will save me unto his heavenly kingdom.' Eusebius (*H.E.*II, 22, 2. 3) and many others interpret this as Paul looking back from a second imprisonment in Rome to his first imprisonment, but there is no reference here either to an imprisonment in Rome or to a release from prison. 'Defence' probably means 'strict cross-examination' in which Paul hopes to hold his own again if it is repeated. This corresponds exactly to the situation in Acts xxiii. 1–11. Paul is on the point of being offered as a sacrifice (iv. 6)—in Rome, presumably. He held his own in Jerusalem— will he be able to do the same in Rome? These thoughts fit in with the account in Acts, but this passage cannot be used in support of the hypothesis of a second Roman imprisonment. The same applies to 2 Tim. i. 16 f. One could just interpret these verses to mean that Paul is envisaged as being in Rome now, where Onesiphorus has visited him, but this would not be in agreement with the observations in 2 Tim. iv. and is therefore part of the fiction which we saw could not be upheld (see 3c above). However, we cannot assume from this passage that it is a reference back to the first imprisonment from which Paul has been released.

We can state quite plainly that the evidence of the Pastorals gives no support at all to the idea of a second Roman imprisonment. We could simply support one hypothesis with the other and say that the Pastorals can have been written by Paul only if he was set free again after a first Roman imprisonment. But we can assume that Paul was released again after his Roman imprisonment only if he is the author of the Pastorals— in other words, we find ourselves arguing in a circle.

Quite apart from the Pastorals, however, we have no convincing evidence of an extensive second period of activity by the apostle in the East. If Acts xx. 25 means that Paul is taking his leave not only of Ephesus but of all the churches in the East, this makes it quite clear that on the contrary Luke knew nothing of the apostle's being released from

Rome and undertaking a further journey to the East. This makes the hypothesis of a second imprisonment in Rome appear at least improbable, if not altogether impossible.

We have therefore no alternative but to consider the Pastorals as pseudo-Pauline. However, this does not make the attempt to understand them more difficult, but easier, because it now becomes possible to explain many things in the light of the historical situation which previously presented difficulties.

(5) *The 'Setting in Life'*. The 'setting in life' of the Pastorals can be described as the situation in which the Church can no longer count on an imminent *parousia* but has to organize its life on a long-term basis. We can see this not only in the conception of the ministry—although so far it is only a matter of instructions to invididuals—but also in the general conception of ethics.

The Pastorals give the outline of an ideal of Christian citizenship. A quiet and sober life is held up as a goal worth striving after (Tit. ii. 12), and good works are to be done (1 Tim. ii. 10). A considerable space is taken up by family ethics. Women are to be saved through child-bearing (1 Tim. ii. 15; v. 14) and children are to be correctly brought up (1 Tim. iii. 4, 12; v. 10; Tit. i. 6). The duty of caring for the older members of the family or the church is stressed (1 Tim. v. 5; viii. 16). All this means that Christians are adjusting themselves to the world, ordering their life in society and reckoning with the continuance of the Church. All these instructions are set out not simply as secular ethics, although a considerable number of them have been adopted from this sphere, but are given a Christian motive. By following this ethical teaching one will at the same time continue in the Christian tradition (2 Tim. iii. 14), direct one's conduct according to the teaching (Tit. i. 9) and so live by grace (Tit. ii. 11).

In this form this teaching is certainly not Pauline. The tension of Christian existence in the new eschatological situation has been abandoned in favour of a Christian adjustment to this world. It would be a mistake of course to describe this simply as a 'falling away', because it is really an attempt to come to terms with the changes in structure that came inevitably with the experience of time. 'If we consider the other possibility of provisionally coming to terms with a continued existence in the world, i.e., the Gnostic solution, then we can see that this citizenship is a genuine representation of an existence in the world based on faith, although the dialectic of eschatological existence is certainly no longer expressed in its original clarity.'[24]

We can see the limitation of this striving for the life of the good citizen in the matter of confession of faith. Here the possibility of suffering emerges, especially for those who hold positions of responsibility in the Church (2 Tim. iv. 5). Within the Church there are heretics, distinguished essentially by Gnostic features (cf. 1 Tim. vi. 20), but we cannot identify them with any of the familiar Gnostic systems. Their heresy is described among other things as 'fables and endless genealogies' (1 Tim. i. 4) and as 'profane and old wives' fables' (1 Tim. iv. 7). As far as their beliefs are concerned we learn that they hold that the resurrection has already taken place (2 Tim. ii. 18). Many of the features of the position adopted by the heretics can only be indirectly deduced from the attack made upon it in the Pastorals. Thus, for example, we can probably surmise that they held an attitude of ethical rigorism (1 Tim. iv. 8); the drinking of wine was probably rejected (cf. 1 Tim. v. 23) and marriage forbidden (1 Tim. iv. 14). The delineation of the heretics is made more difficult by the fact that the attack upon them is conducted in very general terms: they are represented as people who do not know what they are saying (1 Tim. i. 7; vi. 3) and often as ethically defective (1 Tim. i. 9 f., vi. 5, 10; 2 Tim. iii. 13). It is impossible to draw any direct conclusions about the heretics from this because such accusations are part of the style of the polemic against heretics. This of course makes the polemic very simple: one can reject the heretics but refuse to enter into discussion with them, which in any case only leads to strife (2 Tim. ii. 23) and is therefore useless and pointless (Tit. iii. 9). Even the positive instructions, such as those in the sphere of ethics, are not really drawn up on a theological basis. Thus, for example, rigorism in the renunciation of wine is rejected and moderation is recommended as an alternative (1 Tim. v. 23).

We can see the beginnings of an independent theological treatment of current questions in the Pastorals in the emphasis on the idea of tradition, and especially on the apostolic factor, which is still associated primarily with Paul. We can see this even from the literary aspect, in that Paul is claimed as the author of the letters. It is not merely a desire to establish a link with him, the connection is actually established. In 1 Tim. i. 12 f. the author either has Gal. i. 13–16 and 1 Cor. xv. 9 f. in mind or actually uses them as models, and the same can probably be said of Rom. i. 8–11 in 2 Tim. i. 3–5.

These 'Pauline elements' in the letters as well as the often evident

[24] Cf. *ibid.*, on 1 Tim. ii. 2.

similarity in terminology have frequently been quoted as proof of their 'authenticity', but with little justification. This is to jump to conclusions too quickly, for the presence of Pauline elements is to be expected if the aim is to adhere to the Pauline tradition. We can arrive at a correct conclusion only by asking whether the elements that do not fit into the usual Pauline framework can be by Paul. This aspect of development is what is significant here, the adoption of a considerable number of new concepts, the extent of which is without parallel in the New Testament. We cannot explain this in the light of the special situation of the Pastorals (as Pauline letters), as the attack on the heretics does not take the form of discussion and therefore cannot provide the occasion for adopting the new concepts.

It is certain that the Pastorals use older traditions to a considerable extent.[25] We can see the idea of tradition in the fact that the material is employed, and in the editorial treatment of it we can see how it is applied to present circumstances. The attempt to isolate in certain passages by means of literary criticism fragments of genuine Pauline letters can be regarded as having failed; but even if it had succeeded it would not alter the character of the Pastorals as a whole as the editorial work of a third person.

The theme of tradition can be seen most plainly in the sphere of doctrine and ministry. It is of the nature of heresy that it alters old traditions (1 Tim. i. 3; vi. 3), and therefore the vitally important thing is to hold fast to the original tradition. The apostolic teaching is something that has been entrusted to the Church (1 Tim. i. 11; Tit. i. 3); in contrast to the preaching of the heretics it is the 'sound doctrine' (1 Tim. i. 10; vi. 3; 2 Tim. i. 13; iv. 3; Tit. i. 9; ii. 1). The guarantor of this tradition is the apostle and, through him, the office-bearer. In the Pastorals we find three official designations—ἐπίσκοπος, διάκονος, πρεσβύτερος (bishop, deacon, elder), but it is difficult to determine the relationship between them. We certainly cannot speak of a three-fold hierarchy, for bishop and deacons (1 Tim. iii. 1 ff.; Tit. i. 7 ff.) are never mentioned along with the elders (1 Tim. v. 1, 17; Tit. i. 5). It is noticeable that the bishop is always referred to in the singular. We can assume therefore that designations that varied from place to place have been brought together here. This view is supported by the fact that in the Pastorals the offices are not created but assumed to be already in existence.

The emphasis lies on the fact that these existing offices are set out as being in continuity with the apostle. It is for this reason that reference is

---

[25] On these earlier traditions, see Dibelius, *op. cit.*, pp. 5 ff.

made to the practice of the laying on of hands which has mediated ministerial grace (by the hands of Paul—2 Tim. i. 6; by the hands of presbyters—1 Tim. iv. 14). The same purpose is served even more by the letter form with the naming of disciples of the apostle as those to whom the letters are addressed. It is significant that none of the official titles we find in the Pastorals is attributed to Timothy or Titus. They are really just the literary expression of the guarantee of right tradition. Timothy and Titus do the same by organizing new churches (Tit.) and establishing already existing ones (1 Tim.) in the name and by commission of Paul.

Considerably more emphasis is placed on this backward look than on the forward look along the line of succession, although the latter is not entirely absent. One can desire the office of bishop (1 Tim. iii. 1), and Timothy is not to be hasty in laying hands on anyone (1 Tim. v. 22). In other words, it is obviously envisaged that the ministry will be handed on. We can see this particularly in Tit. with its forward orientation, but this really only amounts to a reference to something that is a custom, in other words something that can be presupposed at the time the Pastorals were written. The most important thing, however, is to show that the ordering of the Church as well as its doctrine and offices are in harmony with apostolic authority, for it is this that provides the Church with its decisive argument in the battle against the heretics.

In the light of this we can attempt to determine the time at which the Pastorals were written. They were certainly not written before the third Christian generation. On the one hand, they presuppose a fairly developed form of the ministry, especially as it has already almost become a 'vocation' which one can desire (1 Tim. iii. 1). On the other hand, the letters look back not only to Paul, but also to his disciples, through whom one has a link with the apostolic period. For the time of writing of the Pastorals, therefore, we have to think of a time well into the second century.

The author could himself be an official in one of the churches, but we do not know who it was. It is unlikely that Polycarp of Smyrna[26] was the author.

BIBLIOGRAPHY

M. Dibelius, *Die Pastoralbriefe*, edited by H. Conzelmann (Lietzmann, 3 ed., 1955).
H. von Campenhausen, *Polycarp von Smyrna und die Pastoralbriefe* (1951).
E. Käsemann, 'Das Formular einer neutestamentlichen Ordinations-

[26] H. von Campenhausen, *Polycarp von Smyrna und die Pastoralbriefe* (1951).

paränese', *Neutestamentliche Studien für Rudolf Bultmann* (2 ed., 1957), pp. 261 ff. Reprinted in *Exegetische Versuche und Besinnungen*, I (1960), pp. 101 f.

W. Schmithals, 'Pastoralbriefe', in *RGG*, V, cols. 144 ff.

Commentaries: C. K. Barrett, New Clarendon Bible (1963); J. N. D. Kelly, Black (1964); W. Lock, ICC (1924); E. F. Scott, Moffatt (1936). R. Falconer, *The Pastoral Epistles* (1937).

K. Grayston and G. Herdan, 'The Authorship of the Pastorals in the Light of Statistical Linguistics', *NTS* 6 (1959–60), pp. 1 ff.

P. N. Harrison, *The Problem of the Pastoral Epistles* (1921); 'The Authorship of the Pastoral Epistles', *ET* 67 (1955–6), pp. 77 ff.

B. M. Metzger, 'A Reconsideration of Certain Arguments against the Pauline Authorship of the Pastoral Epistles', *ET* 70 (1958–9), pp. 91 ff.

C. F. D. Moule, 'The Problem of the Pastoral Epistles: a Reappraisal', *BJRL* 47, 2 (1965).

19. THE EPISTLE TO THE HEBREWS

As we shall see later, Heb. certainly cannot be regarded as pseudo-Pauline. We include it here because in the early centuries of the Church and in the Middle Ages it was regularly regarded as a Pauline epistle.

(1) *Its Literary Form.* The title 'to the Hebrews' is undoubtedly secondary. It serves, however—disregarding for the moment the specific reference to the recipients—to characterize the document as a letter and to assimilate it formally to the Pauline letters by referring to recipients in a particular area, which is a feature otherwise peculiar to the Pauline letters. But can we really call it a 'letter'? The conclusion, where we are told that the author has written briefly to his readers (xiii. 22–25), suggests that we can reasonably do so. Besides, quite apart from the greeting, there are a number of observations which clearly suggest a letter. On the other hand, it is surprising that it begins without a preface. It has sometimes been supposed that this is connected with the near-eastern letter form, which was a development from the oral message in which the messenger expressed the greeting and then delivered the substance of the message. If this message was given to the messenger in writing, he would read it aloud after he had delivered the greeting, but if the message was sent without a special messenger the address was written on the cover. In the letter itself, therefore, the preface was sometimes omitted and it has therefore been suggested that it would not necessarily be felt that anything was missing at the beginning of Heb.

This assumption, however, still presents certain difficulties. i. 1–xiii. 21 is really lacking in any features that suggest a letter. The work is described in xiii. 22, i.e. in the conclusion, as λόγος τῆς παρακλήσεως (word of exhortation), and it concludes with a doxology (xiii. 20 f.). If we omit the short section that follows, the description that most readily springs to mind for i. 1–xiii. 21 is that of a 'treatise'. But as the style, train of thought and method of argument show many parallels with the form of the Jewish–Hellenistic homily, an even better description for i.1–xiii. 21 would be that of a 'sermon'. In any case the author was obviously familiar with the rhetorical rules of synagogue preaching. If what we have here is really the form of the homily—and this theory is mostly accepted nowadays—then the lack of a preface is no longer surprising and the ending in xiii. 21 also becomes intelligible.

At the same time we must note that a number of other questions which are closely connected with the points we have just considered still have to be left open. If we assume that the homily was later dispatched and therefore was given an ending appropriate to a letter, we still do not know, for example, whether the author of the homily is to be identified with the author of the conclusion. It is possible that an overseer absent from his church might have added a few personal remarks to a homily which he had either delivered himself or borrowed. In this case when copying out the homily he would no doubt introduce his personal mesasge before the doxology (cf. xiii. 18 f. and xiii. 23). On the other hand, however, we cannot be certain whether this homily was ever delivered orally. It is possible to imagine circumstances in which the author might have composed his work in the literary form of the synagogue sermon, although he thought of it from the start as a 'letter', but if this were the case it would be difficult to understand why his 'homily' says much less about the readers and their situation than one would expect in a document addressed to a particular circle of readers. Finally, we must allow for the possibility that xiii. 22–25 is purely fictitious in character. The problem then would be very similar to the one presented by Eph. (cf. section 18, 2), where a treatise was used for the composition of an epistle, whereas in the case of Heb. it is a homily. In this case we should not think in terms of any particular 'recipients' of the letter who can be geographically located, but of 'readers' whose particular situations vary greatly but have general features in common. In other words, the author is addressing his own times in his homily. We cannot be certain which of these possibilities is the correct one—and it is possible of course to combine some of them—but the last one mentioned seems the most likely.

(2) *The Readers.* The information provided by the closing verses is not at all clear. If it is not fictional, then all we learn is that at the time the writer was away from his own church. xiii. 18 f. could be taken as an indication that the separation was not of his own will. The author is awaiting the arrival of Timothy who has either already set off to come to him or has been released—from prison somewhere—and is on his way (both translations of xiii. 23 are possible). When he arrives the author intends to come with him to the church. The information given in xiii. 23 sounds much more reliable than that given in xiii. 18 f. Was the conclusion written later, or is it simply that the statements are not made to harmonize completely because the letter form is merely a fiction? The readers are thought of—in spite of xiii. 17—as needing encouragement

from outside. The statement that 'they of Italy' send greetings (xiii. 24) does not allow us to draw any definite conclusions about the place to which the readers belonged, as all we are told is that people from Italy are staying with the author. If they were compatriots of the readers, the author would presumably have expressed himself differently. It seems more reasonable to assume that the writer himself is in Italy, as Italians are the only ones from whom greetings are conveyed. We can only leave the question open. The fact that Heb. is quoted in 1 Clem., which was written from Rome, does not really help us, as this would be possible whether the letter was sent to Rome or whether it was written from Italy. There are also other ways in which it could have arrived there.

Although the somewhat colourless conclusion does not allow us to determine where the author is writing to, the 'homily' makes very clear for us the situation in which the author sees his readers: they are in a situation of extreme danger. The reason for this is to be found in the first place in the persecutions which the readers have experienced. Some have had to endure a hard and painful conflict, and others have been witnesses of the sufferings of their fellow-believers (x. 32–34). It is possible that some of the leaders have suffered martyrdom (xiii. 7—but the exegesis of this passage is uncertain). In any case these persecutions have faced the readers with temptation. They have seen that some have already 'forsaken the assembling together' and have therefore fallen away (x. 25). The danger of apostasy, however, also confronts those who have remained in the Church (iii. 12). Such apostasy would mean final loss, for, after the first repentance in baptism or on becoming a Christian, there is no possibility of a second repentance (vi. 4–6; cf. xii. 17). Therefore the author has again to teach the oracles of God to his readers who have already been Christians for a long time and could themselves have been teachers, because they have become dull of hearing (v. 11–13). It is to this situation that the author addresses his 'word of exhortation'.

(3) *The Theme of the 'Word of Exhortation'.* The peculiar concepts in which the author expresses his message, which are to a large extent unique in the context of the New Testament, can only be understood when we remember all the time the particular readers the author has in mind. Attention has often been drawn to the special Christology of Heb. It is true that in many respects it is unusual, but we would be interpreting the author's message wrongly, or at least in an unbalanced way, if we were to assume that he was interested in Christological speculations. His approach is far more from the soteriological angle. His aim is to give direct help to his

readers, and he seeks to achieve this by approaching Christology from the soteriological standpoint. By expounding Christology 'ecclesiologically' he reminds his readers of who they are, namely the 'pilgrim people of God' (Käsemann) who are travelling along the same road that the Son of God has already walked as the High Priest of the Church.

It is obvious that the author makes use of a familiar baptismal confession (cf. iii. 1; iv. 14; x. 19 ff.),[27] which he applies by way of interpretation to the situation of the church. He begins with the declaration of the glory of the Son of God who is now exalted over all, expressed in hymn-like language (ch. i), but he immediately goes on to speak also of his humiliation. He who has now reached the goal was made like men in the days of his flesh (ii. 14) and can therefore call them 'brethren' (ii. 11). He became like them in all things (iii. 17), and was tempted like a man—but without falling into sin (iv. 15). In his suffering he robbed death of its power and won redemption (ii. 14 f.). Then he was exalted, and as High Priest represents his people before God (ii. 17; iv. 15; vii. 26, etc.).

If the readers are obedient to this High Priest, who himself learned obedience in his sufferings (v. 8 f.), and if they hold fast to their confession of faith in him (iv. 14), then together with the witnesses of faith under the old covenant (ch. xi) they are on the way to the glory of heaven. Faith is defined as 'the assurance of things hoped for, the proving of things not seen' (xi. 1), which is not a complete definition of faith but is understandable in the context of the situation in which the readers find themselves, for it is a fact that they have nothing to see. But if they exercise obedience, in other words, if they lay aside everything that is a burden to them and run with patience the course that is appointed them, they will be travelling the same way as him 'who for the joy that was set before him endured the cross' (xii. 1–2). As a result he is the 'captain of their salvation' (ii. 10), the 'author of eternal salvation' (v. 9), the 'author and perfector of faith' (xii. 2).

The standpoint of Heb. has a great structural similarity to that of Rev., but whereas the latter belongs to apocalyptic literature (cf. section 27), Heb. has links with Gnostic mythology. It is not bound by this, because it emphasizes the element of ἐφάπαξ, the once-for-allness of the cross of Jesus and his entry into glory (vii. 27; ix. 12), to which the once-for-allness of the 'sanctification' bestowed upon Christians corresponds (x. 10). The important thing is not to think of the unique events merely as some-

---

[27] G. Bornkamm, 'Das Bekenntnis im Hebräerbrief', *ThBl* (1942), pp. 56 ff. Reprinted in *Studien zu Antike und Urchristentum* (1959), pp. 188 ff.

thing that happened in the past, but to take one's stand upon them now. The readers' gaze is directed to the consummation—in Heb. by the adoption of Gnostic motifs, in Rev. by the adoption of apocalyptic motifs —in order that they will be able to endure in the midst of all that threatens them and continue on their journey with confidence.

When we come to exegesis it is very important to bear this general pattern of the message in mind. If we begin to divide Heb. into 'pericopae' when it is meant to be read as a whole, we fall into the danger not only of losing sight of the unity of its message but also of indulging in a variety of speculations which may be able to claim support in the material the author used or borrowed from, but not in the actual message he expressed with the aid of this material.

(4) *Authorship, Time and Place of Composition.* Heb. has come down to us anonymously. At a quite early date people began speculating about the probable author. The ancient Church of the East considered it a Pauline letter. Clement of Alexandria held that the apostle had written it in Hebrew, and that Luke had then translated it into Greek (Eusebius, *H.E.*VI 14, 2). In the West Barnabas was at first thought to be the author (Tertullian), and it was not until the fourth century that the Pauline authorship was generally accepted—which was an important reason for the admission of Heb. to the Canon. At a later period, however, opinions diverged again. Doubts concerning the Pauline authorship in the sixteenth century (e.g. Erasmus, Luther, Calvin) were dealt with by the Council of Trent, which asserted it afresh, although this was weakened again in 1914 by the Papal Biblical Commission to the extent that it decided that it need not be held that the apostle had given the letter its present form.

We can say without any doubt that Heb. is not a translation from Hebrew, but was written in Greek. There is nothing to indicate any close connection with Paul. Indeed, all the names that have been suggested or could be suggested are mere supposition, and it is unlikely that they would have much bearing on the exegesis of the work. As we know it now Heb. is like Melchizedek (vii. 3), 'without father, without mother, without genealogy' (Overbeck).

Heb. must have been written before A.D. 96, as 1 Clem. quotes it, though without referring to it specifically. It cannot have been written much before then, as it looks back to persecutions that have taken place. The fact that in spite of references to the Old Testament sacrificial cult there is no mention of the destruction of the Temple is no reason to suggest a date before A.D. 70, as the point at issue is theological, not historical.

We cannot be certain about the place of writing or the place to which the recipients, intended or actual, belong (cf. 2 above). The work was most probably described as the Epistle to the 'Hebrews' because it deals with the Israelite–Jewish cult, but this is by no means a compelling argument; nor does the extensive use of the Old Testament justify the assumption that Heb. was intended only for Jewish–Christian readers. It is truer to say that it is addressed quite generally to Christians, regardless of whether their background was Gentile or Jewish.

BIBLIOGRAPHY

O. Michel, *Der Brief an die Hebräer* (Meyer, 11 ed., 1960).

E. Käsemann, *Das wandernde Gottesvolk* (4 ed., 1961).

Commentaries: J. Moffatt, ICC (1924); H. W. Montefiore, Black (1964):
    T. H. Robinson, Moffatt (1933).

F. V. Filson, '*Yesterday*' (1967).

W. Manson, *The Epistle to the Hebrews* (1953).

F. C. Synge, *Hebrews and the Scriptures* (1959).

IV. The Church Epistles

Among the twenty-one letters in the New Testament there are seven that are generally referred to as the 'Catholic epistles'; in contrast to the Pauline and pseudo-Pauline letters these are the letters which are not described by the recipients for which they were intended, but bear the name of the author, or supposed author—i.e. James, 1 Peter, Jude, 2 Peter, 1, 2 and 3 John.

The name 'Catholic' was applied to these letters at an early stage. Eusebius speaks of the 'so-called' Catholic epistles, and so makes it clear that he is merely using the customary name. The word 'Catholic' here is not synonymous with 'Canonical', although this identification was made later in the West, but means 'general', in other words, addressed to all Christians. In *Das Neue Testament Deutsch* these letters have recently come to be described as *Kirchenbriefe* (Church epistles), which is a better description, as it is less open to misunderstanding. It is not altogether appropriate as a title, as some of the letters do define the intended recipients more specifically (1 Pet., 2 and 3 John). Only Jas., Jude and 2 Pet. can be described as truly 'Catholic' at least as far as their prefaces are concerned.

These Church epistles were all written later than the other epistles in the New Testament, in particular later than those of Paul. In the early lists of canonical books we mostly find the following order: Gospels, Acts, Catholic epistles (with James usually placed first), Pauline epistles, Revelation. This is obviously meant to emphasize that the 'early apostles' come before Paul, chronologically at least, and perhaps also in status. In this case, however, it would seem strange that the early apostles should write 'to the Church' whereas Paul only writes to individual churches and people. The development was much more likely to be in the opposite direction. First came the specific letter to particular churches and then the general letter or encyclical addressed to all. This is also in harmony with the observations we made earlier to the effect that Eph. or the Pastorals, in contrast to the Pauline epistles, are 'on the way' to becoming Church epistles—in fact in some respects we could go so far as to include them under this heading. Thus we can see how the letter approaches the epistle, or actually turns into the epistle.

This does not mean of course that no letters were written in the later period. Quite a number of them have in fact been preserved, e.g. 1 Clem., the letters of Ignatius and Polycarp, etc. These, however, are directed to a definite address and are also sent in the name of the actual author. But if one wishes to continue the 'apostolic tradition' in literary form, one can no longer write 'letters' because the old recipients are no longer alive. This means therefore that the Church epistles, precisely because of their literary character, cannot be anything other than pseudonymous documents. Their pseudonymity springs from the underlying theological aim—to keep alive the apostolic tradition in a later period.

We can now see how the Church epistles prepare the way for the Canon, and they do this precisely through the authors' names which they bear. In later times the Church can defend itself against heresies and eccentric traditions by pointing to its own *apostolic* tradition. We can see this happening already in these epistles—although with varying emphasis —in the fact that an 'apostle' is claimed as the author. And later when the problem of fixing the Canon arose this question of authorship played an important part. Although we may wish to question some of the individual decisions that were then made (cf. esp. section 19) the aim was certainly the correct one. Only the apostolic Church can be the Church of Jesus Christ.

Q

20. THE EPISTLE OF JAMES

Opinions concerning this document vary greatly, as regards both its antiquity and also its authorship and literary character.

(1) *Contents.* We are struck immediately by the fact that there seems to be no particular pattern, at least as far as the contents are concerned. After the preface to the letter (i. 1) there follows a variety of exhortations to persevere in the right conduct of life (i. 2 -v. 20). Mention is made of withstanding temptation (i. 2–18) and of hearing and doing the Word (i. 19–27); in dealing with one's neighbour one should not allow oneself to be influenced by bias (ii. 1–13). The most important section for the general assessment of the letter is the passage concerning faith and works (ii. 14–26). The question whether faith without works can save (ii. 14) at first seems very strange in view of the Pauline teaching, but when we read in ii. 19 that even the devils believe it becomes clear that 'faith' is not thought of here in its personal aspect (faith in God) but rather in the theoretical sense as belief in the existence of God (monotheism). This 'faith in certain facts' simply in the sense of holding something to be true is different from the faith of which Paul speaks. The undoubtedly polemical statement in ii. 24 may therefore be aimed against Rom. iii. 28, but it is questionable whether, on account of the different interpretations of 'faith' we can consider it as a real polemic.

iii. 1–12 contains a warning concerning sinning with the tongue; iii. 13–18 speaks of what constitutes true wisdom; iv. 1–12 warns against enmity with God, and iv. 13–17 against the folly of planning too far ahead. The so-called *conditio Jacobea* (iv. 15) is not specifically Christian. There are pagan parallels to it, and it gives a quite general warning about thoughtlessly looking beyond the present in one's plans. After a few sentences about the danger of wealth (v. 1–6) there follow exhortations concerning the *parousia* (v. 7–11), the swearing of oaths (v. 12), misfortune and illness (v. 13–15). There is a command to confess sins to one another (v. 16), a reference to the power of prayer (v. 17 f.) and an exhortation to correct brethren who have gone astray (v. 19 f.). There is no formal conclusion.

It is significant for the letter as a whole that in the 108 verses it contains there are fifty-four imperatives (Jülicher-Fascher). In other words, it is made up of a series of paranetic passages.

(2) *Its Literary Character.* We must note first that Jas. is presented to us in the form of a letter. The preface reads: 'James, a servant of God and of the Lord Jesus Christ, to the twelve tribes which are of the Dispersion, greeting' (i. 1). Apart from Acts xv. 23 and xxiii. 26 this is the only example of a purely Greek preface to a letter in the New Testament. Apart from this introduction, however, the document does not seem to possess anything of the character of a letter. Attempts have been made to discover in it a reference to the actual circumstances of the recipients. Michaelis[1] goes so far as to speak of a 'limited circle of recipients', but the passages he mentions in this connection (e.g. ii. 2 ff; iii. 1 f.; iv. 13; v. 1 ff.) are expressed in much too general a way for them to have arisen from any particular situation. 'It is a didactic and paranetic document made up of series of aphorisms and short treatises' (Feine-Behm). Without altering the general character of the document the title could equally well read: 'Teaching (διδαχή) of James for the twelve tribes which are of the Dispersion',[2] in which case it would have shown a formal similarity to the title of the Didache, which begins with the words: 'Teaching of the twelve apostles'.

The material that is used comes from a great variety of sources. Twenty-six instances of borrowings from material in the Synoptic Gospels have been counted,[3] and in addition there are ancient Jewish sayings, echoes of Proverbs, Ben Sirach and the Wisdom of Solomon. Use is also made of Greek and Hellenistic paranetic traditions, and there are echoes of similar passages in Paul. We cannot of course assume that there was direct dependence in all these cases, for paranetic traditions were very widespread, overlapped in the various cultures and religions and influenced one another considerably. The author succeeds, not least by his gift as a writer—Jas. is written in good Greek—in binding together in a relatively compact way material which is very varied in origin.

The surprising fact that the name of Jesus Christ occurs only twice in the whole document (i. 1; ii. 1), and that it could be removed from the context relatively easily and without causing any disruption—in ii. 1 in fact this would avoid a certain tautology—has led to the supposition that what was originally a non-Christian writing was later 'christianized' by inserting the name of Jesus Christ.[4] The whole document in fact contains no specifically Christian ideas (although ii. 14–26 can only be understood

---

[1] *Einleitung in das Neue Testament* (3 ed., 1962), p. 275.

[2] H. Windisch, *Die katholischen Briefe* in Lietzmann (3 ed., 1951), p. 3.

[3] G. Kittel, 'Der geschichtliche Ort des Jakobusbriefes', *ZNW* (1942), pp. 71 ff.

[4] F. Spitta, 'Der Brief des Jakobus' in *Zur Geschichte und Litteratur des Urchristentums*, II (1896), pp. 1 ff. A. Harnack, *Geschichte der altchristlichen Literatur*, II, 1 (1897), pp. 485 ff.

against the background of Pauline theology), and when the *parousia* is mentioned (v. 7 ff.) the context suggests that the reference is to the coming of the Lord God of Sabaoth rather than to the coming of Jesus Christ, which is very surprising in a Christian document. Therefore there seems to be at least some ground for assuming that there was a pre-Christian source.

There is a further point to be considered regarding the source. A. Meyer[5] made the suggestion that it was a Jewish–Hellenistic document which gave an allegorical interpretation of the names of the sons of Jacob by means of a Jewish onomasticon. For a comparison one could consider the Blessing of Jacob (Gen. xlix.) or the Testaments of the Twelve Patriarchs. Suggested examples are that the heavenly and earthly wisdom (iii. 5–17) are an allusion to Leah and Rachel, that Judah is the κύριος τῆς δόξης (Lord of glory, ii. 1) and Reuben the ἀπαρχή (the first fruits, i. 18). It has to be admitted, however, that these parallels cannot be traced with any degree of certainty, and that it would be very difficult to reconstruct the source with any accuracy. On the other hand, the suggestions are so striking that we must at least consider whether this onomasticon provided the pattern for the assembling of the various paranetic traditions at an early stage of the tradition.

Whatever opinion we arrive at concerning the question of the source, it is undeniable that the final editor has done very little to 'christianize' his traditions. This means that it is possible to make a two-fold exegesis —we can consider the meaning of the source and also the meaning the editor aimed to convey in using the source. There is no doubt that his aim is to give it a Christian interpretation, although he hardly ever, or only rarely, makes it clear how he sees the Christian bearing of any particular passage. Thus, for example, the statement about the *parousia* (v. 7 ff.) is open to misunderstanding, although we can assume that when he speaks of the *parousia* of the Lord the editor has the *parousia* of Christ in mind.

(3) *The 'Readers'*. What can we say about the recipients or readers for whom the letter was meant? It is possible to interpret the phrase 'the twelve tribes which are of the Dispersion' in three ways. It could refer to Jews living outside Palestine (after A.D. 70 or 135 this would mean the whole Jewish people), but this explanation is ruled out by the fact that Jas. is not a missionary document. The other possibilities are that it refers either to the Jewish Christians living in the Dispersion or to all Christians,

[5] *Das Rätsel des Jakobusbriefes* (1930).

thought of as the 'true Israel'. In either case, however, the 'address' is strange for a Christian document.

The difficulty resolves itself if we consider the possibility that parts of the preface may have come from the source. In a Jewish writing about the patriarchs the mention of the twelve tribes could have had a definite significance, but if the Christian editor took over the wording as he found it, then—while still maintaining the wording—he may well have interpreted the twelve tribes of the Dispersion as standing for the Church which lives dispersed—in the theological rather than the geographical sense, as in 1 Pet. i. 1. In this case the address would indeed be 'catholic'.

(4) *The Question of Authorship.* Similar factors have to be considered in trying to determine the question of authorship and that of the time of writing. If we start by considering the name Jesus, then of the five men who bear this name in the New Testament James the son of Zebedee and James the brother of Jesus seem the only possibilities. However, James the son of Zebedee has to be excluded, as he died as a martyr about A.D. 44 (cf. Acts xii. 2) and the letter cannot have been written so early. If, on the other hand, we assume the brother of Jesus to have been the author this gives rise to certain discrepancies between what we know of him and the contents of the letter. It contains no mention of the problem of the ritual laws (whereas, as far as James the brother of the Lord was concerned, see Gal. ii. 12) and speaks quite simply of the 'law of liberty' (i. 25; ii. 12) that consists in morally good deeds and, according to ii. 8, is the royal law. Pure and undefiled 'religion' in the sight of God the Father consists in visiting widows and orphans in need and preserving oneself undefiled by the world (i. 27). In other words, there is no trace of cultic ritualism; the attitude to the Law could be best described as 'prophetic', an attitude akin to that of Amos.

We have already seen some of the difficulties that arise if we assume the Lord's brother to have been the author, but it becomes obvious that this assumption is quite out of the question if we go on to consider the relationship of this document to Paul. The discussion about faith and works (ii. 14–26) is only conceivable in the post-Pauline period, for as far as we know it was Paul who first raised the problem in this form.[6] We have already described ii. 24 as being polemically directed against Rom. iii. 28, and this is made clear particularly by the fact that the word μόνον (alone) which is missing in Paul—but is really understood—is explicitly included here. We have to be clear of course as to what we

[6] M. Dibelius, *Der Brief des Jakobus* in Meyer (10 ed., 1959), pp. 163 ff.

mean by a 'polemical' expression.[7] Faith for Paul always implies obedience. Faith in Christ leads the Christian not only into a new existence, but also into a new way of living not thought of as something separate, but as directly connected with the former—in other words, into a form of conduct resulting from faith. Rom. iii. 28 is valid only on this presupposition. But if the concept of faith changes, so that faith is limited to the acceptance of doctrines (cf. ii. 19), then Paul's formula naturally becomes distorted, for the consequence would be libertinism or at least ethical indifferentism.

It would be quite wrong to make the author responsible for this reduced understanding of faith. This is something that he finds already in existence. What he attacks is the idea that the Pauline formula should be accepted as valid with *this* interpretation of faith (cf. the criticism of antinomianism in Mt. v. 17 ff.; vii. 15 ff.; xxiv. 11 ff.). This polemic could in theory follow two lines. The author could have corrected the concept of faith, or he could correct the existing situation by starting from the current concept of faith and carrying it in its reduced form ad absurdum (N.B. ii. 19). The author adopts the second course and brings out what Paul means by faith by means of an addition. In other words, what Paul signifies by 'faith' can now be expressed only by 'faith *and works*': the element of obedience, which is implicit in the Pauline concept of faith has become separated from the concept of faith and is now added by the author as an independent entity—as 'works'.

There is a danger of course in adopting such a procedure. The question arises as to what the basis of works is in Jas. It cannot be faith, as faith means little more than belonging to the Church and believing the same things (N.B. not: in the same person) as the Church. In this case, however, there is no genuine Indicative to provide a basis for the Imperative. By adding together faith and works in this way the author does not create a real inner connection between the two. Faith is not really anything special, as even devils can have faith. The danger that emerges here, therefore, is that of an isolated ethics, a pure nominalism. Basically faith is only a view of the world, or of God, and one has to allow for the possibility that there can be works without faith—but the author does not raise this problem, therefore we cannot know what his attitude to it is. His aim is to lead believers—i.e. members of the Church—to do good works; but as he cannot base works in faith his ethical teaching runs the danger of becoming mere morality.

[7] For a fuller treatment, see the author's *Der 'Frühkatholizismus' im Neuen Testament* (1958), pp. 22 ff.

There is another respect in which the author's procedure is a dangerous one—that he abandons, though quite unintentionally, Paul's teachings. The false concept of faith is recognized as a possible one—but from this position it is difficult to arrive at a proper understanding of what Paul means.

When we remember these two dangers, we can understand why Luther described Jas. as an 'epistle full of straw'. Nevertheless, however difficult the attempt may be, we must not forget the author's own approach. His aim is to bring back a Paulinism that has been misinterpreted and distorted to the truly Pauline position. He is seeking to make it clear that Christian faith must be living, active, creative faith—he does not go into the reason why, but merely emphasizes the fact that it must be. It is possible that he is restricted, among other things by the fact that he is dependent on an existing paranetic tradition. All the evidence points to the fact that the document in its present—edited—form is much later than the Pauline epistles. The attempt has sometimes been made (by Michaelis, for example) to reverse the order Paul—Jas. and so make Jas. the earliest letter in the New Testament, but this does not really make sense, as there is no question of any polemic against Jas. in Paul.

As the document has to be considered post-Pauline it cannot have been written by James the brother of the Lord, as he died as a martyr about A.D. 62 (cf. Josephus, *Ant.* xx. 200). This does not mean, of course, that we have to assume any deliberate pseudonymity here. If it is correct to surmise that a writing by James forms the basis of the document as we know it, then the name of James rightly belongs to it, and is therefore not a pseudonym in the sense in which the name of Paul is in the Pastorals, Eph., Col., etc., i.e. a pseudonym deliberately chosen, but one that became such only because it was simply assumed. It is possible therefore that the author had a particular James in mind—and there is no reason why it should not have been the Lord's brother that he was thinking of.

For a long time there was no reference to Jas. in the early Church. Neither the Muratorian Canon nor Tertullian nor Cyprian mentions it. The first definite reference to it in the East is in Origen, but Eusebius (*H.E.*II 23, 24 f.; cf. III 25, 3) does not accept it as genuine. It is difficult to suggest a date for its composition, but it was probably written about the turn of the first century.

BIBLIOGRAPHY

M. Dibelius, *Der Brief des Jakobus* (Meyer, 10 ed., 1959).
H. Windisch, *Die katholischen Briefe* (Lietzmann, 3 ed., 1951).

K. Aland, 'Der Herrenbruder Jakobus und der Jakobusbrief', *ThLZ* (1944), pp. 97 ff.

K. Aland, 'Jakobusbrief' in *RGG*, III, cols. 526 ff.

G. Kittel, 'Der geschichtliche Ort des Jakobusbriefes', *ZNW* (1942), pp. 71 ff.

A. Meyer, *Das Rätsel des Jakobusbriefes* (1930).

Commentaries: J. B. Mayor (1892); J. Moffatt (The General Epistles), Moffatt (1928); J. H. Ropes, ICC (1916).

L. E. Elliott-Binns, *Galilean Christianity* (1956), pp. 45 ff.

J. Jeremias, 'Paul and James', *ET* 66 (1954–5), pp. 368 ff.

W. L. Knox, 'The Epistle of St. James', *JTS* 46 (1945), pp. 10 ff.

M. H. Shepherd, 'The Epistle of St. James and the Gospel of Matthew', *JBL* 75 (1956), pp. 40 ff.

21. THE FIRST EPISTLE OF PETER

(1) *Contents.* As the document lacks any obvious arrangement of its material, it is not easy to analyse its structure. The salutation (i. 1–2) and postscript (v. 12–14) in particular give it the appearance of a letter, but much of it reads more like an exhortatory address. The preface (i. 1–2) names as the sender Peter, the apostle of Jesus Christ, and as the recipients 'the elect who are sojourners of the Dispersion in Pontus, Galatia, Cappadocia, Asia and Bithynia', in other words, Christians who live in Asia Minor. The names are those of Roman provinces and regions in Asia Minor.

The letter begins (i. 3–12) with an ascription of praise to God, through whom the readers have been born again to a living hope that cannot be dimmed by suffering, to the hope of a glorious salvation based on the resurrection of Jesus Christ from the dead. This is followed by a series of exhortations. The rebirth should be expressed in holy living (i. 13–21), in unfeigned love of the brethren (i. 22–25) and in putting away all vice (ii. 1–10). Here, as also later, the Imperatives are always based on a variety of Indicatives. From ii. 11 onwards the exhortations become more specific. They deal with the Christian's conduct in the world (ii. 11–12), subjection to the authorities (13–17) and patient obedience which is prepared even to bear injustice (18–25). Women (iii. 1–6) and men (7) are addressed in a kind of list of household responsibilities, and then all the members of the Church are exhorted to deal kindly with one another (iii. 8–12). Such a way of life may possibly lead to suffering (iii. 13–17), but this can be borne (iii. 18–22) if we remember Christ and the path he took (reference to his death for sins and his 'descent'). A complete rejection of the old way of life is called for (iv. 1–3), and one will have to put up with the amazement of one's former acquaintances who have remained pagans (iv. 4–6). The letter now seems to be drawing to a close. After a reminder that the end of all things is at hand, the command to love is emphasized again and the readers are encouraged to exercise hospitality. The message is summed up in the demand that all that one does and says should be done and said as in God's sight, and this exhortation then leads into a doxology (iv. 7–11).

However, the letter starts up again. The churches must hold out in the present fiery ordeal of persecution, for suffering is honour so long as one suffers as a Christian and not as a criminal (iv. 12–19). There follows a further list of duties, in which the 'elders' (v. 1–4) and the younger members (5a) are exhorted and reminded to show humility towards one another, particularly in view of the 'roaring lion' that is going around (v. 5b–9). A blessing and doxology (v. 10–11) are followed by the conclusion (12–14) which mentions Silvanus as the amanuensis and conveys greetings from 'she (i.e. the church) that is in Babylon, elect together with you', and from Mark, who is described as the author's 'son'.

(2) *The Literary Problem*. When we recognize that this 'letter' has the very marked features of an exhortatory address—especially because of the way it uses paranetic material which in part at least was already in existence in oral or written form—the question arises whether the author of this document drew his material directly from the paranetic tradition, or whether we can trace any of the preliminary stages as the tradition took literary form.

A starting-point is provided by the clearly recognizable break after iv. 11. It is striking not only from the literary point of view, for there also seem to be differences in content before and after it. The most remarkable difference is the position as regards suffering. In i. 3–iv. 11 it is described as a possibility (i. 6), arising from the new kind of behaviour of Christians in their old pagan surroundings (iv. 4; cf. iii. 14). There is no suggestion at all that this 'suffering' is the result of persecutions (iii. 17), but after the break the position is quite different. Straightaway in iv. 12 there is reference to the present 'fiery trial', which clearly means persecution, and we are told later that this has befallen not only those to whom the letter is addressed, but Christians everywhere (v. 8 f.). These different emphases can hardly be accidental, and therefore it has been assumed—correctly—that i. 3–iv. 11 represents the original and that it was expanded by iv. 12 ff. at a later stage.

It is possible to characterize this earlier section even more closely. One of its features is the frequent occurrence of baptismal themes and this has led to the suggestion that it was perhaps originally a baptismal homily,[8] in which the hearers were addressed as those whom God has caused to be born again (i. 3, 22 f.) and who through baptism are like newborn children (ii. 2). Previously they were sheep who had gone astray, but now they have been brought back to the 'Shepherd and Bishop of (their) souls' (ii. 25). Finally the salvation of Noah by means of water is described as a type of baptism (iii. 20), and the image is then applied directly

---

[8] R. Perdelwitz, *Die Mysterienreligion und das Problem des 1. Petrusbriefes* (1911).

to the hearers (21). The whole section can therefore be interpreted as a baptismal exhortation, and the peculiar announcement of suffering, not thought of yet as direct persecution but as arising simply from surprise and derision from one's old associates (ii. 7 f.; iii. 16; iv. 4), fits into such a context. The way in which the old and the new way of life are contrasted in this address (i. 14; ii. 1 f.; iv. 2 f.) is also significant, as is also the way in which the new life is thought of as a sojourn in a strange land and as a pilgrimage (i. 17; ii. 11).

The theory that an original baptismal address can be traced in i. 3–iv. 11 has been modified along two lines. On the one hand Bornemann[9] suggested that the baptismal address extended as far as v. 11, but one difficulty is that this would mean that the differences in the treatment of suffering would be present in the address itself. iv. 12 ff. appears to be a later realization of what was previously set out. Preisker,[10] on the other hand, assumes that i. 3–v. 11 is derived from a primitive Christian baptismal liturgy and suggests that the various sections were spoken by different officials in the course of the service: a prayer-hymn (i. 3–12) and instruction (i. 13–21); then followed the baptism, which however is not mentioned because of its nature as a mystery; after the 'baptismal dedication' (i. 22–25) there was a festal song of three strophes (ii. 1–10), an exhortation (ii. 11–12) and a revelation (ii. 13–iv. 7a). The original final prayer has not been preserved, but was exchanged for a 'substitute suggestive of a letter' (iv. 7b–12). The baptismal service was then followed by the concluding liturgy of the whole congregation, which included a further revelation (iv. 12–19), an exhortation (v. 1–9), the blessing and the doxology (v. 10–11). This explanation, however, gives rise to considerable difficulties. Would we not expect the baptism to have been mentioned? It seems rather improbable that it should be left out because it was considered a mystery. And when Preisker goes on to explain the different treatment of suffering by suggesting that first the baptismal candidates are addressed, to whom suffering is presented only as a possibility, and then the whole congregation, who have already experienced suffering, he seems to overlook the fact that 'suffering' in the section i. 3–iv. 11 presupposes a quite different situation in the church from the suffering under persecution in iv. 12 ff.

(3) *The Editorial Process.* In a period when the Church in the world (v. 9) is suffering persecution the author takes up an older baptismal address or

[9] 'Der erste Petrusbrief—eine Taufrede des Silvanus?', *ZNW* (1919–20), pp. 143 ff.
[10] Appendix to H. Windisch, *Die katholischen Briefe*, pp. 156 ff.

exhortation and uses it to bring comfort to his readers. This means that in the context of the document as we know it i. 3–iv. 11 is really a reminder of baptism, which is meant to strengthen the readers to endure and hold fast in the persecution which is now taking place.

It is more than unlikely for a number of reasons that Peter was the author of this work. The contents do not reveal a 'Petrine character' in any way. If the name were missing from the preface, one would be much more likely to suspect that the author was a disciple of Paul on account of the terminology and train of thought. This document is like 2 Thess., Eph., Col. and the Pastorals in that it draws on Pauline theology at a number of points, and we would therefore have good grounds for calling it 'pseudo-Pauline'. This makes it very difficult to conceive of Peter as the author.

It is also striking that the recipients mentioned in the preface live in the missionary region associated with Paul and are clearly thought of as Gentile Christians. It would be difficult to evolve theories to explain why Peter should have written a letter to such people; besides, it would make him appear in a strange light, in view of Gal. ii. 7. The very fluent Greek of this work—and there is no question of its being a translation—and the general use that is made of the LXX are further reasons for doubting the Petrine authorship.

We have still not considered the secretary theory which assumes that Silvanus wrote the letter at Peter's request (v. 12). This would no doubt dispose of certain arguments, particularly those based on the language of the letter which rule out the Petrine authorship, but it would still not explain the reference to the recipients. This in fact presents considerable problems for another reason. The document gives the impression throughout of being written not to a number of churches but only to one. We would expect to find this in ii. 18 ff. and iii. 1 ff., 7, 8 ff. if we suppose that a baptismal address is being used here—but we get the same impression in ch. v. Besides, the preface does not address itself to 'churches' but to 'the Christians in Asia Minor'. In this case, how could a 'letter' have been dispatched and delivered? It is probably better to think of it as a 'manifesto', and then it is easy to understand how at a later date the authority of Peter was claimed for it.

This is underlined by the reference to the place of writing in the conclusion (v. 13). 'Babylon' does not mean either the city in Mesopotamia or the garrison town of the same name in the Nile delta, but stands for Rome (cf. Rev. xiv. 8). This pseudonym arose, however, in connection with the persecution of Christians by the Roman state, which strengthens the supposition that this document came into being as a result of the situation in which the Church was being persecuted. As according to the ancient tradition of the Church Mark served as Peter's companion and interpreter in Rome (cf. section 12), it is not difficult to understand why his name should be mentioned as sharing in the greetings.

The instruction to the elders not to exercise oversight of the church for personal gain (v. 2) also suggests a later date for the letter. The description of Peter as μάρτυς (witness) of the sufferings of Christ (v. 1) could be an allusion to his death as a martyr. The document cannot have been written as early as the time of Nero, as the persecutions of the Christians that took place then were not universal. The reference is more likely to be to the persecutions under Domitian (A.D. 81–96) which afflicted Rome and the East, or even to those under Trajan (A.D. 98–117).

In making an exegesis of this manifesto we need to bear in mind that two lines of approach are possible as far as the section i. 3–iv. 11 is concerned. We can expound it—regardless of its present context—as an address to newly baptized Christians, or—in the framework of the manifesto—as a 'baptismal remembrance', for the author's aim is to encourage Christians to stand firm in their trials by reminding them of their baptism. By presupposing one or the other setting in life, exegesis gives the message different emphases. 1 Pet. in fact is a very clear example of the way in which literary criticism can—and must—bear fruit in the work of exegesis.

BIBLIOGRAPHY

E. Schweizer, *Der erste Petrusbrief* (Prophezei, 1942).

H. Windisch, *Die katholischen Briefe* (Lietzmann, 3 ed., 1951).

W. Bornemann, 'Der erste Petrusbrief—eine Taufrede des Silvanus?', *ZNW* (1919–20), pp. 143 ff.

R. Bultmann, 'Bekenntnis- und Liedfragmente im ersten Petrusbrief', *Coniectanea Neotestamentica* (1947), pp. 1 ff.

E. Fascher, 'Petrusbrief' in *RGG*, V, cols. 257 ff.

E. Lohse, 'Paränese und Kerygma im 1 Petrusbrief', *ZNW* (1954), pp. 68 ff.

R. Perdelwitz, *Die Mysterienreligion und das Problem des 1 Petrusbriefes* (1911).

Commentaries: F. W. Beare (2 ed., 1958); E. G. Selwyn (2 ed., 1947).

F. L. Cross, *I Peter. A Paschal Liturgy* (1954). (Cf. 'I Peter, a Paschal Liturgy?', *JTS*, N.S. 12 (1961), pp. 14 ff.

A. R. C. Leaney, 'I Peter and the Passover: an Interpretation', *NTS* 10, (1963–4), pp. 238 ff.

R. P. Martin, 'The Composition of I Peter in Recent Study', *VE* 1 (1962), pp. 29 ff.

C. F. D. Moule, 'The Nature and Purpose of I Peter', *NTS* 3 (1956–7,) pp. 1 ff.

23. THE EPISTLE OF JUDE

(1) *Contents.* This document contains a forceful polemic against heretics. After an opening greeting (1 ff.), which we shall consider later, the author goes straight into his theme. His aim is to strengthen the recipients in their struggle against the heretics who have crept in and who lead disorderly lives and deny the Lord (4). But the Lord is severe in his judgement on wrongdoers, and as examples the unbelieving Jews in the wilderness, the fallen angels and Sodom and Gomorrha are quoted (5–7). The heretics, who are described in v. 8 as 'dreamers', indulge in slander, debauchery, rioting at the love feasts, scolding and boasting (8–13, 16). Enoch spoke of the judgement that would befall them (14 f.), and the leaders should now remember the words of the apostles, who prophesied that such people would appear (17–19). They must hold fast to their 'most holy faith', but above all show sympathy to the doubters (20–23). The document closes with a doxology reminiscent of Rom. xvi. 25–27.

(2) *The Question of Authorship.* The letter claims to be written by 'Judas, a servant of Jesus Christ, and brother of James' (1). The other brothers Judas and James referred to in the New Testament are the brothers of Jesus (Mk. vi. 3). Whether they are the ones referred to here, and this Judas is meant to be taken as the brother of Jesus, is a disputed point, but it seems probable.

It is impossible however for Judas the brother of Jesus really to have been the author of this document. This is made quite plain by v. 17, where the readers are reminded of 'the words which have been spoken before by the apostles of our Lord Jesus Christ; how that they said . . . In the last time there shall be mockers, walking after their own ungodly lusts'. This means that the author is looking back to the circle of the apostles. They prophesied what is now taking place in the 'last time'. No doubt he includes Judas (and James) among these apostles, even though he does not expressly say so. It is clear that someone is speaking here who wishes to be the bearer of apostolic tradition and is attacking the current heresy by appealing to tradition.

The author is fighting against a libertinist Gnosticism which has found its way into the Church (4) and is evidently meeting with some success (22 f.), and whose representatives still take part in the love feasts (12).

The Gnostics apparently think of themselves as spiritual and look down on those they consider 'carnal' (cf. the polemic in v. 19). As bearers of the Spirit they are not tied to any ethic, and this is evident from their conduct (4, 8, 10–13, 16). However, we need to be cautious in interpreting these verses, as they are expressed in the traditional style of polemic against heretics.

No positive theological standpoint is set out in opposition to the heretics. The argument is simply an appeal to tradition. The Christian faith is the 'most holy faith' (20), which was 'once for all delivered to the saints' (3). In other words, in answer to the spirit of indiscipline an appeal is made to the apostolic tradition, but the content of it is not set out.

A variety of apocalyptic material has been incorporated into this document. 'Enoch' is quoted (14), and this is one reason among others why this 'letter' was for a long time a matter of dispute in the Church; but at the same time it is an indication that the fixing of the Old Testament Canon has either not yet been completed or not yet become established.

The 'recipients' are described in quite general terms as those 'that are beloved in God the Father and kept for (or "through" or "in") Jesus Christ' (1). The address therefore resembles that of 2 Pet. In other words, it is not a letter but—as we already saw in the case of 1 Pet.—a manifesto. It is impossible to say whether it was intended for Jewish or Gentile Christian circles. The edited material gives us no clear indication. The time of writing was probably around A.D. 100. Jude was written before 2 Pet.

BIBLIOGRAPHY

H. Windisch, *Die katholischen Briefe* (Lietzmann, 3 ed., 1951).

E. Fascher, 'Judasbrief' in *RGG*, III, cols. 966 ff.

Commentaries: C. Bigg (with I and II Peter), ICC (2 ed., 1910); J. B. Mayor (with II Peter) (1907); J. Moffatt (The General Epistles), Moffatt (1928).

B. H. Streeter, *The Primitive Church* (1929), pp. 178 ff.

23. THE SECOND EPISTLE OF PETER

(1) *Contents.* The preface (i. 1–2) names as the author Simon Peter, the servant and apostle of Jesus Christ, and as the recipients 'them that have obtained a like precious faith with us'. This reference is again couched in very general terms (cf. Jude, Jas., and also 1 Pet.) and suggests that the document is more of a manifesto than a letter.

Ch. i. deals with tradition, which is a guarantee of the authenticity of the teaching. The author reminds his readers (i. 3–11) of the treasure they possess through the faith that has come down to them. They are to have a share in the 'divine nature' (i. 4). The treasure, however, includes the responsibility of diligently 'making sure' one's election; if this is done, the readers are assured of entrance into the eternal kingdom of the Lord and Saviour Jesus Christ. The author then sets out the reason why he has written (i. 12–15): he wishes to strengthen his readers in the truth they already possess. This is all the more necessary as the Lord has revealed to him that he must be prepared soon to die. The document therefore is in effect the 'testament of Peter'. The author is able to fulfil the task he has set himself because—with other apostles—he was an eye-witness of the majesty of Jesus at his Transfiguration (i. 16–18). This thought then leads to the next, that exposition should not be undertaken arbitrarily, but only with the help of the Spirit (i. 19–21).

Ch. ii. contains Jude, only slightly altered. It is striking that the author 'purges' Jude of material derived from Old Testament apocryphal writings (cf. Jude 6, 9, 10 f.), but at the same time creates certain obscurities by the changes he makes (cf. e.g., Jude 12 f. and 2 Pet. ii. 17). In other words, the author has used Jude—it is not that Jude is an extract taken from 2 Pet., as used to be sometimes assumed.

The transition from ch. i. to ch. ii. is also worth noting. i. 21 attacks the heretics by criticizing their interpretation of Scripture, which must not be arbitrary but can only be carried out with the aid of the Spirit, in other words, along the lines of tradition. Here we can see that tradition is used to attack the adversaries, who themselves claim to possess the Spirit. As they do not stand within this tradition, they cannot have the Spirit. Another reason why they cannot is that they are ethically defective. The adversaries can therefore be taken to be Gnostics, but in considering to what extent we can accuse them of libertinism we have to remember that

R

the charge of evil living is part of the style of the polemic against heretics, and also that this accusation is expressed with the aid of material that was already in existence (Jude).

Now that the author has set out his main theme, he opens ch. iii. on a personal note by saying that he is now writing his second letter. We hear again the theme of remembering the words spoken before by the prophets and the commandments of the Lord delivered by 'your (N.B.) apostles' (iii. 1–2). The fiction of the testament is introduced again with the announcement that mockers will appear (in fact they are already present) who will cast doubt on the coming of the *parousia* on account of its long delay (iii. 3–4). The author sets out four arguments to refute them: that there has already been a great destruction (at the Flood)—on that occasion by water, but the next one will be by fire (iii. 5–7); that God has a different measure of time (iii. 8); that the delay has a positive meaning, in that it affords time for repentance (iii. 9); and finally, that the day of the Lord will come suddenly like a thief in the night (iii. 10). This is followed by an exhortation to holy living, which can in fact hasten the coming of the day of the Lord (iii. 11–13). The readers must therefore see the possibility of salvation in the long-suffering of the Lord, 'even as our beloved brother Paul also, according to the wisdom given to him, wrote unto you' (iii. 14–15). There is then a reference to 'all' the epistles of Paul, which contain many things hard to understand. The ignorant and unsteadfast take advantage of this and twist the meaning of the letters, and they do the same with 'the other scriptures' (iii. 16). The document closes with a renewed exhortation to watchfulness (the false exegetes are 'wicked' and a doxology (iii. 17–18).

(2) *The 'Setting in Life'.* The period of the fathers is a long way in the past (iii. 4). There is already something approaching a *corpus Paulinum* and there is even already a collection of Scriptures (iii. 16). In other words, there is in existence a relatively long tradition, which means that 2 Pet. must have been written quite late. This tradition, however, which the Church possesses—mainly embodied in the Pauline epistles—does give rise to one particular problem. Paul wrote according to the wisdom that was granted him, but there are many things in his letters that are hard to understand (iii. 15 f.). This is not merely an exegetical problem, for the 'ignorant and unsteadfast' take advantage of the position to 'twist the meaning' of the epistles and the other Scriptures.

It is becoming clear that one must engage in exegesis in order to be able to make use of the Scriptures in the present. This is what the adversaries are also doing; they and the author are concerned with the same questions, but come to different conclusions. How can one deal with this newly emerging problem? As one exegesis stands over against the other and each side asserts the correctness of its own interpretation, it is really a matter of one assertion over against another. It is therefore necessary to provide a basis for one's own position, and this is done in two ways.

First it is argued that one must have the 'Spirit' for correct interpretation, as interpretation without the Spirit is arbitrary (i. 21). But the adversaries would use the same argument, and it would again be a case of one assertion against another. It is clear that the appeal to the Spirit cannot be used as a theological argument, because arguments need to be convincing, and it is of the very nature of the Spirit that one cannot prove that his activity is in fact his activity. It is for this reason that the claim to possess the Spirit is supported by a reference to tradition, which is guaranteed by 'Peter' in his capacity as an apostle.

But how can the apostle Peter express himself as regards current problems of a later period? Precisely by the fact that he left behind a 'testament' in which he 'foresaw' the emergence of these heretics. This testament claims to have been written shortly before Peter's death (i. 13 f.).

This argument that one is standing within the tradition is applied not only as regards form but also content. Thus it is argued that the apostle was present when the revelation was made: he was a witness of the Transfiguration on the holy mount. This testimony of ear and eye proves that he (and the other witnesses at the time) and the Church, which now stands in his tradition, have not been following 'cunningly devised fables' as the adversaries have (i. 16–18). In this passage we find for the first time the concept of the *parousia* used not exclusively in the sense of a future coming but of the 'first coming' of Jesus. A distinction is soon made between the first and second *parousia*, the first referring to the Incarnation and the one that is still awaited becoming the second. 2 Pet. therefore represents a transitional stage in this development, as it speaks of the Transfiguration as the first *parousia*. In this way the author not only draws from tradition the proof that this tradition, through the apostle, is on his side, but also at the same time is provided with a relevant argument against the denial of the *parousia* by his adversaries: because there was a first *parousia* there will also be a second one. The argument here is similar to that in iii. 5–7.

The whole argument is very skilfully developed. In opposition to the unhistorical conception of the adversaries, who lay all the emphasis on the presence of salvation, interpreted along Gnostic lines, the author sets out a conception of history which by means of tradition provides a link with the past and a forward look to the future. This represents a legitimate attitude towards heresy. The way in which it is expressed, however, raises certain problems. The idea of the presence of salvation is almost abandoned, or is expressed rather doubtfully in the terminology of Hellenistic piety. The readers are to have a share in the θεῖα φύσις ('divine nature'). Taken to its logical conclusion this could also lead to an abandonment of ethics. It is clear that the author does wish for this consequence, but he can no longer provide a real basis for ethics and merely says that one must be prepared for the future (i. 11). The concept of faith also undergoes a change here. We can see this even from the preface: the document is addressed 'to them that have obtained a like precious faith with us' (i. 1). Faith is something handed down, and in this faith one has to exercise virtue (i. 5). This is very different from the way in which Paul argued against the Gnostic standpoint.

This document gives us a glimpse of the situation of the Church at a relatively late period. The eschatology which looks to an imminent End has fallen into the background, and one has to adjust oneself to living in the world (cf. esp. the Pastorals). The Church is in process of becoming an institution. The Spirit is linked with tradition—and with the ministry —and is passed on by the laying on of hands. The point has now been reached where one has to make clear where one differs from those among whom the Spirit is still 'freely' active. In the post-Pauline period—long after Paul, in fact, for he has already become a 'literary entity' belonging to the past—the futurist eschatology of the Church is attacked by the Gnostics. 'Where is the promise of his coming? for from the day that the fathers fell asleep, all things continue as they were from the beginning of the creation' (iii. 4). Though far removed from the beginnings of the Church, the author is seeking to remain in continuity with these beginnings and sets out an 'apologia for the primitive Christian eschatology'[11] in its apocalyptic form.

The author cannot possibly be Peter, nor is he the same as the author of 1 Pet. We do not know his name. 2 Pet. is probably the latest document in the New Testament, having been written about A.D. 130–140.

---

[11] Cf. E. Käsemann, 'Eine Apologie der urchristlichen Eschatologie', ZThK (1952), pp. 272 ff. Reprinted in *Exegetische Versuche und Besinnungen*, I, pp. 135 ff. (E.T. *Essays on New Testament Themes* (selections from *Exegetische Versuche und Besinnungen*), pp. 169 ff.).

BIBLIOGRAPHY

H. Windisch, *Die katholischen Briefe* (Lietzmann, 3 ed., 1951).

E. Fascher, 'Petrusbrief' in *RGG*, V, cols. 257 ff.

E. Käsemann, 'Eine Apologie der urchristlichen Eschatologie', *ZThK* (1952), pp. 272 ff. Reprinted in *Exegetische Versuche und Besinnungen*, I (1960), pp. 135 ff. (E.T. *Essays on New Testament Themes*, selections from *Exegetische Versuche und Besinnungen*, SCM; Allenson, 1964, pp. 169 ff.).

Commentaries: B. Reicke (The General Epistles), Anchor Bible (1964). See also commentaries on Jude.

G. H. Boobyer, 'The Indebtedness of II Peter to I Peter' in *New Testament Essays in Memory of T. W. Manson* (1959), pp. 34 ff.

E. M. B. Green, *II Peter Reconsidered* (1962).

V. The Johannine Writings

The four documents to be considered in this section occupy in many respects a special place within the framework of the New Testament. We will first give a brief outline of the historical position of this group of writings and so try to give some idea of the purpose they were meant to fulfil.

One characteristic of the 'Johannine literature' is the special eschatological standpoint that we find expressed in it. In the early Synoptic traditions and in Paul we find the imminent expectation of the *parousia*. The Church has the transition from the old age to the new already behind it, and awaits an early consummation. There seems to be no clear awareness of any interval: Christians live in the power of the new age begun in Christ, and therefore are already living the new life of the future. This becomes particularly clear in the matter of ethics, which can be based alternately on the past (e.g. Gal. ii. 19 f.; 2 Cor. v. 14 f.) and on the future (e.g. 1 Thess. v. 4 ff.; Rom. xiii. 11 ff.). These two eschatological 'points' are very close together. Through the preaching of the Gospel one is transported into the new eschatological reality (Paul, Mark), and to believe means to establish oneself here and now in this eschatological event, which comes to man through the 'Gospel'. When a man believes he is not only a new creature, but he also lives as a new creature. This new life is still imperfect—and therefore still needs to be based on an Imperative—only because it has to be lived in the midst of the old age which is passing away and will soon come to an end.

It is obvious that this standpoint could not be maintained when the arrival of the *parousia* was delayed. Time was now experienced as something continuing, and Christians became conscious of it as such. The past became an entity in its own right, and the question arose of the relationship of the present to the past on the one hand and to the future on the other. Matthew and Luke try to deal with this problem in their different ways. By means of their conception of history they maintain the link with the past, and in their teaching concerning the future they use apocalyptic ideas and motifs. The same is true of the pseudo-Pauline and Church epistles. It is mainly by means of the idea of tradition that the attempt is made to maintain the message as time goes by. We can see evidence of this in the Pastorals, for example, in the interpretation of the ministry, the handing down of the different ministries and in ordination, in Eph. in the meaning of the apostolate (the 'holy apostles and prophets'), and in Col. in the emphasis on the succession of Paul—Epaphras—Colossae. The 'baptismal remembrance' in 1 Pet. in view of the persecution that Christians are having to face, and the apologetic argument in Jude and particularly in 2 Pet. are also relevant here. In most cases the aim is simply to preserve the link with the past by means of tradition, but the concept is also applied in the opposite direction to the continuation of tradition in the future.

The inevitable result of all this was that the present was emptied of eschatological meaning, and this was of course often the expression of an 'eschatological impoverishment' in the later period. This proved to be a disadvantage over against Gnosticism in its various manifestations, because Gnosticism claimed to possess to the full what the Church now lacked. It was out of the question for Christians themselves to follow the path of Gnosticism, for they neither wished to nor was it possible for them to renounce the past and the future. These two aspects were emphasized in argument with the Gnostics, but it proved difficult to preserve the present as a period filled with eschatological significance. Of course Christians did not wish to live merely the life of this world, but it was difficult now to give an adequate explanation of this. One could of course fall back on the two considerations, that one should observe the commandments of Christ, and that one must hold fast to the expectation of the *parousia*, and so show that it is frivolous just to live for the passing day. The question that arises, however, is what there is specifically Christian in all this—when we compare it with the earliest period of the Church. What emerges is either a more or less marked legalism—even when one's attitude is based not on the Old Testament, but on Christian tradition, which is itself of course greatly influenced by the paranetic traditions of popular philosophy—or pure apocalyptic.

What was previously a complex eschatology splits up, therefore, into its three component elements: the past and the future, and in between the element that concerns the present, which however can hardly be called eschatological any longer. We can sum up the position briefly as follows: the presence of salvation is preserved by Gnosticism, but at the price of sacrificing past and future. In the post-apostolic Church, on the other hand, a firm hold is kept on past and future, but the presence of salvation is either lost or can no longer be organically linked with the other elements. The position that the post-apostolic Church had to adopt against Gnosticism increased the Church's difficulties, but they were difficulties it would have had to face in any case. In Gnosticism it had to oppose a movement which was able to express something that was a problem for the Church itself, which created a very complicated situation. All the attempts at a solution really only touch the surface of the problem and fail to get to the root of it.

Once we understand this, we can see the exceptional significance of the Johannine conception, particularly its eschatology. As a result of it the present aspect becomes vital again in a way that is quite unparalleled in its time; indeed the reversal is so marked that the future aspect almost disappears and the Gnostic danger emerges again—a danger of which the Church was well aware in its later treatment of Jn. The situation is different as regards the element of the past: the anti-Gnostic trend becomes very clear here in the emergence of a 'Gospel' in which a manifest salvation is presented as being made manifest in Jesus. We are left in no doubt that 'the Word became flesh' (Jn. i. 14). We can therefore describe the Johannine standpoint as the attempt to deal in a quite new and radical way with the problems which apparently could no longer be solved by traditional methods.

24. THE GOSPEL OF JOHN

(1) *Contents.* Jn. describes the course of Jesus' life from the beginning to the Crucifixion and Resurrection, as do the Synoptic Gospels, but there are some characteristic differences. According to the Synoptics—following the Marcan pattern—Jesus went to Jerusalem only once, at the end of his ministry, but according to Jn. he went there on four occasions (ii. 13; v. 1; vii. 10; xii. 12). Each time he is depicted as being there during a feast, on three occasions the feast of the Passover. It is as difficult to draw any conclusions from Jn. concerning the actual length of Jesus' public ministry as it is from the Synoptic outline.

Another peculiarity in Jn. is Jesus' relationship to John the Baptist. According to the Synoptics Jesus does not appear in public until after John has been put in prison (Mk. i. 14 et parr.), whereas in Jn. the two work alongside each other for a time. Jn. iii. 24 seems to be a deliberate correction of the impression given in the Synoptics. Jn. iii. 22 also speaks of Jesus baptizing, but this statement is retracted or modified in iv. 2.

Certain pericopae have a different position in the Synoptics and in Jn. For example, the Cleansing of the Temple comes at the beginning of Jn. (ii. 13 ff.), but at the end of Jesus' ministry in the Synoptics (Mk. xi. 15 ff. et parr.). We do not have to wait until Jesus' Last Supper for a reference to the Eucharist in the Fourth Gospel (xiii. 1 ff.), as it is already mentioned in vi. 51 ff. There is no 'institution' of the Lord's Supper in Jn. There are further differences as regards the day of Jesus' death; according to the Synoptics (Mk. xiv. 12 ff. et parr.) Jesus celebrates the Passover with his disciples at the beginning of the 15th Nisan (the Jewish day begins at sunset); according to Jn. he dies on the afternoon before, on the 14th Nisan (the 'Preparation' of the Passover), at the time when the Paschal lambs are being killed in the Temple (xix. 30 f.).

There is no parallel in Jn. to the great majority of passages in the Synoptics. Of the miracle stories we find in Jn. only the Feeding of the Five Thousand (vi. 1 ff.) and the Walking on the Sea (vi. 16 ff.) similar to those in the Synoptics. The story of the Healing of the Centurion's Servant (iv. 46 ff.) has been expanded compared with Mt. viii. 5 ff. and Lk. vii. 1 ff. On the other hand, however, Jn. contains four miracle stories which have no parallel in the Synoptics (ii. 1 ff.; v. 1 ff.; ix. 1 ff.; xi. 1 ff.).

There are further differences in style. There are none of the short pregnant sayings of Jesus which can still be recognized in the longer

Synoptic discourses (Mk. xiii; Mt. v–vii, etc.). Instead we find long discourses of a mostly meditative character with a steadily unfolding train of thought. It is noticeable that the style of Jesus' discourses and of those of John the Baptist, and also the style of the evangelist's own account are the same, which means that the evangelist himself shaped the style of all the three elements. This gives us the impression of a work composed as a whole, far more than is the case with the Synoptics.

(2) *Sources and Standpoint.* In spite of the formal coherence of the work, on closer inspection we can discern in it various sources, which give evidence of editorial treatment. This problem is still a matter of dispute among scholars. Really there are only two sections that we can separate from the whole with certainty, and the problems in each case are different. The pericope of the Woman taken in Adultery (vii. 53–viii. 11) is undoubtedly secondary in the context of the Gospel. Not only is it missing in a whole series of manuscripts, but it is also thoroughly 'Synoptic' in character; besides, it has been inserted in different positions in Jn. in various manuscripts and codices. Occasionally it even appears after Lk. xxi. 38. We can therefore ignore this pericope here. Ch. xxi presents a different problem. It has come to be assumed that this is a chapter subsequently added by another hand (cf. the conclusion in xx. 30 f.), yet the chapter has not been disputed from the point of view of textual criticism, but it is accepted as belonging to the 'substance' of the 'canonical' Gospel. We can say for certain, therefore, that chs. i–xx have received a subsequent editorial expansion. We shall have to consider later whether this merely involved ch. xxi, or whether chs. i–xx were also affected by way of interpolations. We will deal first with the original work.

The first indication that Jn. i–xx also contains sources that have been treated editorially is to be found in ii. 11, where the miracle at Cana is explicitly referred to as 'this beginning of his signs'. There is mention of further signs (ii. 23; iv. 45), of which no account is given. The healing of the Officer's Son, however, is called the 'second sign' (iv. 54). It seems probable that the evangelist had access to a 'signs source' (cf. also the reference back to ii. 1 ff. in iv. 46). There is a further reference in xii. 37 to Jesus' miracles, and to the fact that they did not lead men to believe. This reads like the ending of the source, to which xx. 30 f. may have been added later.

It is noticeable, however, that the other miracles which are found in Jn. but not in the Synoptics appear before xii. 37: the healing of the Lame Man (v. 1 ff.), the healing of the Man born Blind (ix. 1 ff.) and the

Raising of Lazarus (xi. 1 ff.). Compared with the miracles recorded in the Synoptics, these are on a much larger scale, and they also express a viewpoint different from the one expressed elsewhere in Jn. in that they do not represent faith as being called forth by the miracle, but by the word and proclamation of Jesus. We can therefore suggest the following picture: the basis of the work was probably a 'book' of signs (xx. 30) which contained the miracles Jn. refers to and expressed the view that these miracles were meant to call forth faith (ii. 11; iv. 53; vi. 14; vii. 31; xi. 45, 47b f.; xii. 37 f.; xx. 31), a viewpoint of which there is evidence elsewhere in the early Church (cf. Acts ii. 22). The evangelist, however, modifies this position, as we can see from the editorial comments he makes upon the source (ii. 23 ff.; iv. 48) and also from his own interpretation, which comes out very clearly in the conversation with Nicodemus where the traditional conception expressed by the Pharisee (iii. 2) is corrected by the reference to the birth from above (iii. 3) and to the Spirit (iii. 5 ff.). For the evangelist, in other words, the miracles are not meant to call forth faith in Jesus and proclaim his authority, but are signs which are meant to point to him.

He presents Jesus as One who is sent. Whether he used a further source here—Bultmann[1] suggests a 'discourses source'—is by no means so certain as is the use of the 'signs source'. It is not altogether necessary to assume that there was such a source, even though the 'revelatory discourses' are constructed according to a set pattern, with certain modifications. They begin with the declaration of the revealer—'I am'. After the invitation or call to decision comes the 'crisis saying' containing either promise or warning—or both. We find this pattern, e.g., in chs. iii, v, x and xv. It is quite possible that this is a stylistic device of the evangelist (adopted from elsewhere), by means of which he expresses his viewpoint over against the traditional conception. He depicts Jesus as the One who acts on behalf of God (vii. 1b f.; x. 30; xiv. 9 f., etc.), and he does this with such distinctive subtlety that he can put into the mouth of Jesus words which at one and the same time are sayings addressed to his disciples and are also directed to the Church. What was future for the disciples prior to the glorification and gift of the Spirit is present for the Church (cf. v. 25; xvi. 32). The result as far as the evangelist is concerned is that his account of the past becomes something that is directly addressed to the present.

The same purpose is served by the introduction of the 'disciple whom Jesus loved' (xiii. 23; xix. 26; xx. 2—also xxi. 7, 20). The evangelist is

[1] *Das Evangelium des Johannes* in Meyer (16 ed., 1959). (E.T. in prep., Blackwell).

familiar with the tradition of the Twelve (vi. 67, 71; xx. 24) and also
with some of the names of this group, but he never refers to the disciple
whom Jesus loved by name. It might therefore be correct to assume that
this is a kind of ideal figure. To speak of him as the 'favourite disciple' is
not really accurate, for there is no suggestion of any preference on the
part of Jesus or that he singled him out from the rest of the Twelve. The
disciple whom Jesus loved is for the evangelist the 'ideal type of discipleship according to his view', 'the model of a discipleship which makes
bearers of revelation out of recipients of revelation'.[2] Possibly the
evangelist thought of himself as being such a disciple.

We can see in this an attempt to correct 'tradition' by adopting a
critical attitude to the way in which being a Christian is linked with the
institution, and by emphasizing instead that succession lies in true
discipleship. It is significant that in xx. 19 ff. it is not the Twelve or the
Eleven who are endowed with the Spirit, but 'the disciples'. True
discipleship is manifested not in the following of rules and regulations,
but in the practice of love (xiii. 34). This loving, however, is linked in a
very special way with Jesus, and here again we can see the way in which
the evangelist modifies the traditional eschatology. Such love is possible
for the disciple only because Jesus enables him to exercise it, because the
one sent by God has given him the 'example' (xiii. 15). When a man
practises love, the Father and the Son come to him (xiv. 23): in other
words, the *parousia* takes place now. This explains why the evangelist
thinks of judgement as taking place now. He who believes has life, but
he who does not believe is already judged. With great force and concen-
tration the author brings past and future to bear upon the present reality
of salvation.

(3) *The 'Church Redaction'*. We have so far considered the evangelist's own
standpoint, and we must now turn to the later editorial process that the
work underwent. This does not only concern ch. xxi, but if we start by
considering this chapter we shall then be able to trace the editorial process
in chs. i–xx. We need to note first of all that the style of ch. xxi is for the
most part identical with that of chs. i–xx. In other words, the style is not
a personal characteristic of the author of chs. i–xx, but rather the style
of a circle or 'school', which we also find in the Johannine epistles.
Perhaps we can conclude from this that chs. i–xx are not the work of a
single man who is trying in the outline he draws up to deal with a burning

[2] M. Dibelius, 'Joh. 5, 13. Eine Studie zum Traditionsproblem des Johannes-
evangeliums' in *Festgabe für Adolf Deißmann* (1927), pp. 179 ff.

problem of his own time, but that this man belongs to a 'community', or at least has a circle of disciples.

It is clear that ch. xxi is a supplement. In Jn. xx—as in Lk. xxiv—the appearances of the Risen Lord take place exclusively in and around Jerusalem. Ch. xxi, on the other hand, speaks of an appearance by the Sea of Tiberias, and so gives rise to the question whether it is meant to represent a compromise with the tradition which speaks of appearances in Galilee (cf. Mt. xxviii. 16; for Mk. xvi. 7, see section 12). The commissioning of Peter as leader of the Church in this supplementary chapter (xxi. 15–19) is somewhat surprising, followed by the conversation about the disciple whom Jesus loved (xxi. 20–23). It appears that here again the Gospel is defending itself against a tradition with which its contemporaries were familiar, which was opposed to the historically interpreted or 'historicized' account given by the evangelist. At first this tradition is accepted. Peter *was* in fact commissioned as leader of the Church, but he met martyrdom, and was followed by the 'beloved disciple'. This idea is already present in nuce in the racing of the disciples to the tomb (xx. 2 ff.) and also possibly in the commending of the disciple whom Jesus loved to Mary at the Cross (xix. 25 ff.). However, there is a certain change of tone. Whereas previously the evangelist had presented the 'ideal figure' of the beloved disciple as a disciple of the time of Jesus and as a type of true discipleship by merging together the perspectives, now we see a 'historicizing' of the figure as he becomes virtually the 'successor' to Peter. Something similar takes place when the disciple whom Jesus loved is described as the guarantor of the authenticity of the book (xxi. 24), for this makes the ideal figure in effect an 'eye-witness' (cf. also xix. 35—see below). Nevertheless the standpoint of the Gospel is still maintained at least to the extent that the author thought of himself as the 'beloved disciple'. From the formal point of view, therefore, ch. xxi gives the impression of simply being a supplement; in fact its aim is to preserve for the Church—though in a modified form—the original work that is opposed to the traditional conception of the Church.

We can see the same motif also in a number of passages within chs. i–xx. When it is particularly emphasized in iii. 24 that John the Baptist had not yet been put into prison, this is an assertion of the accuracy of the account, in contrast to the Synoptics. The statement that Jesus baptized (iii. 22), however, cannot be upheld by the redaction, and is retracted or modified in iv. 2. This verse is obviously an editorial interpolation (iv. 3 originally followed directly upon iv. 1), and possibly belongs to the same 'stratum' as ch. xxi. This 'stratum' could be even more extensive, as we can see particularly from those passages where there is a certain discrepancy not only between the statements and their context, but also between the statements and the underlying conception of the work.

This is true in the first place as regards the references to the sacraments. The most important passage in this connection is vi. 51b–58. The discourse on the Bread of Life is in no way sacramental, but it is made sacramental by these verses which speak not only of eating the flesh of Jesus, but also of drinking his blood. There is a similar situation in iii. 5. In the conversation with Nicodemus entrance into the Kingdom of God is made dependent on being born of the Spirit, but the redaction adds: 'of water and'. In this way being born of the Spirit is connected with Baptism; in the context this is not necessary, and is in fact an interruption, but it is understandable against the background of Church tradition. Finally, xix. 34b–35 is also evidently an interpolation which interrupts the continuity. Blood and Water flow from the side of Jesus. If we compare xix. 35 and xxi. 24 we can see that this comes from the same hand as ch. xxi. The redactor is making it clear that Baptism and the Lord's Supper are based upon the death of Jesus.

It would not be true to say that the original author was anti-sacramental. He is familiar with Christian Baptism, and goes so far as to describe Jesus himself as baptizing (iii. 22; iv. 1). In the high-priestly prayer he also seems to allude to the Lord's Supper (xvii. 19).[3] There is no evidence of any polemic against the sacraments, but he places the greatest emphasis on the fact that men are brought to faith when they are confronted by the Word as it is proclaimed, and as a result the sacraments fall into the background. Understandably the 'Church' misses them, and so the redactor has again to effect a compromise.

The same is true, finally, as regards eschatology. In the original Gospel all the emphasis is on the present bearing of eschatology (see above), but in the work as we know it there are certain abrupt statements about the future which counter-balance the one-sided emphasis on the present. There is reference to resurrection and future judgement (v. 28 f.), and the phrase 'I will raise him up at the last day' recurs almost like a refrain in vi. 39, 40, 44 (but contrast the attitude of the evangelist in xi. 23–27). We find the same phrase again in vi. 54, in the middle of a passage we have already seen to be a redactional interpolation. As the Lord's Supper is spoken of as promising eternal life it is presented as the φάρμακον ἀθανασίας (medicine of immortality).

[3] Cf. R. Bultmann, *op. cit.*, p. 391, n. 3.

We can say, therefore, that by means of 'correctional' interpolations the 'Church redaction' attempted to make the original work fit the traditional conception as regards both the sacraments and eschatology. As a result the work lost something of its distinctive character. Originally it represented a protest against the eschatological 'emptying' of the present, and was an attempt at a 'reformation'. This makes it clear that it was not the author's intention—as has sometimes been assumed—to supplement the Synoptics. It is doubtful whether—even improbable that —he was familiar with them, but he was familiar with certain Church sources (a book of signs and traditions of the Passion). He uses these, however, not just as he finds them, but treats them critically, and his aim —like Luke: cf. Lk. i. 1–4—is not to write a work which will stand alongside earlier works, but which will take their place. It is in carrying out this aim that he comes into conflict with Church tradition. The redaction has therefore to bring about a compromise. This makes it plain that one cannot simply by-pass tradition in the Church. It has to be taken into account as a creative force which can not only not be ignored, but also can be corrected only to a certain degree. The original work of the evangelist has to be made to accept this compromise.

Many of the detailed questions have to be left open for the moment, as for example the question whether the arrangement of the text as we have it is original. This is probably not the case. Within the farewell discourses (xiv–xvi) the conclusion in xiv. 31 sounds strange, and its sequel is not xv. 1, but xviii. 1. Did xviii. 1 originally follow straight after xiv. 31? There is a similar situation in vi. 1, to take only one example among many. This verse could well follow directly after iv. 54, which would mean that ch. v is not in its original position.[4] These peculiar circumstances have called forth various theories to explain them, from the assumption that the leaves became interchanged—which no doubt happened quite frequently in those days—to the hypothesis that the Gospel was revised three times by the author (original Gospel, to which discourses were later added, finally developed into a Passion Gospel) and then published by the disciple of the evangelist.[5] Although this theory contains many valuable insights into the way the material grew, it cannot be accepted as it stands, as it does not take sufficient account of the discrepancies in the theological statements at the various stages. As the last alteration to the text was made by the Church redaction, it is quite possible that the 'disorder' of the material arose at this stage. We have

[4] *Ibid., ad loc.*
[5] W. Wilkens, *Die Entstehungsgeschichte des vierten Evangeliums* (1958).

S

to leave open the question whether this was accidental or intentional—in which case we would have to try to explain the reason for it.

We can sum up the position as follows: the 'original evangelist' created a Gospel by using a book of signs and other material (Passion traditions) in which he re-interprets his sources, presents the miracles as signs, relegates the sacraments to the background and strongly emphasizes the present bearing of eschatology. Hearing the word of Jesus, the revealer, confronts men now with the question of belief or unbelief. The believer fulfils the new commandment by loving, in which he experiences the 'coming' of the Father and the Son to him (xiv. 23) and in the same way also becomes aware that the word of the revealer is the word of God (vii. 17). In this work, therefore, the presence of salvation is set out in a way to which there was no parallel at the time—but without the risk of falling into Gnosticism. This viewpoint, however, contradicted the traditional conception accepted by the Church, and so among the circle of disciples of the evangelist an attempt at a compromise was made by means of a 'Church redaction', which though it tried to remain faithful to the approach of the original evangelist, could not leave his standpoint unaltered.

This insight into the literary growth of the Gospel is of great value for exegesis. It can proceed generally speaking in three stages: we can expound the sources which were available to the original evangelist; we can expound his own work; and we can expound the Gospel as we know it, after it has been subject to the Church redaction. It has to be noted that exegesis of the earlier stages can only succeed to the extent that one can with some certainty lay bare the sources by means of literary criticism. On the other hand, the message of the final redaction can really only be brought out if we bear in mind its treatment of the sources, for it is through the process of redaction that this message becomes decisive. This is a vicious circle from which we cannot escape.

In other words, in the work of exegesis we have constantly to bear in mind the particular 'setting in life'. At the same time we have to refrain from any evaluation of one viewpoint over against another—this is the task of systematic theology rather than exegesis. The successive stages of exegesis bring to light an extremely interesting aspect of the development of early Christian proclamation, where we can see it coming to terms with various problems of the time and trying to deal with them.

(4) *The Question of Authorship*. In view of the factors we have already considered, the question of the author is not of great importance, and can

therefore be dealt with briefly. The Church redaction identifies him with the 'beloved disciple' (xxi. 24; cf. xix. 35), but this person is never mentioned by name. By internal evidence therefore the Gospel is anonymous.

Church tradition later attributed it to John the son of Zebedee. Whether this is true of Justin is not certain. Irenaeus explicitly identifies the beloved disciple with John and states that Ephesus was the Gospel's place of origin (*Adv.Haer.* III, i. 1). Alongside this tradition we frequently find the suggestion that the Gospel is the work of a certain John the 'presbyter'. We meet this name in a reference by Papias preserved by Eusebius, which mentions the names of John the disciple and John the presbyter together (*H.E.* III, 39, 3 f.), but as Eusebius adopts a critical attitude towards Papias' statements, and obviously does not reproduce them all, we cannot be certain as to what Papias meant. The historicity of John the presbyter therefore remains doubtful (cf. also section 28, 3).

The early Church tradition showed a great interest in these questions, as we can see in a statement—though historically worthless—in the Muratorian Church, according to which John was requested by his fellow disciples (=fellow apostles) to set down his reminiscences. After a fast of three days Andrew had received by revelation instructions to do this. As a result the book was supposed to have been published in the name of John but at the same time by the authority of all the apostles. We can see here the attempt to underline the historical reliability of the Gospel by the strongest means possible.

A similar attempt has also often been made to prove that the author was an eye-witness, but without success. Even if the author had been an eye-witness, we could not say that he made any use of his experience, in view of his use of sources on the one hand and the style of the Gospel on the other, where, as we have seen, even Jesus' discourses are presented in the style of the author. Even if we were to assume that he was an eye-witness, this would not mean that we had before us a historically authentic source, and so it is really a waste of time to argue the point.

The theological conception underlying the work as a whole rules out the possibility that it is based on the testimony of an eye-witness, and clearly indicates that it belongs to a later period. Our only starting-point is the fact that the author thinks of himself as a disciple whom Jesus loved and who—by means of the shift of perspective which we have noted previously—had a place in the work itself. It was the Church redaction that first made it possible to consider him as an actual figure among the circle of the disciples. The work was probably written in the East towards the end of the first century.

BIBLIOGRAPHY

R. Bultmann, *Das Evangelium des Johannes* (Meyer, 17 ed., 1962).

R. Bultmann, 'Johannesevangelium', *RGG*, III, cols. 840 ff.

E. Haenchen, 'Aus der Literatur zum Johannesevangelium 1929-1956', *ThR*, NF (1955), pp. 295 ff.

W. Wilkens, Die Entstehungsgeschichte des vierten Evangeliums (1958).

Commentaries: C. K. Barrett (1956); J. H. Bernard, ICC (2 vols., 1928); E. C. Hoskyns (2 ed., 1947); R. H. Lightfoot (1956); G. H. C. MacGregor, Moffatt (1928); J. N. Sanders and B. A. Martin, Black (1967).

J. W. Bowker, 'The Origin and Purpose of St. John's Gospel', *NTS* 11 (1964-5), pp. 398 ff.

F. L. Cross (Ed.), *Studies in the Fourth Gospel* (1957).

C. H. Dodd, *The Interpretation of the Fourth Gospel* (1953): *Historical Tradition in the Fourth Gospel* (1963).

P. Gardner-Smith, *St. John and the Synoptic Gospels* (1938).

A. Guilding, *The Fourth Gospel and Jewish Worship* (1960).

A. J. B. Higgins, *The Historicity of the Fourth Gospel* (1960).

W. F. Howard, *The Fourth Gospel in Recent Criticism and Interpretation*, revised by C. K. Barrett (1955).

D. M. Smith, 'The Sources of the Gospel of John: an Assessment of the Present State of the Problem', *NTS* 10 (1963-4), pp. 336 ff.

25. THE FIRST EPISTLE OF JOHN

(1) *Its Literary Form.* As the document lacks not only a preface—like Heb.—but also a letter ending, its literary form is not easy to determine. We certainly cannot describe 1 Jn. as a 'letter', as it lacks all the concrete details which would justify such a description. On the other hand, it is quite plain that the author frequently has in mind a circle of readers to whom he addresses himself directly (ii. 1, 7 f., 12 ff., 18, 21, 26, etc.). The document has been spoken of as a 'homily', an 'admonitory letter', a 'tract' or a 'manifesto', but none of these is a really adequate description. It is a document the form of which has no parallel elsewhere. All we can say is that the author is seeking to address readers with whose particular situation he is acquainted. This means that his writing repeatedly approaches the form of a letter, but he does not actually write a letter.[6]

(2) *The Situation of the Readers.* The author envisages his readers as threatened by a heresy the representatives of which are neither Jews nor Gentiles, but claim to be Christians themselves. From the attack he makes upon them we can conclude that they are Gnostics who deny a real incarnation of Jesus Christ (iv. 2 f.; cf. ii. 22). As it follows from this that the Cross can have no meaning for them (cf. i. 7; ii. 1 f.; iv. 10), they evidently reject the Lord's Supper (v. 6), but not Baptism. The most accurate description of the heretics therefore would be to call them Docetics. In spite of ii. 15 ff. and iv. 5, we cannot say for certain whether they were also libertinists, but they apparently consider themselves sinless (i. 8) on account of their possession of the Spirit (iv. 1). The author regards these heretics as false prophets (iv. 1), and even as antichrists (ii. 18). There has been a split between them and the readers (ii. 19), and the sharpness of this division in the church is underlined by the author's statement that intercession should not be made for those who have committed the 'sin unto death' (v. 16).

(3) *The Unity of the Document.* The author's statements seem to be very disjointed, so that it is difficult to divide the document into sections. The most we can do is to note the alternation—though not a very strict one—between didactic and paranetic passages. It has also been observed,

---

[6] Cf. E. Haenchen, 'Neuere Literatur zu den Johannesbriefen', *ThR* (1960), p. 13.

however, that there appear to be certain contradictions in the material (for example, the relationship between sin and sinlessness is seen dialectically in i. 5 ff., but v. 16 f. on the other hand speaks of two classes of sins). Differences of style have also been noted. As a result, various attempts have been made to trace the author's model by means of separating the sources, but there is a great divergence among the findings. They range from the assumption that the author used a non-Christian source (Bultmann) to the view that he revised and expanded an earlier writing of his own (Nauck). The difficulty in trying to separate the sources with any degree of certainty can be seen clearly in the fact that we have to assume that the author did not merely take over his source but that he altered it by adding his own comments and even more so by re-casting the material so that the original form can be deduced only in a very hypothetical kind of way.

Of course it would be wrong to use the uncertainty of the findings as an argument against using this method. The question is simply whether we are not over-simplifying the question by attempting to solve it by purely—or predominantly—literary methods. It cannot really be disputed that the author is dependent on traditions that have been handed down, but it is very likely that he adapted them independently. If we bear in mind that he is not a very systematic person—as the lack of a general structure seems to suggest—we can probably assume that the variation in style derives from the author himself. In other words, he is a 'practical Churchman, a preacher, who cheerfully constructs a bridge of stock phrases in order to cross from one point to the next, but who succeeds in suddenly coming back again to where he started'.[7]

(4) *The Theological Position of the Author.* The language and style of the document indicate a close connection with Jn., but the question is how we can determine the relationship of the two documents to one another. v. 6 provides the first—and also a very clear—indication. Baptism and the Lord's Supper are spoken of here in the same way as in the 'Church redaction' of Jn. (Jn. vi. 51b–58; xix. 34b–35; cf. section 24, 3). The author seems therefore to belong to the group which incorporated the—original—Johannine viewpoint into the tradition of the Church. In any case he is 'post-Johannine', as we can see—among other things—from the different statement of the problems that arise. Whereas Jn. is concerned with the alternative of faith or unbelief, in 1 Jn. the alternative is that of faith or heresy. The relationship between Jn. and 1 Jn. has been

[7] E. Haenchen, *op. cit.*, p. 15.

compared with that between Paul and the pseudo-Pauline epistles, which suggests that 1 Jn. is to be seen as a 'Johannine pastoral letter', which betrays a number of early Catholic features.[8]

(5) *The Author's Message.* In his confrontation with a Christian Gnosticism the author's aim is to maintain the Church in a true confession of faith (ii. 22). In the first place this means recognizing the full humanity of Jesus Christ. The traditionally formulated confession in iv. 2 is the anti-Gnostic expression in a more pointed form of the older confession in ii. 22. The author also stresses the redemptive meaning of the Cross (ii. 1 f.; iv. 10), but without expounding it in detail; once again he adopts a standard confession (i. 7). Finally, he attaches importance to the fact that one's conduct should be in keeping with one's faith (ii. 3 ff.).

It is significant that the author does not define Christian conduct in any detail, but limits it in the first place to love of the brethren. Thus Jn. v. 24 ('. . . hath passed out of death into life') is continued in 1 Jn. iii. 14 ('We know that we have passed out of death into life') with 'because we love the brethren'. This does not refer to one's 'neighbours', but—in contrast to those who have left the fellowship (ii. 19)—those who have remained in the Church. For it is they—and only they—who believe that Jesus is the Christ. Therefore it is only they who are born of God (v. 1). For the same reason it is not Christian faith simply, but 'our' faith that overcomes the world (v. 4). The 'orthodox' faith holds that Jesus is God's Son (v. 5), and the evidence of it is that one remains loyal to the Church (cf. ii. 19). He who cuts himself off from the Church commits the 'sin unto death' (v. 16).

The author can now assert—and he uses Gnostic terminology to do so —that what the opponents claim to possess is in fact the possession of the Church. At Baptism it received the χρῖσμα (anointing—ii. 20, 27), the σπέρμα (seed) of God (iii. 9); and in this connection the author can go so far as to say—along thoroughly Gnostic lines—that Christians no longer sin (cf. v. 18).

How can we reconcile this, however, with other statements which describe this claim to sinlessness as a heresy (i. 8, 10) and which speak of the forgiveness of sins as necessary—and also possible—even for Christians (i. 9; cf. v. 16a)? The answer is provided by iii. 10, together with iii. 9: for the one who is truly born of God there can be no sin, because he remains a child of God and proves it by loving his brother—in other

---

[8] Cf. H. Conzelmann, 'Was von Anfang war' in *Neutestamentliche Studien für R. Bult-mann* (2 ed., 1957), p. 201.

words, by remaining in the Church. It is true that the Gnostic idea of sinlessness is adopted, but at the same time it is restricted by the insistence that as far as the orthodox faith is concerned there is no sin so long as one does not fall away. If one does fall away this is a proof that one was not really born of God, and one has committed the 'sin unto death' (v. 16b).

There is, however, a sin—but only in the 'orthodox' Church—which need not lead to death. The readers are exhorted not only to remain in the Church, but also to practise love within it (iii. 17 f.). All unrighteousness is sin (v. 17), and the transgression of the law is sin (iii. 4). It is also a sin to fail to practise love, but not a sin unto death (v. 17), for it can be confessed and forgiven (i. 9). He who observes the commandments and does what is pleasing in God's sight (iii. 22) will abide in eternity.

We can see therefore two lines running through the author's message. On the one hand he gives an urgent warning not to fall away into heresy, as this would mean the final loss of salvation. At the same time he is concerned with the practical importance of living in accordance with the commandments within the Church. If his readers prove themselves in both respects to be 'children of God', then one day there awaits them an eschatological future, in which their present existence will be transcended (iii. 2).

(6) *Authorship and Time and Place of Composition.* The document has come down anonymously. We have already seen that it is not possible to regard Jn. as the work of John the son of Zebedee (cf. section 24, 4), and the same is true of 1 Jn. The reference to seeing in i. 1–4 cannot be taken as evidence that the author was an eye-witness any more than the reference in iii. 6 (cf. also 3 Jn. 11). The author continues the Johannine traditions, but he also gives them an ecclesiastical turn—as did the 'Church redaction' of Jn. We can say therefore that he evidently belongs to a Johannine 'school'.

The work probably originated in the East around the turn of the first century.

(7) *The 'Comma Johanneum'.* In a number of manuscripts—mainly early Latin ones—we find a gloss added to v. 7 f., which contains a Trinitarian interpretation of the passage. This so-called 'comma' (section) is certainly not genuine and has no relevance for the exegesis of 1 Jn., although it is of great interest from the point of view of the history of dogma.

BIBLIOGRAPHY

H. Windisch, *Die katholischen Briefe* (Lietzmann, 3 ed., 1951).
R. Bultmann, 'Analyse des ersten Johannesbriefes', *Festgabe für A. Jülicher* (1927), pp. 138 ff.
R. Bultmann, 'Die kirchliche Redaktion des ersten Johannesbriefes', *In Memoriam E. Lohmeyer* (1951), pp. 189 ff.
R. Bultmann, 'Johannesbriefe' in *RGG*, III, cols. 836 ff.
E. von Dobschütz. 'Johanneische Studien I', *ZNW* (1907), pp. 1 ff.
E. Haenchen, 'Neuere Literatur zu den Johannesbriefen', *ThR*, NF (1960), pp. 1 ff.
W. Nauck, *Die Tradition und der Charakter des ersten Johannesbriefes* (1957).
Commentaries: A. E. Brooke, ICC (1912); C. H. Dodd, Moffatt (1946); B. F. Westcott (3 ed., 1892).
W. F. Howard, 'The Common Authorship of the Johannine Gospel and Epistles', *JTS* 48 (1947), pp. 12 ff.
J. A. T. Robinson, 'The Destination and Purpose of the Johannine Epistles', *NTS* 7 (1960–1), pp. 56 ff.

26. THE SECOND AND THIRD EPISTLES OF JOHN

(1) *Literary Form and Contents.* There is no doubt that both these documents are letters. There is no reason for regarding them as fictions, as has sometimes been suggested. In the preface a πρεσβύτερος (elder) is mentioned as the sender, but he is not named. The conclusions of the two letters contain greetings, preceded by a phrase which reads like a stock formula, in which the brevity of the documents is explained by the fact that the writer intends to pay a personal visit (2 Jn. 12; 3 Jn. 13 f.).

2 Jn. is addressed to an elect κυρία (lady) and her children (1), in other words to a congregation. We are told that they are loved not only by the writer but also by all those who know the truth, i.e. by all true Christians. After the greeting (3) the 'presbyter' states that he has got to know certain members of the church he is writing to who are 'walking in truth' (4), and he exhorts them to follow the commandment 'which we had from the beginning' (5). After explaining once again what this means (6) he speaks of Gnostic deceivers (7), of whom the church must beware (8). Whoever does not abide in the teaching of Christ does not have God, but he who abides in the teaching has the Father and the Son (9). If such heretics make their way into the Church, they should not be shown hospitality, should not even be greeted, for even by greeting them one is associating oneself with these people (10 f.).

The aim of the letter therefore is to give a warning about heresies which evidently correspond to those referred to in 1 Jn., for both the heresies and 'orthodoxy' are described in both documents in the same terms (cf. 2 Jn. 7 and 1 Jn. ii. 18; iv. 1–3; 2 Jn. 9 and 1 Jn. ii. 23; 2 Jn.5 and 1 Jn. ii. 7 f., etc.). The letter is written for a very definite purpose, but it takes a long time to come to its real theme (10 f.).

3 Jn. is addressed to a certain Gaius (1). After expressing a prayerful wish for Gaius' well-being (2) the author states how pleased he was that the 'brethren' gave such an encouraging report about him (3 f.). These have apparently been received hospitably by Gaius, for the author now asks him to continue to do the same (5–8). It is necessary for him to make this request because Diotrephes, who is evidently the leader of the church, did not welcome a letter he received from the presbyter (9). He has also engaged in slander against the latter, refused to receive the 'brethren' and drives out of the church those who give them a welcome (10). Gaius is exhorted to imitate not the evil but the good, for 'he that doeth good is of God: he that doeth evil hath not seen God' (11). After commending a certain Demetrius, the presbyter concludes the letter with the announcement that he hopes to pay a visit soon and with final greetings (13–15).

The letter is apparently delivered by this man Demetrius who is himself one of the 'brethren' or at least accompanies them. They are described as Christian missionaries, who, as they refuse to accept anything from Gentiles, are dependent on the hospitality of the Christians (7 f.); but as Diotrephes will not receive them, and even takes disciplinary action to prevent their being received, they have to turn to Gaius for accommodation. He has already given them hospitality once before, and the purpose of the letter is to exhort him to do the same again. There is no direct reference to any heresy in 3 Jn.

(2) *The Situation.* These two very short letters have presented scholars with a number of questions which it is difficult to answer,[9] because the very brief references they contain are not enough to give us a clear picture of the situations from which they arise—although of course they were familiar to the recipients in each case.

Although the first impression may be that 2 Jn. is exclusively concerned with 'dogmatic' problems and 3 Jn. with those of 'Church order' or discipline, the question that immediately arises is whether we can in fact draw such a sharp distinction. In 2 Jn. the dogmatic opposition leads ultimately to the same step that we find in 3 Jn. (the refusal of hospitality); and in 3 Jn. the complaint about Diotrephes' refusal to receive the 'brethren' is followed by an appeal to Gaius not to imitate the 'evil' (i.e. that which Diotrephes has done—11). This could of course simply refer to the way he acted, but it is immediately given a theological connotation, for 'he that doeth evil hath not seen God'. This contains at least an echo of motifs that we find in 1 Jn. Correct conduct emphatically includes love of the brethren. By cutting themselves off from the congregation those who subscribe to heresy show a lack of brotherly love—and so prove that they are not born of God (cf. section 26, 5). In the light of 3 Jn. 11, therefore, we have to ask whether the presbyter at any rate does not interpret Diotrephes' unfriendliness in such a way as to identify him to some extent with the supporters of the heresy.

The circumstances, however, are not at all clear. If we ask, for example,

9 Cf. E. Haenchen, *op. cit.*, pp. 267 ff.

why Diotrephes refuses to receive the brethren, we can find no answer—or not directly, at least. Käsemann[10] thinks there was a doctrinal reason for it. He suggests that Diotrephes was a monarchical bishop and as such the representative of ecclesiastical orthodoxy, and that the author—who was previously one of Diotrephes' presbyters and who Käsemann assumes was the author of Jn. and 1 Jn. as well—was suspected of Gnosticism and excommunicated by Diotrephes. Nevertheless he continued to use his title, and as both 'heretic and witness' he fought on two fronts against Gnosticism and ecclesiastical orthodoxy, hoping for an eventual settlement. This is not a very probable theory, however.[11] There is no mention of any excommunication of the presbyter. If this really had happened, the author would hardly have restricted himself to accusing Diotrephes merely of speaking slanderously of him. And how would he have been able to reckon on the possibility of confronting Diotrephes when he came on a visit? No doubt the latter excommunicated only the members of his own congregation (3 Jn. 10). We cannot discover the reason for Diotrephes' rejection of the missionaries.

On the other hand we must avoid the danger of reading too much into 3 Jn. 11. It does not follow from the fact that the author interprets the behaviour of Diotrephes along the lines of the reproach against the Gnostics that he actually regards Diotrephes as a Gnostic. If this had been the case he would have made it much clearer.

We cannot say anything very certain about the situation. All we can say is that it appears that the presbyter and Diotrephes live in different places. There is a missionary activity centred on the place where the presbyter lives, which evidently spreads out beyond the congregation. It is in competition with the Gnostic mission, of which a warning is given in 2 Jn. Diotrephes was probably a monarchical bishop who ruled with great strictness and saw the activity of missionaries from other places as an intrusion into his congregation, and therefore tried to prevent it. The presbyter, however, is determined to persist with his mission and tries to further it in Diotrephes' church by means of Gaius, who has already shown himself sympathetic to it—maybe because it was through the presbyter that he became a Christian (cf. v. 4). We have no means of knowing whether the presbyter wishes to do this because the congregation itself is not engaged in missionary activity, or only insufficiently, or whether there are other reasons.

[10] 'Ketzer und Zeuge. Zum johanneischen Verfasserproblem', *ZThK* (1951), pp. 292 ff. Reprinted in *Exegetische Versuche und Besinnungen*, I, pp. 168 ff.
[11] Cf. G. Bornkamm in *ThWNT*, VI, p. 671, n. 121.

(3) *Authorship, Time and Place of Composition.* The author's description of himself as 'presbyter' without any indication of his name is strange. That this description does not stand for the 'apostle John' is clear not only from the earlier observations (cf. sections 24, 4 and 25, 6), but also from the fact that it would be difficult to understand how Diotrephes could resist such an authority with so much success in his church. It is also unlikely that in these circumstances the author would have omitted to stress his 'apostolic authority'. In 2 Jn. he has to pursue his aim very cautiously, but in 3 Jn. there is little that he can do. It is a rather improbable solution to suggest that the name disappeared—at the same time?—from the two letters. The presbyter must have been known to his readers, which means that it cannot have been an elder (among others) of the place he belonged to. It is questionable how much weight should be attached here to the office in the constitutional sense. If he was simply a well-known 'older' member of the church who exerted a wide influence through the missionaries he sent out, the omission of his name is not altogether surprising.

We cannot say for certain whether the author is the same as that of 1 Jn. The fact that in this case he writes real letters, whereas in 1 Jn. he uses a different literary form, does not really affect the argument as to his identity. In any case he belongs to the Johannine 'school', and wrote the two letters in the East around the turn of the first century.

BIBLIOGRAPHY

H. Windisch, *Die katholischen Briefe* (Lietzmann, 3 ed., 1961).
R. Bultmann, 'Johannesbriefe' in *RGG*, III, cols. 836 ff.
E. Haenchen, 'Neuere Literatur zu den Johannesbriefen', *ThR*, NF (1960), pp. 267 ff.
E. Käsemann, 'Ketzer und Zeuge. Zum johanneischen Verfasserproblem', *ZThK* (1951), pp. 292 ff. Reprinted in *Exegetische Versuche und Besinnungen*, I (1960), pp. 168 ff.
Commentaries: A. E. Brooke, ICC (1912); C. H. Dodd, Moffatt (1946); B. F. Westcott (3 ed., 1892).
W. F. Howard, 'The Common Authorship of the Johannine Gospel and Epistles', *JTS* 48 (1947), pp. 12 ff.
J. A. T. Robinson, 'The Destination and Purpose of the Johannine Epistles', *NTS* 7 (1960–1), pp. 56 ff.

T

VI. Apocalyptic Literature

After the decline of Israelite prophecy and against the background of the difficult political situation of the Jewish people during the Hellenistic period there developed the 'late Jewish apocalyptic', a movement which is linked both with prophecy and also Wisdom literature. As the name implies, it is concerned with the unveiling of secrets which deal particularly with the future course of the world and are meant to give to those who are initiated information concerning future events.

The works written by the apocalyptic writers—the apocalypses—are full of dark mysteries, which constitute a large part of their attraction. They are published under the names of great men of faith of the past: Enoch, Abraham, Jacob and his sons, Moses, Daniel, and others. The apocalypse written under the name of Daniel is the earliest one that has come down to us; it is also the only one to be included in the Canon of the Old Testament, apart from which there are only short apocalyptic sections such as Is. xxiv–xxvii.

Together with the fictional authors' names there is often linked the idea that after the works were communicated to their authors by means of secret revelations, dreams, visions, etc. they were then 'sealed' (Dan. viii. 26; xii. 4; cf. Rev. xxii. 10), to be discovered and opened at a later time. When this happens the reader realizes that the ancient writers have 'foreseen' the course of history up to the present moment with remarkable accuracy, and is therefore strengthened in his confidence in the correctness of any further foreseeing of the future.

The apocalyptic conception of history is thoroughly dualistic. This period of the world is followed by that which is to come and which is imminent. The events which have to take place first are set out in a kind of time-table. The reader therefore knows, or can work out by observation of the signs of the times, at which point in the course of history he is living. The period of salvation that is to come will be preceded by catastrophes of world-wide proportions. The various concepts are not made to harmonize with one another in detail, so that we find different Saviour figures (Messiah, Son of Man), and the expectations also vary (salvation only for Israel or for all nations). This arises partly from the fact that sometimes when one apocalyptic programme was outstripped by events another had to be conceived. The basic aim, however, remains the same:

in the tribulations of the present a knowledge of the glory that is to come has to be imparted to the reader in order that he should not waver but faithfully observe the law and so have the prospect of being acquitted in the judgement that is to come.

Apocalyptic ideas were very widespread. We find them among other things in the Qumran documents found by the Dead Sea, and also in the New Testament. We need to take care, however, in judging the contents of the New Testament. There is an apocalyptic conception present in 2 Thess. ii. 1–12, for example, but although we quite often find such apocalyptic material in Paul's letters (1 Thess. iv. 16 f.; v. 2 f.; 1 Cor. xv. 23 f., 52), he himself was not an apocalyptist, but merely used this material to express his own eschatological message. The same is true of Lk. xii. 8 f. (cf. Mk. viii. 38). Mk. xiii presents a special problem: it seems that the evangelist had before him an apocalyptic document[1] to which he seeks to give not an apocalyptic but an eschatological interpretation, as we can see from his editorial work. Later the apocalyptic element comes to the fore again (e.g. Lk. xvii. 22–37). Such passages have to be expounded with great care, for it does not follow from the presence of apocalyptic ideas that the author himself shares this viewpoint. We have to examine the context carefully before we can draw any firm conclusions.

[1] Cf. G. Hölscher, 'Der Ursprung der Apokalypse Mrk 13', *ThBl* (1933), pp. 193 ff.

The work itself claims to be an apocalypse, or revelation (i. 1). However, we need to consider to what extent its message is really determined by apocalyptic ideas, or whether it is merely couched in these terms.

(1) *Contents.* The key to the structure of the whole work is probably to be found in i. 19. The seer is given the task of writing down (a) what he has seen, (b) what is, and (c) what is to come.

(a) In a vision in which he receives his call (i. 9–20) the seer sees the Son of Man with seven stars in his right hand in the midst of seven golden candlesticks. The latter touches John who had fallen down as though he were dead when he saw the vision and declares himself to be the Lord of death and of hell. The seer is told to write down what he has seen.

(b) The account of the vision is preceded by an introduction like that to a letter (i. 1–8), in which the author addresses seven churches in the province of Asia. The main content of the work is indicated with great brevity: 'the things which must shortly come to pass' (i. 1—cf. i. 3). Then each of the seven churches receives its own open letter, in which the characteristics of each one are described (ii, iii).

(c) The main section (iv–xxii) deals with 'the things which come to pass', and in the course of it the emphasis changes from time to time. First we have the announcement of the judgement that is to come (iv–xi); this is followed by the battle against the enemies of Christ and the Church, ending with the fall of Babylon (xii–xviii), and then comes the final triumph (xix. 1–xxii. 5). The details of the account are set out in images and visions which are very varied in origin, but have many parallels in apocalyptic literature. We frequently meet the number seven (vision of the seven seals: iv. 1–viii. 1; vision of the seven trumpets: viii. 7–12; ix. 1–21; xi. 15–19; vision of the seven bowls: xv. 1–16, 21; also the seven churches: i. 4, 11; cf. iv. 5; v. 6; the seven thunders: x. 3, etc.). The numbers four (iv. 6; vii. 1; xx. 8) and twelve (xii. 1; xxi. 12 ff.) also have special significance.

The concluding section (xxii. 6–21) contains a further command to proclaim what has been seen, but there is no command to seal it—as is usual in apocalypses—as the End is near (xxii. 10; cf. xxii. 20).

(2) *The Author's Standpoint.* For an understanding of the message of Rev. two facts need to be borne in mind: firstly, that the churches to which the author is writing are being persecuted by the State (i. 9; vi. 9–11; xi. 11 ff.; xiii. 1 ff.); and secondly, that the End of the world is expected in the immediate future (i. 1, 3; xxii. 6, 10). In other words, Rev. is a highly topical document, written with the immediate situation in mind which we should not attempt to interpret without reference to its context, by relegating to the future the *parousia* which has not yet taken place and by trying to identify the author's vision of the future with events in the history of the world which—from our standpoint—have either taken place already or are still to come. This would inevitably lead not only to a misunderstanding of the author's message, but also to a misuse of the document itself, such as has taken place in the history of the Church, both past and present, particularly at the hands of sects and fanatics. The author's aim was not to address himself to later generations, but to his own troubled times.

By adopting the literary form of the apocalypse the author makes plain how close he stands to the apocalyptic viewpoint, the aim of which was to turn the reader's eyes from the tribulations of the present to a glorious future, so that he might remain faithful and have the prospect of being acquitted at the judgement and of sharing in salvation. There is an apocalyptic element in this dualism which we find in Rev. Over against the Church, represented as a woman (xii. 1 ff.) or as the bride of the Lamb (xix. 7 f.; xxi. 9) there stands the harlot Babylon (xvii. 1 ff.), over against Jerusalem the city of God that is to come (xx. 9; xxi. 2, 10 ff.) there stands the fallen city (xiv. 8; xvi. 19; xviii. 2 ff.). A further apocalyptic note is to be seen in the great variety of concepts we meet, although it should be noted that in the whole work there is no direct quotation from any apocalypse that is known to us.

It would be a mistake, however, to place an exclusive and one-sided emphasis upon the author's connection with late Jewish apocalyptic. He adopts the same pattern, but he fills it with a fresh content, in particular with a considerable number of Christ sayings. The replacement of the figure formerly associated with the End by Christ would not of course of itself break up the apocalyptic framework; but the significant thing is that the One who will come in glory is identical with the Lamb that has been slain (v. 6; xiii. 8), was crucified outside the gates of the great city (xi. 8) and has redeemed with his blood those who believe in him (i. 5; v. 9). The Church therefore not only knows the One who is to come as present here and now: the Church is also his possession.

What this relationship means for the present age is not brought out at all fully, and almost the only aspect of it that comes to the fore is the theme of the forgiveness of sins as an accomplished fact (xxii. 14). What does come to the fore as far as the present is concerned is the element of decision. Time after time we hear the call to perseverance (viii. 7; xiv. 12), to watchfulness (xvi. 15) and to maintain one's witness till death (ii. 10; xiv. 13). This is what matters in the present trials, but we are given no details of what it actually implies.

The author's gaze is fixed almost exclusively therefore on the future. He is certainly convinced that final events will take place very much as he has described them, and yet he does not really set out a 'time-table', especially as that which is presented as belonging to the future (particularly in chs. xiii and xvii) already belongs to the present—in its initial stages at least—as far as the author is concerned. This underlines once again the fact that the author's aim is to show that his own period is the period immediately before the End. By pointing his readers beyond the confusions of the present to the great End he seeks to inspire them with hope (xix. 9). Here we can see a great similarity between the standpoint of the author and that of Heb. (cf. section 19), and also with Luke's standpoint, although in this case the point of reference is reversed. Whereas Luke based his hope on the 'centre of time' that belonged to the past and which he described as a foretaste of the final consummation (cf. section 14), the author of Rev. bases this hope on the future, in which the Church will live with the Christ who appears in glory and who, as the Lamb that was slain, bestowed the forgiveness of sins upon the Cross. All the various themes from the different traditions are meant in the last resort to serve to bring out this message. Properly understood, therefore, the author does not seek to encourage us to indulge in fanciful speculations; his aim rather is soberly to kindle into new life the hope that is growing faint under the oppression of the forces of the State—without extenuating or denying in any way the present distress that is still to come—and at the same time to issue a call to loyalty and perseverance.

(3) *Authorship, Time and Place of Composition.* The author presents himself to his readers by the name of John (i. 1, 4; xxii. 8), and goes on to describe himself as 'your brother and partaker with you in the tribulation and kingdom and patience which are in Jesus' (i. 9). He evidently does not write anonymously, therefore, as other apocalyptic writers do, for it is unlikely that a later writer would issue the work under the authority of the apostle John without expressing himself more explicitly on the point.

The question is who this seer John can be. From the second century onwards Church tradition identified him with John the son of Zebedee, but the idea never won universal acceptance. But as these divergent views are polemical, the tradition which seeks the author among the disciples of Jesus is no doubt earlier. Even if it were historically reliable, however, it does not really carry any weight, for the author neither appeals to his connection with the Twelve nor does he make any use of the fact that he was an eye-witness of the life of Jesus.

The ancient tradition also presents certain difficulties. In xviii. 20 the 'saints, apostles and prophets' are mentioned as a definite group, and in xxi. 14 the apostles by themselves, but there is no indication that the author includes himself among them. It can hardly be his aim to suggest that he himself has 'seen'. The impression we receive is rather that he is looking back to the apostles as an entity belonging to the past, who will have their definite place or function in the course of the events associated with the End.

It has often been assumed that the author is the same as the presbyter John who was active in Asia Minor (Papias, quoted by Eusebius, *H.E.* III, 39, 4; cf. *H.E.* VII, 25 ,16). This theory is questionable, however, as it is by no means certain that there ever was such a person. As far as we are concerned therefore—but not his readers—the author of Rev. remains anonymous, although we know his name. There seems little doubt that he was of Jewish origin: this is indicated not only by his familiarity with apocalyptic ideas and with the Hebrew Old Testament, but even more by the fact that a number of sections of the work give the impression of being a word for word translation from the Hebrew.

As the author places his vision and call on Patmos, a small island off the west coast of Asia Minor (i. 9) it is quite possible that he also wrote the work there. Indirect support for this idea could also be seen in the fact that this island was used by the Romans as a place of exile.

It is difficult to suggest a time for its writing, as there are in the work a number of allusions which could be interpreted as referring to a considerable variety of historical events. As the author is obviously looking back to persecutions that have already taken place and awaiting still more severe ones, it seems reasonable to assume that the work was written at a time when the situation was becoming worse for Christians. This was the case at the time of Domitian (A.D. 81–96), who had statues of himself erected at many places in the Empire—in Ephesus, for example—before which homage had to be paid to the Emperor. The vision of 'another beast' (xiii. 11–18) seems to presuppose those practices associated with

278   THE REVELATION OF JOHN

Domitian—the persecution and killing of those who would not 'worship the image of the beast'. It follows from this that Irenaeus' statement (*Adv.Haer.* V, 30, 3) that Rev. was written towards the end of Domitian's reign could well be correct.

BIBLIOGRAPHY

E. Lohmeyer, *Die Offenbarung des Johannes* (Lietzmann, reprinted with additions, 1953).

E. Lohse, *Die Offenbarung des Johannes* (NTD, vol. 11, 9 ed., 1960).

E. Lohmeyer, 'Die Offenbarung des Johannes 1920–1934', *ThR*, NF (1934), pp. 269 ff.; (1935), pp. 28 ff.

O. A. Piper, 'Johannesapokalypse' in *RGG*, III, cols. 822 ff.

Commentaries: G. B. Caird, Black (1966); R. H. Charles, ICC (2 vols., 1920); M. Kiddle and M. K. Ross, Moffatt (1940).

A. M. Farrer, *A Rebirth of Images* (1949); *The Revelation of St. John the Divine* (1964).

D. S. Russell, *The Method and Message of Jewish Apocalyptic* (1964).

C. C. Torrey, *The Apocalypse of John* (1958).

It is almost accidental that the New Testament breaks off at this point. The early Church certainly did not stop writing letters or producing other documents in the early part of the second century. One approach would be for us to examine all the documents which came into being later in the same way as we have examined those that have been brought together in the New Testament. At the same time, however, we have to recognize that not all the writings produced in the 'New Testament period'—i.e. between about A.D. 50 (1 Thess.) and A.D. 130 (2 Pet.)—were included in this collection. This is certainly true of 1 Clem., a letter from Clement sent from Rome to the church at Corinth about A.D. 97, and probably also true of the Didache (The Teaching of the Twelve Apostles), a kind of manual of Church order, which probably originated at the beginning of the second century. This raises the question as to the criteria by which these twenty-seven documents—and only these—were selected from the realm of early Christian writings and brought together in the New Testament.

This process of selection followed a complicated course which is not always easy to trace. The first stage we can recognize is that of separate collections. 2 Pet. iii. 15 f. is one of the earliest witnesses to the fact that there was a 'corpus Paulinum' alongside other writings, as to the extent and compilation of which however we have no information. The Church lived by its 'writings' and appealed to them, and included among them of course was the Old Testament, the Canon of which was not fixed until the last decade of the first century. A collection was also made of the Gospels. The first indication of this is in the references of Papias to Mk. and Mt. around the middle of the second century (cf. sections 12 and 13). We can deduce that such a collection was in existence also from the fact that Tatian produced a harmony of the Gospels (*Diatessaron*) in the second half of the second century which was used in the Syriac Church until the fifth century. In the middle of the second century Justin reports that the 'reminiscences of the apostles' were read in the Sunday worship along with writings from the Old Testament (*First Apol.* 67, 3). There is no evidence yet, however, of any exact fixing of a 'Scriptural Canon'.

The first evidence of a clearly defined Canon is in Marcion, who founded a congregation in Rome about A.D. 140 which deliberately stood apart from the rest of the Church and soon spread throughout the Empire. Marcion rejected the· Old Testament. His Canon was in two parts and contained on the one hand Lk. (abbreviated and purged of Old Testament quotations particularly) and on the other hand ten Pauline epistles, in the following order: Gal., 1 and 2 Cor., Rom., 1 and 2 Thess., Laodiceans (=Eph.), Col., Phil., Phm. There is no other evidence elsewhere of such a clear definition of the Canon so early in the Church. It is probably true to say that Marcion's Canon made it necessary for the Church to press on with its own definition.

The earliest list that has come down to us from within the Church is the Muratorian Canon that came into being in the second half of the second century and is preserved as a fragment in a manuscript of the eighth century. It is named after the Milanese librarian L. A. Muratori, who discovered the fragment and published it in 1740. The manuscript begins with observations on Mk. (we can assume that Mt. was mentioned previously), followed by Lk., Jn. and Acts. Thirteen Pauline epistles are recognized (1 and 2 Cor., Eph., Phil., Col., Gal., 1 and 2 Thess., Rom., Phm., the Pastorals), Jude among the so-called Catholic epistles and two Johannine epistles, and then the Wisdom of Solomon and Rev. Mention is made of a similarly titled Apocalypse of Peter, but with the reservation that its acceptance is disputed. Heb., Jas., 1 and 2 Pet. and one of the Johannine epistles appear to be unknown. The Shepherd of Hermas and apocryphal Pauline epistles are rejected, but again this view is said to be disputed. The Muratorian fragment is valuable in so far as it brings to light the criteria by which the selection of books is to be made: a document can be counted as canonical only when it is intended for the whole 'catholic Church'—and when it is derived from an apostle. It was this second criterion in particular which determined the subsequent process of selection.

At this point, however, we find a divergence of opinion as regards many of the documents. At different places and at different times varying views were adopted as regards the apostolic authorship of Heb., 2 Pet., 2 and 3 Jn., Jude, Jas. and Rev. in particular, whilst at the same time many writings were acknowledged which later came to be considered apocryphal. A relative unification was first brought about by the more or less authoritative Festal Letter XXXIX of Athanasius of the year 367, which declared the twenty-seven books which still make up the New Testament as we know it to be canonical. This did not by any means put an end to varieties of opinion, but critical revaluations—among others, for example, by Luther—have not been able to change it. The question whether such criticism is possible, and in certain circumstances even necessary, depends on the theological significance one attaches to the process of drawing up the Canon.

From the historical point of view the fixing of the Canon of the New Testament is accidental. This is true in two directions: in the first place it is an accident that only those documents could be admitted to the Canon which had been preserved. This fact is often hardly noted, but it should not be overlooked. It is not as important where the lost Pauline epistles are concerned (on 1 Cor. v. 9 see section 7, and on Rom. xvi. section 9), as where the lost sources are concerned which provided the material for the Synoptic Gospels (cf. section 12) but have not come down to us. The second accident is that the historical judgement on the authorship of the documents sprang from the insights of each particular period. It is not at all surprising that in making historical judgements various opinions were arrived at, for a definite decision simply could not be made, particularly with the means that were then available. The authoritative definition was therefore the only possible solution of the problem in view of the fact that a historical judgement was now called for.

In view of the fact that 'Popes and councils can err', Athanasius' definition, as well as subsequent definitions, is open to revision. There would be little point, however, in placing too much emphasis on the element of criticism. The early Church was certainly concerned with the question of authorship. If we can establish nowadays that, for example, Heb. was definitely not written by Paul and 2 Pet. not by Peter, then we would be acting in accordance with the mind of the early Church if we excluded these two books from the Canon. The only objection to this is to reply that the early Church did not take its own criteria seriously, but we have no real reason to object. There can really be no doubt about the fact that the early Church would not have accepted these documents into the Canon if it had been in a position to pass such definite historical judgements upon these documents as most scholars feel able to do today. Nevertheless, we must not give too much prominence to this kind of criticism of the Canon.

It is more important to ask why the early Church made the apostolic element a criterion of canonicity. There is no doubt about the answer. Faced with heresies and in particular with claims to later revelations, the early Church wanted to hold fast to the once-for-allness of the revelation of God that was made in Jesus Christ. But as this was a revelation in history, the direct witnesses were the first not only in time but also as regards the substance of their testimony. The concept of the apostle is used in various senses in the New Testament, but as far as the question of the Canon is concerned it can be defined in terms of the direct witness of ear and eye to the revelation of God that took place in Jesus. From this point of view, however, there is not a single document in the New Testament that is really of apostolic origin. Even Paul can be counted as an apostle in this sense only indirectly, as he did not know Jesus during his earthly life.

Although this may seem to mean the breakdown of the concept of the Canon—simply by carrying to its logical conclusion the intention of the early Church—we have to note straight away that it is still true that the apostolic testimony, which alone has normative authority, can only be arrived at by working back through the New Testament. The real Canon is prior to the New Testament, and we are nearer to it in the sources the Synoptists used than in the Synoptic Gospels themselves. We have seen previously that the pre-Synoptic tradition presents us with a history of proclamation which is then continued in the Synoptic Gospels and in which the apostolic testimony was proclaimed afresh to each new situation. This of course inevitably meant variations. This history of proclamation can be traced along different lines of tradition through the New Testament, and it does not stop with the New Testament, but goes on further. The aim is always that the apostolic proclamation should be set out afresh in such a way as to reach each new situation as it arises. The New Testament could therefore be described as the earliest volume of sermons in the Church that has come down to us, but we need to note that later sermons cannot be directly linked with the original apostolic proclamation and so to the 'Canon'. Their 'text' is in fact an earlier sermon. Matthew and Luke build on Mark's proclamation; the pseudo-Pauline epistles are similarly based on Paul; and the Johannine literature presents a similar history of proclamation. The Church epistles also use older traditions of various origin.

It is possible for the exegete to determine the traditions on which the various authors drew and also the situations to which they were addressing themselves when they set out their message. This is his task, and the purpose of New Testament Introduction is to help him to do this. He needs to remember all the time, however, that their messages are not addressed to him but were addressed to earlier readers. And as the New Testament is made up of sermons, we always need to ask—as indeed with all sermons—whether the preacher has remained true to his subject. This cannot be decided simply by determining whether a document belongs to the New Testament. It does not follow that post-New Testament sermons are false or less valuable proclamation because they are not to be found in the New Testament, nor does it follow that the value of a sermon is determined solely by the fact that it was included in the New Testament. The test is whether the preacher has preserved the original apostolic testimony in such a way that his own testimony declares the 'matter of Jesus' in the new situation to which he is addressing himself. Ideas and ways of expression may change, and the preachers may follow very different traditions—but if their preaching declares the 'matter of Jesus' to their time, it is theologically legitimate. Or, to be more exact, we should say: their preaching was theologically legitimate for their time, for it cannot subsequently be simply repeated but has to be actualized afresh for each new situation.

It is not the task of exegesis, however, to apply this test, for its work is not to evaluate, but to bring out the original message. It is necessary for such a test to be made, however, if exegesis is to prove faithful for the work of proclamation. In view of what has already been said, it is not a question of continuing to declare thoughts about the text, but rather of translating into terms relevant to the present situation the original messages which were addressed by means of the texts to specific situations at the time. But this cannot be done without guidance, and so it becomes clear that the historical-critical task of going back beyond the New Testament in search of the apostolic testimony is of great theological importance.

It is impossible, therefore, to describe the New Testament as it stands at present as the Canon, for in the strict sense only the apostolic testimony to Jesus as the Divine revelation can be described as canonical. On the other hand, however, this Canon can only be arrived at via the New Testament. Even if we were to keep the limits of the New Testament open for subsequent Church history, as the history of proclamation does not stop with the New Testament sermons, it is from this later proclamation that we must always start, for the enquiry concerning Jesus always leads us back through one of the lines of proclamation present in the New Testament to the Canon which is prior to the New Testament.

The question that arises is whether in these circumstances the present-day reader can find anything of value in the New Testament. The question has to be answered in the negative if he is seeking a message addressed directly to himself. But as no book in the New Testament aims to speak directly to the present-day reader, to use the New Testament in this way would be to use it against the intentions of those who wrote it. The question therefore needs to be phrased differently. It is not a question of whether Paul, Mark, Matthew, Luke or John have something to say to me, but rather whether what these writers sought to say to their readers can become something that is addressed to me as well. In doing this we are adopting what has always been the attitude of the Church, which has never said that it believes in the New Testament, for such a belief would be a Docetic heresy. The Church's confession of faith is rather: I believe in Jesus of Nazareth as the Christ of God. This faith is a faith shared with the apostles and also with the post-apostolic witnesses within and without the New Testament. To stand four-square on the Church's confession of faith means to see the writings of the New Testament in their original function as a summons to share this faith in Jesus; it does not mean to put the New Testament in the place of Jesus as *the* revelation.